DRIVER REHABILITATION

ACROSS AGE AND DISABILITY

DRIVER REHABILITATION ACROSS AGE AND DISABILITY

An Occupational Therapy Guide

Sue Redepenning, OTR/L, CDRS

AOTA PRESS
The American Occupational Therapy Association, Inc.

AOTA Staff
Frederick P. Somers, Executive Director
Christopher M. Bluhm, Chief Operating Officer
Audrey Rothstein, Director, Marketing and Communications

Chris Davis, Managing Editor, AOTA Press
Barbara Dickson, Production Editor

Robert A. Sacheli, Manager, Creative Services
Sarah E. Ely, Book Production Coordinator

Marge Wasson, Marketing Manager
Elizabeth Johnson, Marketing Specialist

The American Occupational Therapy Association, Inc.
4720 Montgomery Lane
Bethesda, MD 20814
Phone: 301-652-AOTA (2682)
TDD: 800-377-8555
Fax: 301-652-7711
www.aota.org
To order: 1-877-404-AOTA (2682)

ISBN: 1-56900-214-2

Library of Congress Control Number: 2006920219

Composition by Laura J. Hurst, Grammarians
Printed by Versa Press, Inc., East Peoria, IL

Contents

Tables, Figures, Exhibits, Personal Experiences, and Appendixes

Introduction

My goal in writing this book is twofold. The first is to have all occupational therapists address driving as an instrumental activity of daily living (IADL) with their clients within their level of training ability (generalist and specialist). The second is to educate medical professionals to value the lead of occupational therapists and to increase their awareness of the need to address driving so that a client receives the proper services or referral for driving to be addressed. This book explains the importance of this awareness and of collaboration among a team of rehabilitation professionals with occupational therapists as the lead. My main goal is for the IADL of driving to be a main factor discussed and addressed in the medical community for all clients receiving services so that they know if they can drive; if they need to wait to drive and for how long; if they need a driving evaluation and, if so, whom to go to; and if adaptive equipment is needed, that they receive training on the properly installed equipment.

I emphasize the value of having occupational therapists lead this team; they are professionals who are well suited to specialize in the field of driver rehabilitation. Occupational therapists also need to recognize their role and to value what they can provide as generalists. Occupational therapists must realize their importance in driver rehabilitation, working with those individuals who wish to return to driving after an illness or injury or as they grow older.

The cost of a driver evaluation is usually paid privately by clients, but it is worth the expense. Medical professionals must understand what is covered and, most important, value this service, or they will not refer their clients and patients for a driver evaluation. This book discusses the in-depth analysis that occurs in a driver evaluation for people with a variety of disabilities and for senior citizens. The expertise needed to provide this service and the outcome of completing the evaluation are reviewed so that occupational therapists, along with medical professionals, will have the resources to explain this service to patients and clients.

This book is not meant to train occupational therapists to become driver rehabilitation professionals; that takes years of experience, continuing education, and mentoring. Instead, it is meant to help generalists and specialists understand the importance of driving as an IADL, to provide ideas for addressing the goal of driving, and to value the need for a collaborative effort among occupational therapists and medical professionals.

As the profession of driver rehabilitation grows, it will be important for everyone who works with people with mental or physical disabilities of all age groups, or with senior citizens, to feel comfortable asking clients or patients about driving and providing resources to fully address this IADL. It will be important for facilities to look at how they are addressing driving so that consistent policies and practices are put in place. Adding the IADL of driving to an initial evaluation is one way to ensure that every client is asked about this skill set.

Occupational therapy assistants have an important role in the field of driving, both as generalists and as specialists. As the profession grows, the roles will become more clearly defined. In this book, the role of occupational therapy assistants is touched on, but role delineation is not specified while these roles are being examined. The collaboration between the occupational therapist and occupational therapy assistant is important in driver rehabilitation, and both professionals have a role as this area develops. Following the American Occupational Therapy Association's (AOTA's) Practice Guidelines is essential in all areas of practice (see, specifically, Stav, Hunt, & Arbesman, 2006).

My hope is that this book will be a learning tool for a variety of medical professionals and that it will raise the awareness of the skills needed for driving. Readers are encouraged to help work to build this new practice area to serve those who need occupational therapy services.

Thanks to the AOTA for asking me to write this book. It has been a great experience.

—Sue Redepenning, OTR/L, CDRS
Occupational Therapy Solutions, Inc.
Minneapolis, MN

Reference

Stav, W. B., Hunt, L. A., and Arbesman, M. (2006). *Occupational therapy practice guidelines for driving*. Bethesda, MD: American Occupational Therapy Association.

Acknowledgments

I thank my husband and four boys for allowing me the time to write this book. I also thank my parents for teaching me to work hard at what I do and strive to be my best, and my mother-in-law and father-in-law for reading over the book, editing the grammar, and providing feedback. This has definitely been a family project.

I thank the many facilities that have loaned pictures for the book and information on research they have completed. Their time and effort are what makes this book special.

- Adaptive Mobility Services, Inc., Orlando, FL
- Anne Forrest Clark, St. Luke's Hospital, Duluth, MN
- Braun Corporation, Winamac, IN
- Complete Mobility, St. Paul, MN
- Courage Center, Driver's Evaluation and Training Program, Minneapolis, MN
- Cynthia Owsley, Department of Ophthalmology, School of Medicine, University of Alabama at Birmingham
- Delta Integration, Inc., Lancaster, PA
- The Division of Vocational Rehabilitation Services, St. Paul, MN
- Easter Seals Crossroads Rehabilitation Center, Indianapolis, IN
- Frederik R. Mottola, National Institute for Driver Behavior, Cheshire, CT
- Linda Hunt, Project Director, Training for Health and Education Opportunities, Flathead Valley Community College, Kalispell, MT
- National Institute for Driver Behavior, Cheshire, CT
- National Older Driver Research and Training Center University of Florida, Gainesville
- Occupational Therapy Solutions, Inc., Minneapolis, MN
- Therapeutic Mobility Services, Fort Wayne, IN
- University of Minnesota, Minneapolis

Thanks also go to the AOTA Expert Panel, which includes

- Mary Frances Gross, COTA, CDRS, Licensed Driving Instructor
- Linda Hunt, PhD, OTR
- Dennis McCarthy, MEd, OTR/L
- Susan Pierce, OTR, CDRS
- Wendy Stav, PhD, OTR/L, CDRS
- Carol Wheatley, OTR/L, CDRS
- Elin Schold Davis, OTR/L, CDRS, *AOTA Staff Liaison*

Rehabilitation and the Component of Driving

Rehabilitation professionals play an important role in helping to ensure that driving is included in the early development of the general rehabilitation intervention plan.

—Wheatley, Pellerito, and Redepenning (2005, p. 105)

The term *instrumental activities of daily living* (IADLs) is used in the occupational therapy profession to describe the daily living tasks that require advanced skills (e.g., driving, work, parenting, and community mobility; American Occupational Therapy Association [AOTA], 2002). IADLs are usually addressed late in the rehabilitation process or after the first stages of rehabilitation are complete. Sometimes the client has been discharged from rehabilitation for a period of time before his or her IADL skills develop more fully.

Driving and community mobility too often are overlooked in occupational therapy practice (Pierce & Hunt, 2004); however, these IADLs should be introduced to some extent early in the rehabilitation process, even though they usually are addressed fully during later stages of rehabilitation. Clients may have questions about driving, the family may want a client's driving evaluated, or driving may be an activity that the client can no longer do. How questions are answered and what information is provided will set the tone for driving as it is addressed in all areas of rehabilitation for that client now and in the future. The more clients and their families understand ahead of time, the better prepared they will be and the more accepting they will be of the results.

Importance of Addressing Driving and Community Mobility

Rehabilitation professionals should always work together as a team and should be aware of effective interventions as well as the limitations of occupational therapy for the task of driving analysis and intervention (Hopewell, 2002). All rehabilitation professionals—including speech therapists, physical therapists, nurses, social workers, physician assistants, and physician residents in the hospital—should have some comfort level in addressing driving and community mobility as an integral part of the rehabilitation process. For example, if a speech therapist working on cognitive retraining notices a significant processing delay and knows that the client plans to return to driving, he or she should be able to discuss this concern with the client. The therapist should be able to direct the client to resources and notify the team to develop a plan. In another example, a physical therapist working on balance might observe that the client has decreased sensation and reaction time in the lower extremities but is still driving; the therapist should be able to inform the physician and rehabilitation team and perhaps provide referral information for driver rehabilitation. Physician assistants and residents often have more time to spend with the patient to gather information and provide necessary resources.

Rehabilitation professionals often benefit from visiting a driver rehabilitation company or accompanying one of their clients to a driver evaluation appointment; by seeing firsthand what takes place during a driver evaluation, they can better prepare their clients for the evaluation. Rather than seeking a specific test to predict driving ability, the rehabilitation team should adopt a multidimensional and multistage decision-making model that is based on a risk–benefit decision paradigm (Hopewell, 2002). Together, the team analyzes the risk of the skill and prepares for driving throughout rehabilitation. In this way, the work with the driver rehabilitation specialist can be completed in a timely manner consistent with clients' needs.

> *The rehabilitation professional must address driving within the scope of [his or her] practice area, but not beyond. Knowing the appropriate level of intervention and following it is important to ensure that the client obtains accurate information about his or her driving skills and limitations.*
>
> —Pellerito (2005, p. 59)

The task of driving should be consistently included on all initial evaluations of activities of daily living (ADLs), even if it is just to ask whether the client had recently been a driver (Davis, 2003). This approach has a twofold purpose: (1) to determine whether the client has or can develop the skills to drive and (2) to ensure that he or she knows not to drive now, if doing so is not appropriate.

Discussions about driving bring up many fears for clients if they are not handled in a consistent, caring, and informative manner. Clients want to know why the rehabilitation professional is asking about driving, because it may not be apparent to them that this area should concern that person. Clients may ask whether this is a routine question or if they have been singled out for some reason, and they may check with other clients to make sure that they were also asked about driving. Consistently asking about driving allows the rehabilitation professional to honestly say that all clients are asked about driving to determine any needs related to this skill, thereby decreasing the client's anxiety about being asked about driving and maintaining a fair process.

Most people initially feel threatened when driving is discussed, especially if the outcome is to recommend driving cessation. Consequently, the rehabilitation professional must be prepared and have the resources to address this topic in a knowledgeable, reassuring manner. The recommendation to take away a person's ability to drive should not be taken lightly: Studies have shown that losing the ability to drive causes feelings of regret, loss, isolation, and depression along with a feeling of missed "independence, convenience, and mobility" (Stav, 2004, p. 15). As a result, referral to a driver rehabilitation specialist (DRS) needs to be a communications pathway for the rehabilitation professional and a member of the team, even if it is a referral relationship, so that driving ability is evaluated in a thorough manner.

Clients and the facility are well served by adhering to a fair process: At least one hospital in Minnesota has been brought into litigation because the facility did not have a consistent procedure for addressing driving. The hospital assessed driving for one of its patients and reported his inability to drive to the state. Another man with a similar disability did not even have the question of driving arise in his case. The first patient found out about the inconsistency, and the hospital admitted that it did not have a policy for addressing driving.

Many hospitals are reluctant to develop policies to address driving skills out of concerns over potential litigation; however, this case highlights that addressing driving for some clients and not others can be just as damaging. If the facility develops a policy around driving and educates staff about it, then this important IADL will be fairly and consistently discussed with clients (Kaplan, 1999).

When rehabilitation professionals ask about the function of driving, it sends the message that the professional values the tasks that were important to the client before the disabling incident. It reassures the client that driving goals will be addressed indirectly, through other, more basic ADL goals. The rehabilitation professional can emphasize how the client's short-term goals affect the client's driving goals and explain the steps in the driver rehabilitation process. The prospect of driving in the future can motivate clients to complete the smaller steps needed to accomplish their ultimate IADL goals. Once baseline driving skills are attained, long-term driving goals can be established.

Gathering baseline information on the function of driving for each client is important. The rehabilitation professional should ask the client whether he or she could drive before the disability. Does the client drive for leisure? To run errands? To commute to work? At what times of day does the client drive? What equipment must be stowed in the vehicle? Can the client get to and from the vehicle safely in all types of weather? This conversation will encourage the client to talk about his or her past experiences and demonstrate his or her understanding of how the situation may have changed. The answers to these and other questions provide important insight into the function of driving for that client and help determine whether driving is a client IADL.

The process for returning to driving should be explained so that the client is not surprised that the physician and rehabilitation team play a role in the decision. What often happens is that the client does not understand the clinicians' role until his or her driver's license has been cancelled following a report from the physician or rehabilitation professional to the state. This is not the way a client should find out that he or she is not fit to drive; instead, the rehabilitation team should play an active role in providing the right information, ensuring the right outcome, and involving the client and family in the process so that they understand and value why driving fits into the role of rehabilitation. The more the client and his or her family know ahead of time, the better prepared the client will be for either ceasing to drive or undergoing driver rehabilitation when the time comes.

The rehabilitation professional may screen for driving skills within his or her scope of practice; refer the client to an occupational therapist, if appropriate, for further clinical screening regarding driving and IADL skills; or refer the client to a driver rehabilitation program when the time is right. Before the client starts driving again, a thorough driver evaluation should take place. In some cases, this evaluation will require a physician's screening in addition to the rehabilitation professional's input; in others, it may require clinical and on-the-road assessments by a driver rehabilitiation specialist, which may be an occupational therapist who has specialized in this field (OT/DRS). In the meantime, the rehabilitation team (e.g., occupational therapists, physicians, psychologists, nurses, physical therapists, speech and language pathologists, recreation specialists), with the occupational therapist generalist taking the lead, should identify alternative transportation options and work with the client to ensure that he or she can use those options. Usually, an outpatient occupational therapist or family member (with guidance from the occupational therapist) takes the lead on this task.

The client and his or her family need to know the rehabilitation team's plan for addressing driving and community mobility and should be part of the process from the beginning. They should have opportunities to voice their opinions and concerns at all levels, from generalists to specialists. Discussing the types of patients the facility usually treats, the diagnoses and age groups, typical issues related to driving needs, and the policy of the facility for addressing driving will help create a uniform team approach. The facility should take a good look at what it can provide to address the activity of driving; it will likely need to refer the client to a specialist for analysis of driving skills.

Rehabilitation professionals who are not DRSs should not tell clients to return to driving. Without input from a DRS, some clients may be told that they cannot drive when they perhaps could, given the right equipment or techniques; others may be given the go-ahead to drive but are not safe. Occupational therapists can take the lead on the rehabilitation team to address the activity of driving because driving is a functional task, but matching the skill of the rehabilitation professional to the needs of the client will provide the best outcome. Analyzing the activity of driving—that is, road performance—requires specialized knowledge and skill. This analysis should be carried out only by professionals with the appropriate skills and training, or the accuracy of the results will be affected. The DRS plays the central role in providing efficacious driver rehabilitation and, more recently, community mobility services to clients and their caregivers (Pellerito, 2005). Involving the entire team in the process will ensure that all rehabilitation professionals at the facility continually send a consistent, unified message to the client and family members about the driver rehabilitation process. All rehabilitation staff should be able to consistently describe how driving is addressed at their facility (Tewfik & Sabel, 2004).

Driving affects all practice areas and age groups. For example, the pediatric client's family may want to know whether adolescents with disabilities have the potential to learn to drive. A psychologist may wonder whether a mental health client is emotionally stable enough to drive. A young adult with a spinal cord injury may want to drive to get back to work. A senior citizen may have vision changes but want to continue driving.

To complete an accurate performance analysis, it is critical that the rehabilitation team and the occupational therapist know what skills are involved in driving, such as the ability to activate the accelerator and brake with a smooth, coordinated motion; the ability to visually process information seen so that the appropriate response can be put into action; and the ability to get in and out of the vehicle and stow any needed equipment. The rehabilitation professional should have a basic knowledge of adaptive equipment options to help prepare the client for what he or she will need to do to drive safely. The rehabilitation team, led by the occupational therapist, must fully screen a client's potential skill for the driving activity and ability as they relate to his or her specific medical condition. The intervention chosen must directly benefit the client in the area of driving so that this skill may be possible in the future.

It is important that rehabilitation professionals know that some occupational therapists can provide DRS services. A professional who values the role of an occupational therapist DRS can be a great advocate for this service. If professionals do not value this service, however, then it is unlikely that clients will value it.

Clients should be matched to the appropriate driver rehabilitation program. Some programs provide in-car, low-technology evaluations. Rehabilitation professionals must understand the differences among driving programs: what they offer, who does the evaluation, what the evaluator's background is, and how satisfied rehabilitation staff and clients have been with the services. Some use adaptive equipment only to the extent that the vehicle in which the evaluation is completed has simple safety devices such as dual brakes, cushions for seating, and mirrors for the instructor. Others provide van, minivan, and high-technology evaluations. The training that DRSs receive is not uniform; not all specialists have a medical background, not all are occupational therapists, not all are licensed driving instructors, and not all are certified. Clients will not know the right questions to ask, so rehabilitation professionals should match referrals to each client's specific needs.

Not all occupational therapists have the same background and skill level to address driving at the specialist level (OT/DRS). Some are driving instructors, some have a certified driver rehabilitation specialist (CDRS) credential, and some have experience in the field. Currently, no criteria or standards are in place because the field is too new. A variety of services and models exist, but no way exists to compare and rate those services. The AOTA DRS certification for occupational therapists, currently under development, will give occupational therapists criteria for good practices in the area of driver rehabilitation and spur continuing education to help occupational therapists meet those requirements (Finn, 2004). Once AOTA has the OT/DRS certification process in place, occupational therapists providing driver rehabilitation will need this specialty certification to obtain AOTA approval of their role in this field (AOTA, 2005). The OT/DRS certification will help improve the services provided and the skills of providers who meet the criteria. The AOTA certification process will help ensure the quality of driver rehabilitation services offered by occupational therapists. High-quality services are important in a profession that involves a complex task that could kill or injure someone who cannot safely perform the task.

A blending of medical and driver training backgrounds is needed to be a successful DRS. A medical understanding of disabilities of all types and age groups, a background in vision and vision problems, an understanding of cognition and how it affects driving, and the knowledge of the physical requirements for driving are all needed when working with clients with a disability or senior citizens in driving-related evaluation or training. The OT/DRS has these unique skills. For example, clients with left neglect (i.e., an inability to see objects on the left side or impaired left-side vision) can be mistaken for having sloppy driving habits; clients who fixate on an object in front of them to prevent vertigo can seem like they are tailgating; and clients who are not positioned correctly to see out the front window may appear to have poor judgment of where they or their vehicle is in relation to the environment or to have visual deficits. It is all a matter of interpretation, and an OT/DRS will have an appropriate frame of reference. Occupational therapists who are driving specialists also need to understand the rules of the road, safe road performance habits, techniques for controlling the vehicle, adaptive equipment for the vehicle and the client, how to evaluate previous driving skill and knowledge for safe driving after an injury or disability, and how to teach driving to a new driver.

Driving as an IADL

Driving is the ultimate IADL because it is so complex; it requires quick response and smooth, coordinated movement patterns. Skills in vision, cognition, and motor movements are necessary. Some components of driving can be carried out with adaptation, and some cannot. For example, if a client can no longer drive using the right leg because of amputation, he or she can use a left-foot accelerator instead. If a client does not have the neck and trunk range of motion to be able to check blind spots for traffic, then adapted mirrors can be used. People who cannot scan and process information quickly enough to react to the driving environment, however, cannot drive, because this problem cannot be adapted for. Likewise, people who do not have the memory to get to and from a destination are not able to drive safely.

Many people, including rehabilitation professionals, take driving skills for granted because they have driven for a long time. It is an "overlearned" skill that most of us do not think about consciously when in the process of doing it. If we look at the task and what is involved in safe driving, however, we can see that driving is always a complicated and risky proposition. Yet, generalists (e.g., occupational therapists, physical therapists, speech therapists, physicians) often tell clients to resume driving, but to do so carefully: "Ease back into the task, and bring someone with you."

Driving is not easy and can cause injury or death if the driver does not have the skills to succeed and be safe on the road. Bringing family members along does not make driving any safer because they have no way to control the vehicle if something were to go wrong. Many family members have terrible stories of the first drive after a client's illness or injury. In my practice, clients have told me that when they tried driving on their own, they hit a parked car because they hit the accelerator instead of the brake. One woman told me that her husband became so confused by road construction that he could not maintain his lane; another client rolled his vehicle the first time he tried to get onto the freeway because he could not maintain control of the vehicle and check the blind spot. All of these events could have been prevented if a driver evaluation with a trained OT/DRS had taken place.

If a client does not appear to have the skills for driving at the initial evaluation or intervention, rehabilitation specialists often do not address the task, thinking that the client could not possibly drive or even attempt to do so. A client may get behind the wheel, however, even though he or she is still healing and does not yet have safe skills. Clients often cannot assess their skills in an objective manner and do not understand how their illness or injury affects driving, even if it seems obvious to the rehabilitation professional. Clients who need help getting dressed, have an unsteady gait, and cannot safely stow their walker have tried driving. If the team or physician does not directly tell the client not to drive, the client may assume that it must be all right to do so. The client may say "No one told me I could not drive. I still have a license." The physician or team may say "The client should have known not to drive because he cannot walk on his own yet (or is on certain medications, or has not recovered from surgery)."

Rehabilitation Professionals and Driver Rehabilitation Specialists

Many rehabilitation professionals are confused as to whose role it is to address driving and what they need to do to address this skill. Again, it is important that the question of driving be discussed and that the client knows whether he or she should be driving. Consequently, the rehabilitation professional taking the lead on the team should plan to raise the issue with the client.

Once this discussion occurs, it is important to obtain the physician's input on a plan to address driving as the client progresses in rehabilitation. The issue of driving can be raised throughout rehabilitation to show the client the skills he or she may be lacking, the skills he or she is developing, and how the areas on which the client is focusing will affect driving. The client will appreciate the rehabilitation professional for keeping this task in mind as they work together on the more basic ADL areas.

Gathering Information From Multiple Sources

In all areas of practice, it is critical to ask about driving on the initial evaluation. To ensure that driving is not overlooked, the skill should be listed on the occupational therapist's evaluation form as well as on the forms of other professionals (e.g., physical therapists, speech therapists, physicians, social workers, psychologists). If driving is a client goal and the client is not currently in occupational therapy, the rehabilitation professional who includes driving on his or her own evaluation will be able to make a referral at the appropriate time. The occupational therapist to whom the client is referred may be a generalist who may first screen the client's skills or an OT/DRS who can evaluate driving as a whole. Note that generalists sometimes cannot obtain reimbursement for driver evaluation if the client is seen by both the generalist and the specialist.

The rehabilitation professional and team members can gather information in their specific practice areas related to the function of driving. The occupational therapist may ask about where the client usually drove, the physical therapist may ask about how he or she got to the vehicle and if he or she transferred independently, and the physician may ask about any previous accidents or incidents while driving. Getting the conversation going among the rehabilitation team, the client, and the family will help provide the most accurate and complete picture of the occupation of driving in the client's life. By working together, the team can help ensure that the client receives accurate information that is reinforced on many occasions. The client should hear the same information from all members of the rehabilitation team.

Involving the Family or Caregivers

It is important to gather information from the client; it also is important to obtain the client's permission to get information from family and caregivers. It is often hard for clients to analyze their skills objectively and to focus on how those skills relate to the activity of driving. The family and caregivers often are able to see the big picture and provide relatively objective information and examples. This information is important both for letting the client know why he or she cannot drive and for choosing appropriate goals in the driver rehabilitation process.

The client may perceive that if he or she has never had an accident, his or her driving skills have been safe. The family, however, may report that the client has had near misses, caused someone else to get in an accident, or takes 2 hours to get somewhere that is only 10 minutes from the client's home. The client may tell you that he or she only drives to and from the store, bank, and doctor during daylight hours; if the therapist does not talk to the family, he or she may not know that the client lives downtown and cannot avoid busy streets, heavy traffic, and confusing intersections, regardless of the time of day.

In many instances, the rehabilitation team or physician feels that it is the family's role to address driving skills and driving cessation with the client. This is a difficult task, and making it the family's responsibility is not a good idea. Family members often are unable to be objective; moreover, they need to maintain a good relationship with their loved one into the future and not be perceived as the ones who "took my license away." They do not have the ability to analyze their loved one's driving skills from a medical perspective. The family needs support in this process, along with information from the state department of motor vehicles (DMV) on license requirements and procedures for reporting an unsafe driver in that state. The family often appreciates having the objective opinion of the rehabilitation team, the support of working with the team, and resources on how to handle this task further when it is time.

Working with the family benefits the client, the team, and the family itself; the family is an integral part of the rehabilitation team. The family also is more apt to accept the team's recommendations and reinforce them with the client if family members have been part of the process. With the help of the rehabilitation team, the client and his or her family can make some decisions about driving. If too many red flags exist for the client to continue driving, and if family members have the right information, they can be a critical link to getting the unsafe driver off the road. The client who is driving unsafely often is unaware of his or her decline and

Personal Experience 1.1. My Grandfather

My grandfather drove in his neighborhood, but unsafely. After following him home one day, I noticed glaring mistakes he was making that could have led to an accident or injury. Although I had the background to address the problem with my grandfather, I felt it would be best to involve the family and his physician in the process. After discussions with professionals and family members (who provided concrete examples of his driving errors), my grandfather was able to decide on his own that it was time to get someone else to drive him wherever he needed to go.

benefits from examples provided by the family in combination with intervention from the rehabilitation team.

In addition to helping with decision making, gathering information at the occupational therapist generalist level will assist in getting the client the proper referral when he or she is ready. Often the client and family do not know the correct timing for a driver evaluation, whether one is needed, or even what choices are available to them. It is important that the generalist review the evaluation options with the family.

The rehabilitation professional needs to understand the reporting structure for the DMV in the state in which the client hopes to be licensed to drive (see Appendix C). Information must be reported to the correct authority and by the correct person. The regulations vary in each state: Some states place driving restrictions on people who have seizure disorders or diabetes, and others require physicians to report situations in which patients have any disability or injury that may affect driving. Some states recommend reporting but do not require it. Some state DMVs have a medical evaluation unit that may work with DRSs and refer drivers to them; some do not. All states have vision requirements for drivers, but they vary from state to state. Some states issue licenses with restrictions (e.g., limiting drivers to roads with speed limits of 45 mph or lower); other states do not have such provisions.

The rehabilitation professional's understanding of these pieces will help guide the client and family. Professionals can see the statutes for each state in *The Physician's Guide to Assessing and Counseling Older Drivers* (Wang, Kosinski, Schwartzberg, & Shanklin, 2003), a free publication available from the American Medical Association. The publication includes contact information for each state's DMV. (Contact information for all company and product recommendations can be found in Appendix A, "Resources"). The guide was written primarily for physicians, but it provides helpful information for rehabilitation professionals and the physicians on their team.

Simply gathering information places the topic of driving front and center and allows the issues to be addressed in an open, informed manner. The rehabilitation team, with the family, can establish expectations for the client and outline the rehabilitation steps toward the goal of driving or alternative transportation. Overlooking driver rehabilitation can lead to injury or death, which are preventable in the context of appropriate rehabilitation. The rehabilitation team as a whole must address the IADL task of driving.

Discussion of the Task of Driving

Unfortunately, many rehabilitation professionals do not view driving as an activity that they should or can discuss with the client. In my practice as a DRS, other rehabilitation professionals often tell me that they do not feel comfortable discussing the skill of driving with their clients. Their reasons vary: They feel that they cannot answer the client's questions, worry that the client will be so angry that he or she will not come to therapy or work with that therapist, or believe that the family and client should make those decisions separately from rehabilitation. They do not see their responsibility in the matter or understand that they can be a big help to the client and family. They often do not know to whom to refer clients who want to resume driving. Many rehabilitation professionals do not know that occupational therapists can address the activity of driving in general practice or that some occupational therapy specialists are involved in driver rehabilitation.

Mobility—A Meaningful Activity

In the United States, people who are not mobile in the community are not treated as active members of society and do not feel independent. Mobility includes the ability to drive and much more. If a client is not yet ready to drive or needs to give up driving permanently, transportation alternatives must be available. These often are difficult to find, especially in rural areas. The rehabilitation professional's objective outlook on the client's skill sets and choices can help solve the problem.

The client and family often are too close to the situation to find solutions on their own. The assistance that the rehabilitation specialist provides can be of great value to the client and family as they face tough decisions. It is important to provide the client with options for independence instead of limitations. The IADL of driving and community mobility can affect the client's outcomes in all areas, including where to live, what supports are needed, what activities are appropriate, and whether mental health services are needed.

Analysis of Driving Components

Dividing the task of driving into its components will help the rehabilitation professional learn what skills the client needs and what ongoing deficits will affect the task. Each rehabilitation professional should focus on the components that he or she has the ability and training to analyze. For example,

- The physical therapist looks at the client's ability to walk or to use a wheelchair, scooter or cane, or walker; he or she also provides input as to the client's ability to transfer in and out of a vehicle safely.
- The speech and language pathologist examines how the client will communicate in the community and whether his or her level of cognitive abilities permits functioning independently.
- The physician focuses on the client's medical stability and the effects of medications in evaluating the client's ability to go into the community. When the time is appropriate for the client to return to driving, the physician should approve the client's progression to community skills and the activity of driving.
- The recreation specialist weighs in on leisure options that are important to the client and where he or she will want to go for recreation in the community.
- The nurse provides information on the client's bowel and bladder program and the ability to go out for extended periods, given the complexity of the requirements.
- The vocational counselor provides input as to the client's work activities.
- The occupational therapist takes the lead on gathering and compiling information.

Working as a team provides a comprehensive picture of the client and his or her skills for community mobility and driving. It also helps clarify which areas each team member will focus on.

Driving and community mobility are examined in unison on the IADL evaluation. It is important that the client who cannot drive, even for a short period of time, remain independent in the community. Conditions vary and may change from day to day, so alternatives to driving may be necessary for safe community mobility.

This task analysis should be conducted both for driving and for alternative transportation options that will maintain the client's safe independence in the community. Alternative transportation options must be examined using the same task analysis as driving to ensure that the client has the skills to safely use the various options. The bus, train, taxi, subway, and disabled persons' transportation all require specific skills. For example, to use a bus the client must be able to read and follow a schedule, be able to get on and off the bus safely, and behave in a safe manner while on the vehicle. If the client uses a taxi or transportation for people with disabilities, he or she must be able to plan for when the ride is needed, call ahead and schedule the ride, and be able to get in and out of the vehicle safely. For some modes of transportation, clients need to be flexible in their schedule because the wait can be an hour or more in some areas, and transportation is not always on time. The rehabilitation professional must understand and divide driving and alternative transportation skills into their components. The best option is the one that the client can use safely, given his or her skills, and that meets the goal for community involvement.

The task of driving should be analyzed not only for the actual driving skills required but also for the client's ability to access the car in any weather he or she may encounter; to get in and out of the car; to stow disability-related equipment and other cargo; and to handle associated skills, such as obtaining fuel. If the rehabilitation professional fully analyzes the task and its components, then it will be easier to talk to the client about driving as an IADL and his or her skills in relation to this task.

Summary and Conclusion

Community mobility is not just for people with disabilities. As we age, we should plan for and learn to use alternative options so that we are well versed in how to use them before doing so becomes necessary. Driving is not always the best way to be independent with community mobility, depending on alternatives available in that area. Examples of solutions to transportation that do not involve driving include living in a large city that has good public transportation or in an apartment complex that provides its own transportation. In cities such as Washington, DC, New York, and Chicago, the subway and train systems often are cheaper and easier options than driving. Public transportation is a safer option when road conditions are bad or during rush hour. Local social clubs or churches may have volunteers who provide transportation to people who cannot drive. People often hire drivers—sometimes a college student looking for extra money. Many unique and creative options can be identified if the right team is looking at these skills.

All rehabilitation professionals must play an active role in placing driving on the ADL and IADL evaluation checklist and ensuring that driving is not overlooked in the rehabilitation process. They also must take an active role in identifying alternative transportation options for the client. All rehabilitation professionals will have clients or client families who raise the issue of driving in an effort to find answers or resources. In addressing driving skills, rehabilitation professionals will have more protection legally if they stay within their skill level than if they do not address driving at all with the client.

Knowing the limitations of one's professional skills is critical to appropriately handling driving and community mobility for individual clients. All professionals must value their skill level and that of specialists so that they can work together to provide the best resources and outcome for each client (Pellerito, 2005). Analyzing driving as an IADL clarifies the rehabilitation professional's role. Driving involves the very activities rehabilitation specialists work on each day, modified to the performance of the driving task. It is a high-level skill that requires integration of multiple skill sets to be performed safely. It is the ultimate rehabilitation goal for safe, independent function in life and community. Driving should not be the forgotten IADL; rather, it should be the IADL that is addressed with every client, no matter what the age or disability.

References

American Occupational Therapy Association. (2002). Occupational therapy practice framework: Domain and process. *American Journal of Occupational Therapy, 56,* 609–639.

American Occupational Therapy Association. (2005). Driving and community mobility: Statement. *American Journal of Occupational Therapy, 59,* 666–670

Davis, E. S. (2003, January 13). Defining roles in driving. *OT Practice,* pp. 15–18.

Finn, J. (2004). *Driving evaluation and retraining programs: A report of good practices.* Bethesda, MD: American Occupational Therapy Association.

Hopewell, C. A. (2002). Driving assessment issues for practicing clinicians. *Journal of Head Trauma Rehabilitation, 17,* 48–61.

Kaplan, W. (1999). The occupation of driving: Legal and ethical issues. *Physical Disabilities Special Interest Section Quarterly, 22*(3), 1–4.

Pellerito, J. M., Jr. (2005). *Driver rehabilitation and community mobility: Principles and practice.* Chapter 6 authors Carol J. Wheatley, Joseph M. Pellerito, Jr., Susan Redepenning, page 105. Philadelphia: Elsevier Mosby.

Pierce, S. L., & Hunt, L. A. (2004). *Driving and community mobility for older adults: Occupational therapy roles* [Online Course]. Bethesda, MD: American Occupational Therapy Association.

Stav, W. B. (2004). *Driving rehabilitation: A guide for assessment and intervention.* San Antonio, TX: PsychCorp.

Tewfik, D. B., & Sabel, R. (2004, November 8). Testimony advocacy in action. *OT Practice,* pp. 13–16.

Wang, C. C., Kosinski, C. J., Schwartzberg, J. G., & Shanklin, A. V. (2003). *The physician's guide to assessing and counseling older drivers.* Chicago: American Medical Association & National Highway Traffic Safety Administration.

Wheatley, C. J., Pellerito, J. M., Jr., & Redepenning, S. (2005). *The clinical evaluation.* In J. M. Pellerito (Ed.), *Driver rehabilitation and community mobility: Principles and practice* (pp. 103–164). St. Louis, MO: Elsevier Mosby.

The Occupational Therapist's Role in Driver Rehabilitation

The occupational therapist's involvement in driving is an expanded practice area that has received much attention and focus in recent years. The American Occupational Therapy Association's (AOTA's) work to promote driving as an instrumental activity of daily living (IADL) has provided a new awareness of the specialty in the fields of occupational therapy and rehabilitation (AOTA, 2002).

Occupational therapist generalists are in a key position to take the lead on the rehabilitation team for identifying and handling driver rehabilitation, referring to a specialist as needed. The generalist has the medical knowledge, skill analysis, and focus on activities of daily living (ADLs) that are critical to this task. The generalist takes the lead to address the components of driving, to work on skills that affect the ability to drive, and to refer the client to the driver rehabilitation specialist (DRS) at the appropriate time.

The generalist must work within his or her scope of practice and funding reimbursement. If driving is one of several skills addressed in the IADL plan, Medicare or insurance often will cover the clinical screening and treatment sessions. If driving is the only goal for the client, however, referral to an occupational therapist driver rehabilitation specialist (OT/DRS) may be most appropriate and may actually save the patient time and money for the needed service.

It is important for the rehabilitation team leader to start the driver rehabilitation process and keep it focused. The occupational therapist is a resource for driving issues for the rehabilitation team. Educating the team on addressing the skill of driving is an important part of the occupational therapy generalist's role; no client should fall through the cracks where this task is concerned.

To say that everyone with a particular type of disability should not drive is not the right solution, even if it may be safer. Such generalizations often happen when a driving program does not specialize in the areas of aging or disability or when the evaluator does not understand the purpose of a driver evaluation. It also happens when the driving evaluator or instructor does not understand the unique medical issues of a client or is unfamiliar with how aging or the client's disability may affect driving. Even if the program uses a DRS, if that person does not have the right practice skills and driving background, clients will not have their needs met. Many people over- or underemphasize how age and disability may affect driving, but only a driver evaluation can determine a person's ability to drive safely. Performance on all components of the evaluation—the clinical and the road portions—should be the determining factor in whether a client returns to driving.

Only occupational therapists who are DRSs should complete driver evaluations, which consist of a clinical assessment and an on-the-road driving assessment. States have different rules about who can practice in the area of driver rehabilitation. The state may require the OT/DRS to be a licensed or certified driving instructor, may require that he or she work for a driving school, and may have requirements for the amount and type of insurance needed to practice in the field of driver evaluation and training. This additional training and licensing can ensure that the OT/DRS has the combination of skills critical to the job: occupational therapy combined with an understanding of techniques for teaching driving. The Association for Driver Rehabilitation Specialists (ADED) offers certification that can be completed once the occupational therapist has a certain amount of experience (currently 1 year of full-time occupational therapy experience or an equivalent number of hours over a 3-year period; see www.aded.net). An OT/DRS can establish a driver rehabilitation practice in many ways, but the first steps are to know what the state requires, what types of clients will be served, and what types of deficits the client base will have.

Driver rehabilitation fits perfectly with occupational therapy. To analyze driving, the context of the activity must be evaluated in conjunction with information on the client and his or her disability. Occupational therapists are trained in activity analysis and in understanding the impact of visual deficits on function, cognition, and physical skills. All the

Personal Experience 2.1. Woman With Diabetes

A client with diabetes was fitted for and trained to use a left-foot accelerator because she could not drive with her right leg. However, the health of the left leg was not taken into consideration. Her husband felt her left-leg driving was not smooth, and within months the left leg deteriorated and was eventually amputated. If a medical assessment had been done right away, it would have been determined that the left leg was not an option for driving because that leg did not have good sensation and had poor circulation.

The client was referred to me, and I assessed her clinically. She had good day vision, poor night vision, good sensation in her upper extremities, and intact cognitive skills. She quickly adapted to hand controls, and she noticed right away that they were a much safer option for her than the left-foot accelerator had been. The medical knowledge that occupational therapists have, along with a driver rehabilitation background, is needed to clearly analyze these types of conditions. Had this client initially seen an OT/DRS, she would have been a candidate for hand controls from the start. She would have been safer, and she would have saved money. As it was, she ended up paying for two driver evaluations, installation and removal of a left-foot accelerator, and installation of hand controls.

occupational therapist's skills and training are needed to perform an accurate analysis of the IADL of driving.

Analyzing driving and performance for a person with a disability requires a medical background; it is what the OT/DRS uses to properly evaluate and interpret a driver evaluation. It is helpful if the OT/DRS has experience working with a variety of disabilities and age groups. The OT/DRS must be able to analyze the discrete skills that are needed for driving and help the client integrate those skills.

Many professionals who work as DRSs are not occupational therapists; however, those who are occupational therapists are best suited to manage the driver evaluation and training process for clients with medical conditions. Such OT/DRSs may work with other driving services, such as driving instructors or driving educators, but it is important that the occupational therapist who has specialized in driving take the lead in deciding the best avenue in pursuing driving for the client, including determining which type of professional would best suit the client's needs. The driving instructor or educator who works with the client should be selected according to the client's unique needs and medical diagnosis. For example, a client with an amputation as the result of a farm accident but who does not have any other impairment may be well served by a driving instructor who has had training in the controls that client needs. A client who has an amputation as the result of diabetes, for example, may have complex medical problems. The occupational therapist will need to carefully screen that person before determining whether someone other than a DRS could meet his or her needs. The occupational therapist has an understanding of how diabetes can affect bodily functions, vision, circulation, and cognition. Those effects need to be understood to determine whether the client is a candidate for safe driving, what type of equipment will be best for his or her needs, and what type of training will be needed.

Occupational therapists who want to become DRSs must have the right skills and qualifications to meet the job demands (Glomstad, 2005). The practice area of driving is receiving much attention, but one risk of the higher profile is that people will get into the profession too quickly, before they have the right skills or obtain the needed training. If the occupational therapist does not have broad rehabilitation skills (i.e., experience in a variety of settings with a variety of age groups and diagnoses), it is important to gain those skills before going into a driving practice. The other alternative is to confine the driving program to a specialized area that is consistent with the occupational therapist's skills. For example, if the occupational therapist has extensive background with the geriatric population but does not have experience with other age groups or disabilities, his or her driving practice would do best to specialize in the needs of senior citizens.

The AOTA expert panel on driving recommended that occupational therapists who want to specialize in driver rehabilitation should have at least 3 years of rehabilitation experience along with continuing education and specialized education in advanced practice skills of vision and cognition. The panel recommended that, to obtain a DRS specialization, an occupational therapist should have proficiency in the areas of vision, cognition, physical skills, safe driving skills, and teaching methods for driver's training. After practicing for several years, the occupational therapist can receive further specialized education and apply activity analysis to the task of driving. Again, although other rehabilitation professionals could pursue the profession of DRS, the occupational therapist has perhaps the best foundation for this field.

Many OT/DRSs include the expertise of driving educators and driving instructors on their team. Team members need to understand the strengths and limitations of each client so that the right professional with the right training is matched with the client. The blending of both professions—occupational therapy DRS and driver education or instruction—can be an effective model.

It is critical that the occupational therapist generalist and OT/DRS understand the state laws and regulations governing driving. They need to know who takes the lead in that state for reporting (i.e., the physician, family, or other parties) and what training or level of expertise is required for occupational therapists practicing in the area of driving in that state. Each state has a department that administers these regulations; often it is the department of motor vehicles (DMV). The DMV most often does not differentiate between what is expected from a driving instructor and what is expected of a DRS. In fact, many DMVs do not know that the specialized profession of driver rehabilitation exists.

Occupational Therapist Generalist's Client Interview

Occupational therapists use screening tools, or assessments, in the evaluation process to determine whether a client needs occupational therapy services. These tools include questions about ADLs and IADLs. The initial evaluation includes an interview in addition to the performance assessment of the skills in question. During this initial interview, much information can be gathered on the client's past and present functioning and what areas need to be addressed. The interview allows the occupational therapist to obtain a full medication profile of the client and how he or she is managing ADLs and IADLs. If the client has not addressed dressing, cannot get around in the home safely, or demonstrates severe memory loss, he or she is not ready to focus on driving. The initial evaluation gives the team information to explain to the client why driving is (or is not) being addressed.

Predriving Clinical Screen and Clinical Evaluation

The predriving clinical screen and the clinical evaluation are the tools that occupational therapists use to further the client's driving goals. They are used to educate the client, the client's family, the team, and the physician about the client's status and the appropriateness of referring the client for an on-the-road evaluation. The occupational therapist generalist uses a predriving screen to evaluate driving readiness or appropriateness of driving as an IADL task. For example, some patients no longer drive or rely on alternative transportation and do not plan on driving in the future. The OT/DRS uses the clinical test to gather information to plan the on-the-road assessment and develop a list of the client's strengths and limitations.

The predriving clinical screen is a recurring part of the entire therapy process, not just a one-time test to determine client readiness for driving. It does not indicate whether a client can or cannot drive. Rather, it is a process that starts with the occupational therapist generalist from the initial occupational therapy evaluation (Pellerito & Davis, 2005).

All areas of occupational therapy practice have a role in the screening phase, beginning with identifying driving as one of many IADL goals. No battery of tests has shown direct ability to predict driving. Although various assessments provide information about a client's skills, only the on-the-road assessment can conclusively tell whether a person is safe to drive or not (Stav, 2004). The predriving clinical screen is never performed to confirm or rule out driving (Pellerito & Davis, 2005). Driving is a complex, high-level task that changes from day to day for everyone, for internal and external reasons. For this reason, it is difficult to evaluate driving without an on-road assessment. "One of the best ways to determine [whether] an individual is capable of performing the complex task of driving is to give a behind-the-wheel assessment" (Stav, 2004, p. 7). As a result, it is vital to use an OT/DRS when it is time to evaluate driving.

During the screen, the goal of driving is raised with the client and rehabilitation team and the client's driving-related skills are assessed. For example, the client may have good use of his or her right arm and right leg (allowing him or her to operate the vehicle once in it) but poor left-side balance (making it difficult to enter and exit the vehicle safely). The client may have decreased cognitive processing speed or visual deficits that must be addressed before dealing with the potential to drive. Providing quick screens during ordinary occupational therapy sessions reaffirms the goal of driving for the client, the team, and the family. It helps motivate the client and add value to the rehabilitation process.

Screening the client entails reviewing the occupational therapist evaluation results and highlighting which skills will help in driving (strengths) and which skills related to driving are needed (deficits). Reevaluation, which includes readministration of assessments and other tests, may take place at regular intervals in the occupational therapy process. If the client is unable to drive or will never be able to drive, the goal then becomes community mobility (see Chapter 3).

The tests that screen for driving skills are the tools clinicians use every day in therapy. For example, range of motion

Figure 2.1. Dynavision is a useful screening tool, both for driving and in therapy, to address an individual's visual scanning ability.

Source: Courage Center, Minneapolis, MN. Used with permission.

is measured using a goniometer; it is important to make sure that the client has the active range of motion to drive with either normal or adapted controls. Manual muscle testing, in which the client holds his or her limbs in a certain position and the therapist applies pressure to see whether the client can maintain the hold, also is an indicator of whether the client will be able to drive.

Other routine tests include testing sensation (e.g., hot/cold, sharp/dull) in upper and lower extremities, screening for visual deficits (e.g., eye charts, confrontation testing), and short-term memory tests. Because no standardized tests predict driving ability, referral to a specialist ultimately is needed for task-sensitive testing (Stav, 2004).

Other equipment options that occupational therapist generalists use in the clinic are the Dynavision and Useful Field of View (DRSs do not always use these tools, however, because they are expensive, are not portable, and have components that relate to many ADLs other than driving). The Dynavision (Figure 2.1) is a wall-mounted unit with red buttons that light up; the client must then touch the buttons as they light up. The unit is adjustable for a sitting or standing position. The device has different modes that assess visual processing speed and divided attention. Results on the Dynavision have been correlated with safe driving (Klavora, Gaskovski, Martin, Forsyth, Heslegrave, Young, et al., 1995).

The Useful Field of View (Figure 2.2) is a computer-based assessment and training tool that assesses how clients use their vision and teaches them to build deficient skills. The device consists of a variety of slides; the client looks for an object on each slide, tries to remember what was seen, and indicates the object on the touch screen of the computer when asked. The task becomes progressively more difficult in terms of background information that must be filtered and speed with which the client must complete the task. Results from the Useful Field of View correlate with safe driving (Mestre, 2001). The Useful Field of View also has slides that can be used in occupational therapy intervention.

Some assessment tools correlate with driving ability and are used on a regular basis for driver evaluation; they should be completed by a specialist trained to administer the test—someone who understands the implications of the results for driving and can analyze the results of on-the-road performance to obtain a complete picture. The specialist has the skills to analyze the assessment tools and understand that they are not definitive but simply augment the on-the-road evaluation. The assessment tools help the specialist plan the on-the-road evaluation.

Many clinical occupational therapist generalists work closely with specialists and sometimes administer correlative tests in preparation for referral. In such cases, the generalist and specialist must understand their respective roles and what information from the assessments is important to planning the evaluation. It is helpful when a relationship of training is established so that the generalist comes to understand which driving tasks the assessments are analyzing, how the client's disability will play a factor in driving, and what value the on-the-road evaluation will provide. It is important to not treat the assessment tools as more than they truly are or can be.

Ideally, rehabilitation professionals working with clients who want to drive are using the following model:

- Client sees an occupational therapist generalist, who screens the client for potential ability to drive.
- The generalist either asks the client's physician to refer the client to an OT/DRS for further evaluation or informs the client that he or she is probably not ready to drive yet.
- If the client is not ready to pursue driver rehabilitation yet, the generalist designs a rehabilitation plan that includes driving as an eventual goal. Community mobility options are explored.
- If the client is referred to the OT/DRS, the OT/DRS conducts a clinical and on-the-road evaluation of the client's driving ability. If the client has skill deficits that can be remedied with occupational therapy, the OT/DRS refers the client back to the occupational therapist generalist. If the deficits can be remedied with equipment, the OT/DRS works with the client to obtain the equipment and train the client in its use.

If the generalist does not value the on-the-road evalua-

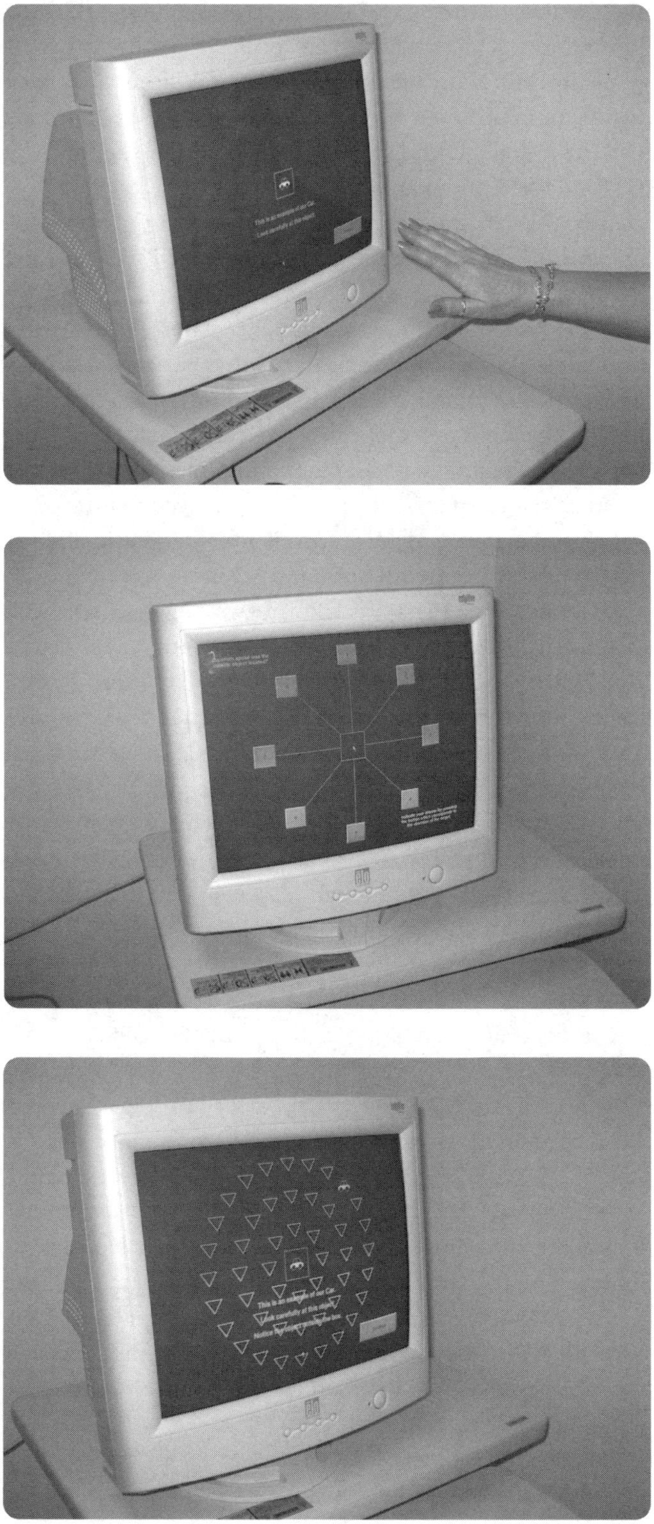

Figure 2.2. Useful Field of View is a computer-based screening tool that tests visual memory, visual processing speed, visual attention, and visual recall. It can be used as a screening tool or clinical assessment and has slides that can be used in treatment.

Source: Courage Center, Minneapolis, MN. Used with permission.

tion, this model will not be successful. The model of using the OT/DRS instead of other paraprofessionals in the area of driving is that the OT/DRS can understand the effects of the medical aspects of the client's disability, illness, medications, and secondary conditions on the task of driving, the function of driving for that client, and the demands of the driving activity. Consequently, the OT/DRS is in a good position to determine whether the client can drive safely. The OT/DRS uses clinical screening to get the needed medical information, strengths, and areas of limitation related to driving before analyzing on-the-road driving ability. This information allows the OT/DRS to plan the on-the-road evaluation to test the client's limitations and determine whether the client can compensate for those limitations safely. If the driving evaluator lacks this level of understanding, the on-the-road assessment may not be safe: It may challenge the client too quickly or be beyond what the client can handle, even with the driving instructor. The on-the-road evaluation may miss critical pieces of information because the driving instructor did not understand the need to test those areas or did not notice unsafe compensation strategies (e.g., the driving instructor may not notice that the client is using other vehicles to gauge where the car is in the lane). The OT/DRS's knowledge permits an accurate, safe analysis of driving skill for a variety of disabilities, age groups, and situations (Pellerito & Davis, 2005). If this model is understood and valued by occupational therapist generalists, they will refer their clients to an OT/DRS because they can explain how the referral will benefit the client.

The generalist also needs to understand the complexity of the driving task so that he or she does not think too lightly about allowing the patient to return to driving. Otherwise, the generalist will make recommendations regarding driving or add restrictions without a road evaluation. This approach is too risky for the client, his or her family, and others on the road. Occupational therapists do not send clients home to live on their own without evaluation of kitchen safety, dressing skills, and ability to shower; we cannot send someone back to driving until that, too, has been evaluated in the context of safety.

Driving can severely injure or kill someone. Family members do not have the training or equipment to keep the driver and passengers safe when riding with their loved one. If the client has any deficits that may affect driving, family members often say they do not want to be the first one to go with them in case something happens they cannot control. Occupational therapist generalists must be careful not to minimize how the client's first driving experience might go or to expect family members to ride with the client. At the very least, the generalist should use the findings on the predriving clinical screen to help the physician see the client's strengths and limitations regarding driving, ask the physician to review all medications as they relate to driving, and ensure that the physician has the resources to make a referral to an OT/DRS if one is needed.

Most driver rehabilitation services are private, and the client will have to pay for the service unless he or she qualifies for state vocational services funding or has a nontraditional funding source (e.g., worker's compensation, waivers that some states provide for non-Medicare-covered services, school services, social clubs such as the Lions Club or the Rotary Club).

If the occupational therapist generalist and rehabilitation team value the driver evaluation and what it provides, they will be able to help the client see the need to complete the service. Many clients who are referred to an OT/DRS never make an appointment: The client or physician may not see the need, the state may not have any rules around completing this type of evaluation, or no one may be tracking whether the client made the call. The generalist and specialist can help physicians understand the value of driver rehabilitation services and encourage them to advocate for the service. They also can work with the team to follow up with the client following referral.

Importance of Acquiring Specialized Training

The profession of driver rehabilitation is inherently risky, and if the occupational therapist is not trained properly, the level of risk is greatly increased. It is therefore of utmost importance that the OT/DRS obtain the best credentials and training possible, following all state requirements. The OT/DRS is the most important asset or tool in the driver evaluation process. His or her understanding of the client, the disability, and the driving task is critical. The ability to analyze the task of driving and break it down into its components is fundamental to an accurate driver evaluation (i.e., one that combines clinical and on-the-road evaluations).

Training to become an OT/DRS should take place in stages and should not be rushed. It will vary somewhat according to the occupational therapist's experience. The generalist's training should begin with learning the screening process and include direct work with an OT/DRS so that the trainee can see how the screening information is used in the next step of driver rehabilitation. The trainee should obtain continuing education in the areas of vision (e.g., low vision, visual difficulties after brain injury) and cognition (e.g., executive skills dysfunction, memory deficits related to Alzheimer's disease, dementia). The importance of learning the driving instructor role should not be minimized. Good books and teaching materials are available (see Appendix A). A mentorship with an OT/DRS who is a licensed driving instructor or who has been trained in how to teach driving will help the generalist who wants to transition to an OT/DRS role. The Association for Driver Rehabilitation Specialists (ADED) and the American Occupational Therapy Association (AOTA) offer resources for generalists who want to obtain DRS training (see Appendix A).

It is important for occupational therapist generalists to take the time to develop skills in a variety of age and disability groups and in multiple areas of rehabilitation before moving to the next level of driver rehabilitation. Obtaining appropriate training, credentials, and mentorship before stepping out as an OT/DRS is vital to the success of the occupational therapist, program, and clients. Not developing the appropriate skills can kill or injure a client.

Occupational therapists who are working as OT/DRSs for a licensed driving school may be required by state law to complete a specific number of hours of training with a licensed driving instructor and pass written and on-the-road tests of driving instructor skills. If a state does not have those requirements, it is still a good idea to seek this type of training if it is available. The OT/DRS should have an instructor's knowledge and ability to evaluate and teach driving. Being an OT/DRS requires all the skills of a seasoned therapist and the skills of a driving instructor.

OT/DRS Driver Evaluation

The driver evaluation is conducted by the OT/DRS and contains two parts: (1) the clinical assessment and (2) the on-the-road assessment.

The clinical assessment comprises tools that measure vision, cognition, and physical skills as they relate to driving. It assists the OT/DRS in identifying the client's skills for and limitations regarding driving. The OT/DRS then can use this information to plan for the on-the-road evaluation to ensure that all skills are examined and the best environment is used. The clinical evaluation rarely results in a determination that the client is unable to drive unless the results prohibit driving under state regulations.

Clinical assessment tools vary greatly by site and by OT/DRS. This section reviews some commonly used assessments. Note that no standardized assessment tool covers driving; however, this situation may change as more research is completed in this field.

Medical History and Profile

The OT/DRS should consider any medical conditions and associated medications that may affect the client's ability to drive. The client's physician should review a list of the

Personal Experience 2.2. Training to Become an OT/DRS

Before becoming an OT/DRS, I had 13 years of occupational therapy experience in rehabilitation settings, including hospitals, long-term-care facilities, and outpatient and inpatient rehabilitation programs. My clients had ranged from ages 2 to 98 with a variety of disabilities. I had taken many vision courses over my career, including courses on low vision and brain injury. I also had taken continuing education courses on cognition, congenital disabilities, learning disabilities, mental health disorders, spinal cord injury, and stroke care management. I took an advanced driving course in the state of Minnesota and attended continuing education coursework on vehicle modification from vendors in my state and at the Association for Driver Rehabilitation Specialists (ADED).

Along the way, I worked in a facility whose driving program used licensed driving instructors. The occupational therapy department was separate from the driving program at first and did not provide any input or referrals to the driving program. Understanding the needs of the staff occupational therapists, I worked hard with the driving instructors to develop a team process whereby the occupational therapists completed the clinical assessment and were involved in the outcome of the total evaluation.

In the course of this team process, I completed several ride-alongs, during which I was in the back seat while the driving instructor completing the road evaluation was in the front seat. This experience helped me officiate the road evaluation and see how the clinical assessment led to the success of the on-the-road testing. It also taught me to appreciate the importance of getting the proper training before being in the front seat. The safety and control of the vehicle are crucial, as is having the medical background and understanding to provide the best on-the-road testing environment.

The more I worked in this team process, the better the understanding I had of the role I could play as the occupational therapist. After working in the occupational therapist/driving instructor model for 3 years, I left to become a consultant OT/DRS for a driver rehabilitation company.

To become an OT/DRS, I knew I needed to first become trained in driving instruction and become a licensed driving instructor. My state required 40 hours of training with a licensed driving instructor, passage of a 100-question essay test about driving instruction, and a 2-hour on-the-road assessment of my training skills. In addition, I read everything I could find online that was related to driving instruction, purchased several books on teaching driving, and completed ADED's certified driver rehabilitation specialty (CDRS) certification before I started completing on-the-road evaluations as an OT/DRS. I taught several teenagers of my friends so I could first learn how to teach without adaptation. I also made sure I found an experienced licensed driving instructor with a defensive driving background to mentor me.

The skills I gained through years in occupational therapy practice have allowed me to complete the best possible evaluations for my clients and reduce my inherent risk. Every day, I use my full range of occupational therapy skills and my knowledge as a driving instructor. The blending of the two fields has given me the skills to analyze a client's potential related to driving.

I have now practiced as an OT/DRS for about 4 years. During that time, I have worked extensively on my skills, taking driving instruction and association-sponsored classes. I also have attended courses offered by adaptive equipment vendors to understand how the adaptations to vehicles are completed and what is possible with various vehicles.

client's medications and assess their potential effects on driving. The client's limb length and use of extremities need to be analyzed so that the OT/DRS knows whether the client will need adaptive equipment such as pedal extenders, hand controls, left-foot accelerator, or accessory controls. The client's driver's license number and the status of the license should be documented to determine whether the client is currently a licensed driver and, if so, in what state.

Social History

It is important to gather information on the client's past driving skills and habits, including the function driving served, any driving restrictions, the driving history (e.g., accidents, traffic tickets), and any problems that the client or client's family noticed prior to this current medical condition. It is important to ask both the client and the family about any accidents or moving violations the client has had over the past 5 years. The OT/DRS should ask the client whether he or she uses or has used alternative transportation options to ascertain his or her skills in this area. Finding out where the client lives and spends time in the community will help identify possible transportation options if driving is not possible temporarily or permanently.

Vision Assessments

Safe and defensive driving requires the use of basic and complex visual skills. The evolution of driver visual performance standards, testing procedures, and periodic evaluations has been guided by a clear need to ensure public safety in a task so obviously dependent on vision (Decina & Staplin, 1993). It is important, then, to assess visual skills and identify visual limitations in the clinical testing. The basic visual skills that need to be assessed are scanning, acuity (especially distance), peripheral vision, contrast sensitivity, depth perception, and accommodation and convergence. If deficits are identified, the client may need to see an eye specialist before proceeding with the on-the-road assessment. If the client does not meet the state vision requirements for driving, a referral to an eye specialist will be needed for vision correction.[1]

The following methods can help assess vision:

- *Optec vision testers.* These portable vision testers can be set up with a variety of slide packages and can test for relevant vision characteristics such as visual acuity (near and distance), peripheral vision, depth perception, color discrimination, sign recognition, and contrast sensitivity. They are available through Stereo Optical Company.
- *Confrontational assessment.* This testing is completed with the therapist seated in front of the client. The only equipment a therapist usually uses is a dowel or pencil with a bright eraser or object on the end of it. The therapist has the client hold his or her head still and move the eyes to follow the dowel as the therapist moves it in front of the client, using set patterns that test vision muscles and eye movements. The therapist checks for weakness and watches coordination of the eyes and eye alignment; he or she is looking for smooth, coordinated eye movements and to see that the client can visually attend to the object. Anything unusual (e.g., jerky eye movements) is documented. Confrontational assessment can test for peripheral vision: The client looks at the therapist's nose, and the therapist moves an object from behind the client and asks him or her to state when it comes into his or her visual field. Ocular motor control (e.g., saccades) can be tested by asking the client to look from one object to another while the therapist watches to make sure the client can accurately locate the objects each time. To test convergence, the therapist brings the pencil toward the client's nose and asks him or her to state when the object becomes blurry; the therapist watches to ensure that the eyes converge equally. To test accommodation, the therapist slowly moves the pencil away from the client (toward the therapist) and observes whether the client's eyes can follow the movement. The tests are screens, not specific measures, but they are nevertheless a useful way to assess for deficits that should be evaluated more closely by an eye specialist.
- *Snellen eye chart.* This is the standard vision chart used by optometrists. The chart is used to measure visual distance acuity (i.e., how the person sees into the distance). One chart is designed for viewing at 20 feet, and one is designed for viewing at 10 feet (when space is tight). It is important to use the Snellen eye chart according to the instructions, which specify the proper room lighting and distance between the chart and the client. Many states have laws that require a certain amount of distance visual acuity to obtain a driver's license. If any deficits are noted in visual acuity, especially if it will affect a client's ability to drive in that state or jeopardize safe driving, a referral to an optometrist or eye specialist is needed. The Snellen eye chart is available from a variety of sources.
- *Contrast sensitivity chart.* The Pelli–Robson contrast chart is a portable, letter-based, wall-mounted chart that, like the Snellen chart, requires proper illumination to be used effectively (Pelli, Robson, & Wilkins, 1988). The size of the letters and their contrast (i.e., how dark or light the letters appear) vary. The client begins by reading the larger, darker letters and then goes on to the smaller, lighter letters. The chart measures the contrast necessary for the client to see objects adequately. Contrast sensitivity is needed in driving to see objects in low light, at night, or against similar backgrounds (e.g., a gray car on a gray road on a gray day). The chart is available from Richmond Products.

Visual–Perceptual Testing

- The *Motor-Free Visual Perception Test* (MVPT; Colarusso & Hammill, 2002) measures components of visual skills without the need for a verbal or motor response. It assesses visual recognition, visual closure, visual memory, figure ground, form consistency, and visual matching skills; can be conducted at a tabletop; and is timed. This assessment tool, which takes 20 to 30 minutes, does not require speaking; the client can use a finger or other method to point to or look at the correct answer to the question. The client is scored on speed of response and accuracy of answers. One study correlated this tool with driving skill, but it used the older MVPT, which uses a different layout (Bouska & Kwatny, 1982). Occupational therapists are encouraged to read the study to learn how the MVPT was administered and find out more about the

[1]Contact information for all company and product recommendations can be found in Appendix A.

results (Owen & Stressel, 1999). The MVPT is available from Pro-Ed and AOTA.

- *Trials A and B,* a two-part, pencil-and-paper test, measures the client's ability to remember and follow specific verbal directions and assesses for visual attention, visual search, mental flexibility, and speed of processing information. Part A measures the ability to follow directions and visual scanning speed and accuracy. Part B measures divided attention along with visual processing speed. It is important that the evaluator follow the standardized protocol (Pellerito, 2005). The tool has been overused in clinics by rehabilitation professionals to the point that clients recognize the test and remember how to do it, so it is best used by the OT/DRS, not a generalist, to prevent future overuse. It can be ordered from Reitan Neuropsychology Laboratory.
- *CLOX* is a tool for assessing executive planning that some OT/DRSs are using instead of or in addition to Trials A and B. It is useful when the client has completed Trials A and B several times and may have memorized that tool. In CLOX 1, the client is first asked to draw a clock from memory. In CLOX 2, the client copies a clock that is presented to him or her. This tool is especially helpful in working with clients with Alzheimer's disease or other dementia (Royall, Cordes, & Polk, 1998).

Cognitive Assessments

The following methods can help assess cognition:

- The *Short Blessed Test* (Walls, 1999) asks questions about familiar information, has the client repeat information to the tester immediately and again after a few minutes, and has the client perform mental manipulations involving numbers and months of the year. This test is part of the Mobility Assessment Program (MAP) test battery. The test is available to copy through the Mobility Assessment Program at Maryville University, St. Louis, Missouri.
- The *Cognitive Linguistic Quick Test* (CLQT; Helm-Estabrooks, 2001) is a 30- to 40-minute assessment of five domains of cognitive function: attention, spatial skills, language, memory, and executive function. The test was designed for clients who have cognitive deficits as a result of a cerebral vascular accident, acquired brain injury, or dementia. It is available to order from Harcourt Assessment.

Physical Assessments

The following methods can help assess the client's physical capabilities:

- *AAA reaction timer.* This tool is no longer available, but if a facility has one, it can be used to measure accelerator-to-brake reaction time (see Figure 2.3). Note that the accelerator and brake pedals for this test do not have the same pressure and are not spaced the same as in a vehicle. The results can provide preliminary information to help guide the road evaluation, but they do not simulate actual accelerator-to-brake reaction time.

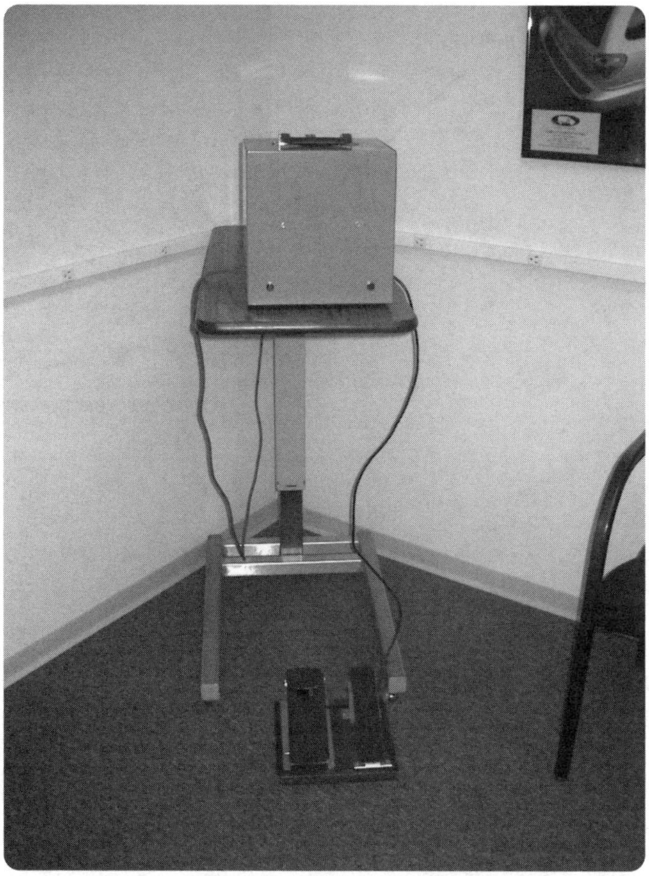

Figure 2.3. The AAA's brake reaction timer is no longer manufactured, but the device is still used as a diagnostic tool in many clinics.

Source: Courage Center, Minneapolis, MN. Used with permission.

- *Clinical reaction timer.* This new tool (Figure 2.4A, B, and C) uses a gas pedal, brake pedal, and red and green lights to measure gas-to-brake reaction time. The company developed norms for male and female reaction times. This product is available from Delta Integration, Inc.
- *In-vehicle reaction timer.* This tool, which is used in the evaluation vehicle, measures gas-to-brake reaction time for speeds from 25 to 35 miles per hour (mph) while the client drives in an empty parking lot. One brand is available from Vericom Computers.
- *Range of motion.* Measuring range of motion of the neck and extremities is important to ensure that the client has the physical skills to drive. If the client has decreases in range of motion, he or she may need adaptive equipment. If the client is very short or very tall, limb length

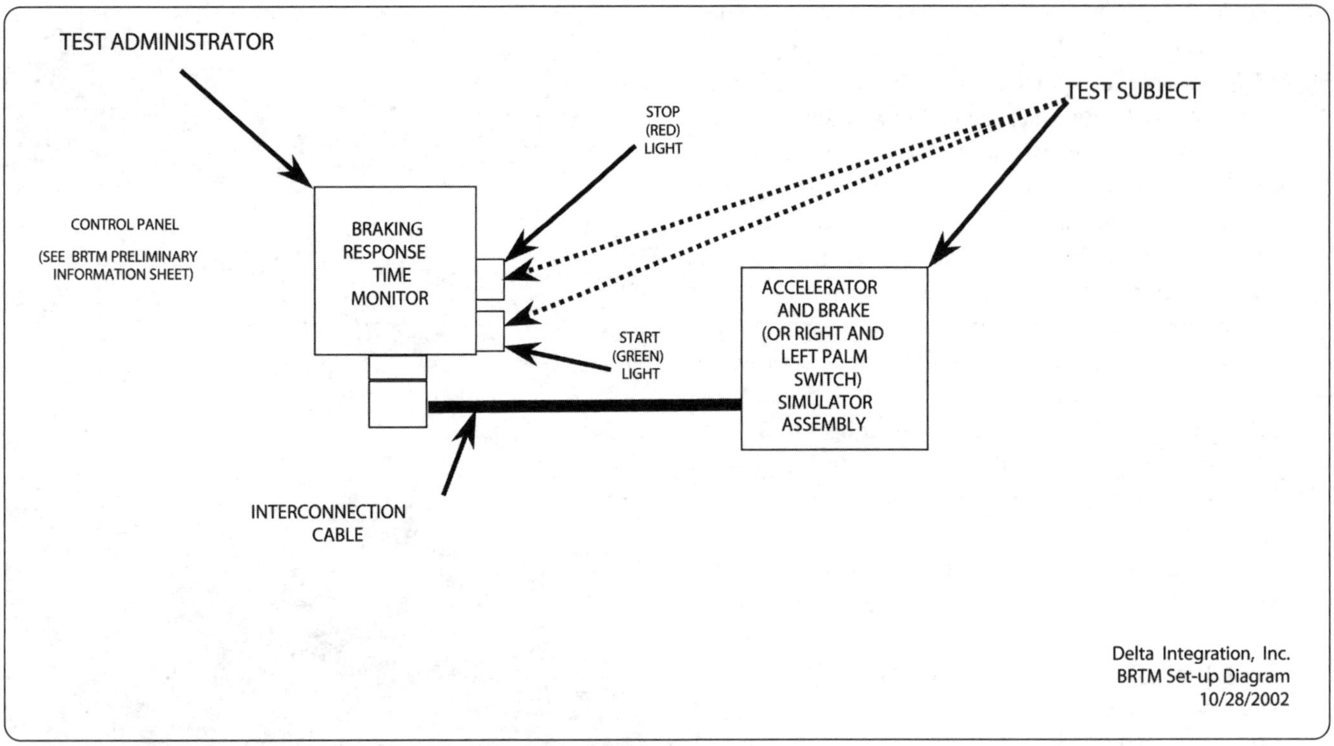

Figure 2.4A. Delta Integration's in-vehicle reaction timer: Braking response time monitor set up—General.

Source: Delta Integration, Inc., Lancaster, PA. Used with permission.

RESPONSE TIMES FOR MEN

GRADE	AGE 16-35	AGE 36-55	AGE 56-65	AGE 65+
A	< 0.59	< 0.61	< 0.63	< 0.65
B	0.59 – 0.62	0.61 – 0.63	0.63 – 0.65	0.65 – 0.69
C	0.63 – 0.67	0.64 – 0.68	0.66 – 0.73	0.70 – 0.83
D	0.68 – 0.69	0.69 – 0.73	0.74 – 0.75	0.84 – 0.86
E	> 0.69	> 0.73	> 0.75	> 0.86

THIS CHART, BASED ON ACTUAL TESTING OF 100 MALE VOLUNTEERS IN VARIOUS AGE GROUPS, HAS BEEN DEVELOPED ONLY AS A GUIDE.

RESPONSE TIMES FOR WOMEN

GRADE	AGE 16-35	AGE 36-55	AGE 56-65	AGE 65+
A	< 0.61	< 0.62	< 0.63	< 0.66
B	0.61 – 0.63	0.62 – 0.64	0.63 – 0.65	0.66 – 0.71
C	0.64 – 0.68	0.65 – 0.69	0.66 – 0.74	0.72 – 0.84
D	0.69 – 0.70	0.70 – 0.74	0.75 – 0.82	0.85 – 0.92
E	> 0.70	> 0.74	> 0.82	> 0.92

THIS CHART, BASED ON ACTUAL TESTING OF 100 FEMALE VOLUNTEERS IN VARIOUS AGE GROUPS, HAS BEEN DEVELOPED ONLY AS A GUIDE.

Revised 3 July 2003 to incorporate more recent time studies.

Figure 2.4B. Delta Integration's in-vehicle reaction timer: Response time charts.

Source: Delta Integration, Inc., Lancaster, PA. Used with permission.

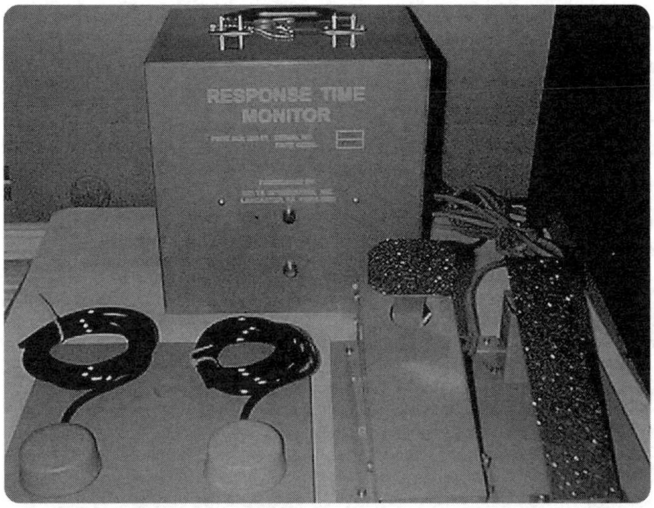

Figure 2.4C. Delta Integration's in-vehicle reaction timer. (2.4A shows the product purpose, 2.4B shows the norms, and 2.4C is the product.)

Source: Delta Integration, Inc., Lancaster, PA. Used with permission.

Figure 2.5. Specially placed mirrors allow the occupational therapist DRS to monitor both the student driver and the traffic flow around the vehicle.

Source: National Institute for Driver Behavior, Cheshire, CT. Used with permission.

should be measured and the appropriate adaptive equipment selected.

- *Manual muscle testing.* Manual muscle testing should take place according to the facility's protocol for measuring clients' strength. It is important to pay attention to the leg used for driving as well as to the arms and hands in case the client needs hand controls or spinner knob adaptations.
- *Sensation testing.* Testing for sensation can be completed by using deep pressure and touch while the client's vision is obscured. In driving, the ability to feel and use the extremities is important. If the client lacks sensation in all extremities, driving may not be safe. The client will need to know where his or her body is in space (i.e., proprioception); judge what the feet, hands, and arms are feeling; and sense how much pressure is needed for the accelerator and brake.

On-the-Road Evaluation

The equipment needed for road assessment will vary depending on the program and the types of clients it will specialize in serving. The basic equipment required is a car, a trainer brake for the DRS, student and instructor mirrors, and any adaptive equipment the client needs. Such equipment includes seat cushions, crossover blinker attachments, spinner knobs, accessory controls (either on a touch switch or mounted on a spinner knob), hand controls (it helps to have them on quick release and have several types for clients to try), left-foot accelerators, cones and sticks for practice parking, and gas guards to block the client from accidentally hitting the accelerator instead of the brake. It is helpful to have a tool kit to adjust adaptive equipment, an emergency kit with reflective signal in case of breakdown, and a cell phone. Of course, it is necessary to have insurance for the vehicle and the driver rehabilitation organization; the DRS should be able to provide proof of insurance in case an accident occurs. If the client is a van user or uses high-technology aids, an adapted van or minivan is needed. Other equipment may include a ramp or lift, a mini-steering wheel, electronic accelerator and brake, joystick control, or accessory controls that are button or voice activated. Developing a plan and researching the client's equipment needs are important to successfully and safely serve clients.

The on-the-road evaluation involves analyzing the client and his or her abilities as they relate to the task of driving. The driving task and client analysis must be evaluated together to determine the client's potential for driving. On-the-road evaluation is vital because that is where the task is performed. The OT/DRS generally uses an adapted instructor vehicle to complete the road assessment. The instructor vehicle is equipped with a trainer brake (a brake on the passenger side that the OT/DRS can use to stop or help the client if necessary) and additional mirrors, usually a student eye-check mirror and an instructor mirror (Figure 2.5). These mirrors enable the OT/DRS instructor to see where the client's eyes scan during driving and to see what is behind the vehicle. It is important to determine whether the driver is scanning properly and using quick, smooth movements. The driver should use all mirrors and regularly check blind spots (e.g., checking over the shoulder before switching lanes). Drivers should be able to go through dark areas, such as tunnels, and

Exhibit 2.1. Elements of an On-the-Road Driver Evaluation

Predriving Readiness
- Having key in hand
- Getting to the vehicle
- Looking over the vehicle before entering (checking for safety of vehicle and surroundings)
- Being able to unlock and open the door
- Getting into the vehicle
- Stowing mobility equipment

Basic Abilities
- Understanding the dashboard and gauges
- Using primary and secondary vehicle accessory controls
- Shifting the vehicle and applying the emergency brake
- Accurately adjusting mirrors
- Fastening and unfastening the seat belt
- Smoothly starting and stopping the vehicle

Basic Road Knowledge
- Recognizing signs
- Knowing rules of the road (e.g., what side to drive on, courteous driving)
- Understanding the meaning of road signs
- Stopping for intersections, stop signs, and lights accurately
- Using parking skills (parking lot, parallel, right back, and turning around in narrow street area)

Basic Road Skills
- Using turn signals
- Using mirrors
- Scanning
- Performing right and left turns
- Maintaining lane position
- Using turn lanes
- Changing lanes
- Parking
- Driving in a parking lot
- Driving on one-way streets

Advanced Road Skills
- Driving with traffic
- Driving in distracting environments
- Merging
- Changing lanes in moderate to heavy traffic
- Driving on a highway
- Scanning for environmental information near and far (accommodation and convergence skills)
- Driving in unfamiliar areas
- Having passengers in the vehicle
- Having a light conversation while driving
- Listening to the radio while driving
- Using defensive driving techniques

Other Important Factors
- Reaction speed and accuracy
- Path-finding skills
- Memory for items seen in the driving environment (both traveling to destination and upon return)
- Ability to listen to the radio or have light conversation while driving
- Client insight on driving performance (ascertained through self-rating)
- Visual scanning skills (i.e., does the client use mirrors and perform blind-spot checks safely and accurately?)

cope with the bright light as they emerge from the dark area. They also should be able to read road signs and respond appropriately. Drivers need to be able to scan intersections as they approach them and continue to do so as they proceed through.

The elements of the road evaluation vary even more widely than those of the clinical evaluation, in part because the profession is so new and in part because the demands of driving vary from client to client and from location to location. Certain items must be assessed on the road for all clients because they are the basic skills for safe driving (see Exhibit 2.1); additional skills may need to be assessed in light of a driver's particular disability or perceptual deficits. The client is tested only within safe measure: If he or she is safe on roads up to 35 mph but unsafe at 40 mph, the road assessment will not continue to more complex levels or faster speeds because doing so would be beyond what the client can safely do.

The road assessment is completed in a progressive fashion. It begins in a parking lot so that the client can get used to the trainer vehicle, then progresses (if and when the client is ready) to quiet side streets, then to busier side streets, and then to multilane roads and highway driving. Stop signs, traffic lights, and construction all add levels of complexity to the task. Starting in an empty parking lot gives the OT/DRS an idea of what to expect or watch for as the client progresses to roadways and enables a comparison of the client's clinical

Personal Experience 2.3. Driver Evaluations

I have not used a standard road test in my practice as an OT/DRS because I go to a client's community to perform the driver evaluation. Although the driver evaluation must address certain skills and abilities for everyone, the individual demands of a client's driving function must be examined, too. By going to a client's community, I can tailor the road evaluation to his or her driving demands. Some people must drive on busy streets that cannot be avoided; others can take quieter routes. Some people live in areas with many pedestrians, adding people, bicyclists, and rollerbladers to the equation.

If state regulations impose restrictions, I can determine whether a client will be safe with those restrictions by having him or her drive within those restrictions. What does it mean for a client to have a 10-mile-radius restriction? Can the client adhere to a restriction of not driving on roads above 45 mph, or does he or she have to drive on a street that requires a higher speed limit? In this way, I can assess whether various restrictions are realistic and safe for the client.

My evaluations add demands that I feel could be a problem for individual clients in light of the clinical assessment results. I require clients with poor contrast sensitivity to drive under bridges or through tunnels (where there is reduced light) and assess how they recover when emerging from the situation. I challenge clients who have visual impairments with a variety of extra tasks to ensure that they can drive safely in different situations. I choose tasks on the basis of objective information gathered in the clinical evaluation so that a client's driving needs, strengths, and limitations are considered.

Although standardizing all road evaluations may be helpful to research and, some may argue, might be fairer than the current situation, doing so would ultimately be a disservice to clients. Driving is different for everyone, and the demands change on the basis of many factors, all of which must be considered when analyzing a client's ability to do the driving they need to be able to do. Some programs that have tried to standardize driver evaluations are not serving the needs of clients and are receiving many complaints from clients, state DMVs, and occupational therapists, who can see the limitations of evaluating clients in a standardized manner.

The process of tailoring a driver evaluation to the unique needs of the client is what makes the driver evaluation so important. The OT/DRS's understanding of the client allows the evaluation to be done in a manner that is fair to the client and truly tests his or her abilities.

and task performance. Beginning with simple skills and building to more complex ones keeps the testing safe, increases the comfort of the client, and helps build rapport between the OT/DRS and the client. The road assessment is stopped if the client is not able to perform safely. In other words, if the client cannot maintain his or her lane on a four-lane road with moderate traffic, then attempting heavy traffic or freeway driving is not indicated.

Some facilities use a standard course for the road assessment so that maneuvers are consistent for each client and the areas that are tested are standardized. Other facilities are community-based and incorporate standards into the assessment; the tests are different for each client, but they incorporate the client's actual driving setting. Some facilities use both approaches. Whatever the testing method, the goal is to ensure that the client meets state requirements, can pass the state driver's license road test, and drives safely.

The scoring of the clinical and on-the-road assessments will vary from facility to facility or program to program. Whatever the scoring method, it is important to clearly define it. Good interrater reliability should be demonstrable: In other words, if several OT/DRSs in a facility were to test the same client, their scoring should be as consistent as possible. For each task component, scoring can be a simple pass–fail; "within functional limits" or "below functional limits"; a number rating; or a check, check-plus, or check-minus system. The driver evaluation form should clearly indicate the grading system and what it means in objective terms. The scoring system should be included in the facility's policies and procedures manual and provide examples of what each score means clinically and on the road. It also is helpful for the staff working in the area of driving to meet periodically to update any policies, procedures, and protocols to ensure consistency in all aspects of the operation.

Ideally, the OT/DRS works as both a driving evaluator and a driving trainer. It is important, however, to know when to use each skill separately. Some driver rehabilitation settings use a team consisting of an OT/DRS and driving evaluator or instructor. Each team member's role must be clearly defined, and both professionals must work closely together to provide the services the client needs. Some programs use the OT/DRS for the clinical portion and the driving evaluator or instructor for the on-the-road assessment. Some have the OT/DRS complete the clinical portion and then ride in the back seat for the road assessment while the driving evaluator or instructor takes the lead. The OT/DRS should take the lead on the driver rehabilitation team to clinically assess the client, determine his or her needs, and match the client to the team member with the most appropriate skills for meeting the client's needs. The OT/DRS should always provide the clinical assessment for the medical needs to be addressed. The best alternative is for the OT/DRS to complete the clinical and on-the-road assessments of the driving evaluation and to use the driving educators or instructors as a resource as needed.

Driver Evaluation Outcome

The clinical and on-the-road assessments together take approximately 2 to 3 hours. Subsequent client training time (if necessary) varies with the equipment needed, the learning abilities of the client, and the rate at which the client picks up new skills. Training is not necessary for the already-licensed driver who has passed the driver evaluation with the OT/DRS, safely demonstrating ability, and who has physician permission to return to driving (unless the physician had some concerns to identify before giving the client the clearance to drive). It is important to see consistent progress during driver training to know that the client is acquiring the skills needed for safe driving.

It is important to give the client time to get used to the training vehicle. If possible, using a vehicle the client is used to driving can help put the client at ease once he or she has demonstrated safe skill in the OT/DRS trainer vehicle. The client should have time to get used to how the vehicle handles and feels. The OT/DRS should review all the gauges with the client and have him or her use all the controls before going out on the road. It is helpful to start in a large, empty parking lot or, if a parking lot is not available, a quiet side street.

Once the client has control of the vehicle and is comfortable, the evaluation begins. The road evaluation should start slowly and progress as the client demonstrates the ability to do so. The road evaluation needs to progress to full function if the client is to drive without restrictions or if restrictions are not allowed in the state.

When the OT/DRS evaluates a client for driving ability, it is important that he or she give the client directions to complete the task only, with no feedback or cues. The OT/DRS needs training to do this successfully. Therapists of all kinds often do not realize that they are cueing someone unless they analyze the task and their directions closely. For example, telling the client to "turn right at the stop sign ahead" provides a cue. If the client had not been told that a stop sign was ahead, would he or she have stopped? Likewise, telling someone to "change lanes after looking" offers a cue. Would the client have checked if the DRS had not mentioned it? As with clinical evaluations, the OT/DRS must be careful not to give hints or cues. Doing so will change the outcome of the assessment.

The outcome of the driver evaluation should be determined by the end of the clinical or road assessments, unless there is a reason to require further testing. For example, some clients may have a disability that affects their performance differently on different days. In such cases, it may be important to see the client on two different occasions to obtain a clear picture of their abilities. It is important that this be determined after the first evaluation session so that the client does not feel as though he or she is being strung along without an answer.

If there is no need for another evaluation session, then the outcome of the driver evaluation should be explained to the client—and his or her family—at the end of the evaluation. This important part of the evaluation should be carried out in a clear and compassionate manner. If the client does not pass the driver evaluation, it is important for him or her to know why and whether it is an area that could improve with further rehabilitation. Discussing community mobility is important at this time so that the client does not become isolated. The client may not be ready to listen that day, but getting the process started is important. Giving the information to the family is helpful because they are more able to "hear" the results of the evaluation and can give the information to the client in the days to come.

Many OT/DRSs find it difficult to review the results, especially when a client fails. People do become angry, and some will get emotional, but it is still important to provide accurate information for that client's safety. It is hard to tell the client that he or she cannot drive, but it is better to do that than to give the client approval simply because it is hard to say no. Occupational therapists have training in helping clients and their families process information about their safety. This step is critical to giving closure to the task of presenting the results of the driver evaluation.

If the client has never driven before or needs adaptive equipment, the OT/DRS must combine evaluation and training skills. The client will complete the clinical assessment, which will help the OT/DRS determine the client's skills and any limitations that require adaptation. The OT/DRS can then plan to adapt the trainer vehicle with the correct equipment and prepare for any specific verbal direction the client may need. The client needs to work in a large, empty parking lot when trying new equipment or if he or she is new to driving and needs adaptive techniques. It is important that the client has room to maneuver and that mistakes do not cause an accident. All equipment takes time to learn; even though the DRS's vehicle has dual brakes, giving the client plenty of room will help ensure the client's comfort in case he or she does make a mistake.

The evaluation data will help determine what type of equipment and how much training the client will need. At the end of the evaluation, the OT/DRS should provide the client with a short outline of possible equipment needs and costs, along with the amount of training each piece of equipment requires. Doing so will let the client and his or her family know what to expect and how much the service and equipment will cost. The OT/DRS should emphasize that costs may vary depending on the client and his or her skill. The experienced OT/DRS will be able to provide more accurate predictions.

Summary and Conclusion

Being an OT/DRS is a complex endeavor. It is important that occupational therapists do not jump into the profession without the right skills and training. Programs developed over time with trained staff will best be able to safely, successfully evaluate a client. Appropriate training is critical to meeting the needs of the client and to the outcome of the evaluation. Understanding of what safe driving is and how to teach it is important to evaluation and on-the-road training. As the profession of occupational therapy gains recognition in the area of driving and as more programs develop, it will be important that programs be developed for the right reasons and in the safest way to provide quality service. All occupational therapy and rehabilitation professionals must understand the value of the on-the-road evaluation.

If the OT/DRS and the occupational therapist generalist work with the rehabilitation team, they will be able to value what each specialty provides and advocate for the services the client needs. The OT/DRS should consider building these relationships to meet the needs of the people they serve and to educate others of the value of on-the-road evaluations. Having the occupational therapist generalist or members of the rehabilitation team ride along during driver evaluations allows them to see what the DRS does and the outcome of the DRS evaluation.

References

American Occupational Therapy Association. (2002). Occupational therapy practice framework: Domain and process. *American Journal of Occupational Therapy, 56,* 609–639.

Bouska, M. J., & Kwatny, E. (1982). *Manual for the application of the motor-free visual perception test to the adult population* (6th ed.). Philadelphia: Temple University Rehabilitation Research and Training Center.

Colarusso, R. P., & Hammill, D. D. (2002). *Motor-Free Visual Perception Test* (MVPT–3; 3rd ed.). Austin, TX: Pro-Ed.

Decina, L. E., & Staplin, L. (1993). Retrospective evaluation of alternative vision screening criteria for older and younger drivers. *Accident Analysis and Prevention, 25,* 267–275.

Glomstad, J. (2005, June 27). Ready for the road? *Advance for Occupational Therapy Practitioners,* pp. 16–19.

Helm-Estabrooks, N. (2001). *Cognitive Linguistic Quick Test (CLQT).* San Antonio, TX: Harcourt Assessment.

Klavora P., Gaskovski P., Martin K., Forsyth, R. D., Heslegrave, R. J., Young, M., et al. (1995). The affects of Dynavision on behind-the-wheel driving ability and selected psychomotor abilities of persons after a stroke. *American Journal of Occupational Therapy, 49,* 534–542.

Mestre, D. R. (2001). Dynamic evaluation of the useful field of view in driving. In *Proceedings of driving assessment 2001* (pp. 234–239). Iowa City: University of Iowa.

Owen, M. M., & Stressel, D. L. (1999). Motor-Free Visual Perceptual Test as a screening tool for driver evaluation and rehabilitation readiness. *Physical Disabilities Special Interest Section Quarterly, 22*(3), 3–4.

Pellerito, J. M., Jr. (2005). *Driver rehabilitation and community mobility principles and practice.* Philadelphia: Elsevier Mosby.

Pellerito, J. M., Jr., & Davis, E. S. (2005, March 21). Screening driving and community mobility status: A critical link to participation and productive living. *OT Practice,* pp. 9–14.

Pelli, D. G., Robson, J. G., & Wilkins, A. J. (1988). The design of a new letter chart for measuring contrast sensitivity. *Clinical Vision Science, 2,* 187–199.

Royall, D. R., Cordes, J. A., & Polk, M. (1998). CLOX: An executive clock drawing task. *Journal of Neurology, Neurosurgery, and Psychiatry, 64,* 588–594.

Stav, W. B. (2004). *Driving rehabilitation: A guide for assessment and intervention.* San Antonio, TX: PsychCorp.

Walls, B. S. (1999, September.) Time to stop? The dilemma of driver rehabilitation weighs quality of life against public safety. *OT Practice,* pp. 24–31.

3

Community Mobility

When discussing driving with a client, it is important to also discuss community mobility, an important instrumental activity of daily living (IADL; American Occupational Therapy Association, 2002). Community mobility is the ability to participate in one's community for leisure, social activities, and work and to obtain needed goods and services (e.g., groceries, medical appointments). If a client is unable to drive, whether for the short term or the long term, it is vital that alternative transportation options be identified and addressed. People who lack community mobility or who attempt mobility without appropriate supervision are at risk for depression and injury (Stav, 2004). The rehabilitation professional and occupational therapist play a big part in helping clients with community mobility.

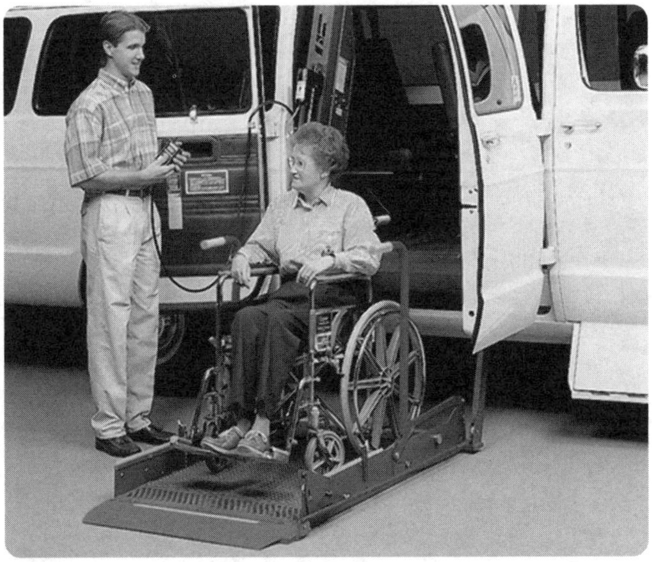

Figure 3.1. Alternative transportation van for seniors.

Source: Braun Corporation, Winamac, IN. Used with permission.

Community mobility fits into the occupational therapy framework and is a reimbursable service if done as an IADL. How it is addressed depends on the setting and the occupational therapist's skill set. Some occupational therapists address community mobility in function (which works best); others work creatively in the clinic and with the family to complete the transition to the community. Many occupational therapists will partner with independent living skills services, vocational rehabilitation services, or other nonmedical entities in developing and implementing a community mobility plan for the client.

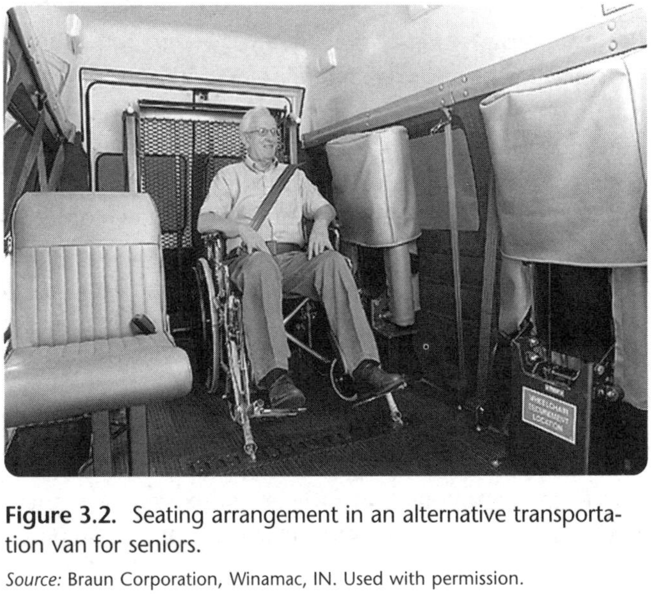

Figure 3.2. Seating arrangement in an alternative transportation van for seniors.

Source: Braun Corporation, Winamac, IN. Used with permission.

Alternative transportation options must meet the clients' needs (Figure 3.1) and match their skills (Figure 3.2). Therefore, involving the client in the process is vital. The client should be asked to describe his or her transportation needs and preferred modes of transport. Cultural and personal preferences need to be considered. The more that the client is involved in this process, the more he or she will value the end result (Pellerito, 2005).

Community mobility is interwoven with driving and must be addressed with the utmost skill and given a high priority. Getting clients into the community again, whether or not they are the driver, will improve their mental wellbeing and self-worth (Stav, 2004). People are afraid to give

Personal Experience 3.1. Woman With Physical Injuries

I had the opportunity to work as a home health occupational therapist with a 38-year-old woman after she sustained physical injuries in a motorcycle accident (I work in home health, in addition to working on driving issues). I worked with this woman in the nontraditional community-based setting through private insurance in a unique model whereby approval is obtained for hours that are needed on a weekly basis. The hours can be used all in one day or over the course of a week. The client does not need to be homebound to qualify for services, so I can work with clients in their homes and communities on functional tasks.

This client had been discharged from a rehabilitation facility with a rental wheelchair, because the team did not know whether her injuries would be permanent or temporary. The rehabilitation team had the woman get used to the chair in the rehabilitation setting, had her demonstrate the transfer into her vehicle, and showed her husband how to load the chair into the vehicle.

The woman had been home for 1 week when home health services started. At home, she required moderate assistance to push her wheelchair because of carpet and inclines. The client's husband had a bad back and drove a sport utility vehicle (SUV). The woman's wheelchair was a rigid, nonfolding chair that was heavy and needed to be lifted into the back of the SUV to be stowed. Lifting the chair was causing problems for her husband. In the community, she was unable to negotiate the chair in snowy conditions, she could not propel through close quarters while shopping, and the weight of the chair caused fatigue on even surfaces after about 10 minutes. She was not able to use the chair on inclines.

The problems with the rental chair did not become apparent until the client was at home and in the function of using the chair. The rehabilitation team demonstrated insight by holding off on purchasing a chair. Their plan was to first see the progress in her recovery and long-term need for the chair, but this approach also was helpful in that, until the client was in function, the type of chair she needed could not be fully identified. Before selecting a new rental wheelchair, the home health team had the client try out chairs in a variety of functions in her home and community. A list of requirements was identified so that she and the rehabilitation team could select the correct wheelchair to meet her needs in the community and home and as a passenger in a motor vehicle (e.g., car, accessible bus, or transportation for people with disabilities).

The rehabilitation team identified a lightweight chair that could fold easily. She was able to propel this chair in her home and community, in all weather conditions, and on inclines, and her husband could stow it in the SUV without hurting himself. The chair had a positive effect on her function.

up driving because they equate it to stopping living (Gourley, 2002). To many, driving is an IADL necessary for a full and productive life (Pellerito & Davis, 2005). Where alternative transportation options are limited, occupational therapists must seek creative solutions. At the rehabilitation center where I held my first job in the area of driving, volunteers gathered information on alternative transportation options in our state. They listed the options by county to further aid the client. Many clients used church volunteers, neighbors, or friends to provide transportation. One client hired a college student to drive her to her appointments, to the store, and to social activities. There are many creative options, but the client and his or her family may need assistance to identify these.

The client may need to consider moving to an area that better meets his or her needs. There are senior high-rise or assisted-living options that include transportation in their services or are built in areas where many of the community needs (e.g., grocery store, pharmacy, doctors' offices) are in the building or close by. Ageless Possibilities (www.agelesspossibilities.org) is developing a pilot program in the Minneapolis area for a community living environment, called connective living, for a variety of age groups to live together and assist each other in life plans (e.g., babysitting needs, driving needs).

Planning for the future should include not only finances, skills needed in the home, and layout of the home but also options for alternative transportation (Gourley, 2002). Fully addressing and successfully implementing alternative transportation options can make the idea of not driving less catastrophic in the minds of clients. Critical roles in rehabilitation are matching transportation options to the client and, if necessary, teaching the client how to use those options.

Roles of the Rehabilitation Professional and Occupational Therapist Generalist

It is vital that questions about driving be asked early in the rehabilitation process; to do otherwise is a disservice to the client. The occupational therapist should gather information on the role that driving or community mobility played in the client's life; identify whether the client is a candidate for driving, either now or in the future; and address community mobility issues. The point is to start the conversation with the client right away, at the same time driving is discussed; the rehabilitation professional should not talk about giving up driving without addressing community mobility. In this way, the client's safety in the community is addressed, along with the issue of driving and alternative transportation options.

All rehabilitation professionals will play a role in assessing community mobility options and training the client to use them safely. Transportation modes that ensure the client's safety and independence within the community must be identified. Training should take place not only in the clinic but also in the community.

The family may work with the client on community mobility, but their efforts should be planned and led by the rehabilitation team. The family should not try to introduce community mobility options before the client has the skills and strategies to stay safe. For example, the client may be able to walk with a cane safely in the clinical setting and even in the parking lot of the facility. But from the community mobility perspective, the client also needs to be assessed as to his or her ability to walk with a cane safely in a variety of weather conditions (e.g., rain, snow, heat), on flat as well as uneven surfaces, over curb cuts and regular curbs, and in a distracting environment. It is important to take this approach, or the client may leave the rehabilitation phase at discharge independent only in certain situations (see "Personal Experience" boxes).

Considerations in Choosing Community Mobility Options

Adaptive devices often are picked early in rehabilitation, even though the client's needs will probably change and the client's needs in the community may not be taken into account. It is therefore important to think of options such as renting equipment or borrowing equipment from loan programs; when it is time to order the equipment, the occupational therapist should think about its use in relation to the client's life at home, in the community, and into the future. Often, insurance companies, Medicare, and other funding sources will only allow equipment to be ordered every year or two unless the client undergoes a drastic change. Planning and thinking about community mobility into the future for the client is therefore critical.

In addition to mobility device options, the rehabilitation professional needs to consider whether the client has the cognitive and visual skills to use the transportation options safely and independently. How will the client solve problems if he or she gets lost or becomes confused when out in the community? The speech therapist, occupational therapist, social worker, independent living skills specialist, and even psychologist should consider factors such as these.

Public transportation options depend on the area in which the client lives and may include buses, trains, a subway system, or taxicabs (see Figures 3.3 and 3.4). In some areas, rides are provided specifically for the elderly population or for people with disabilities; those options

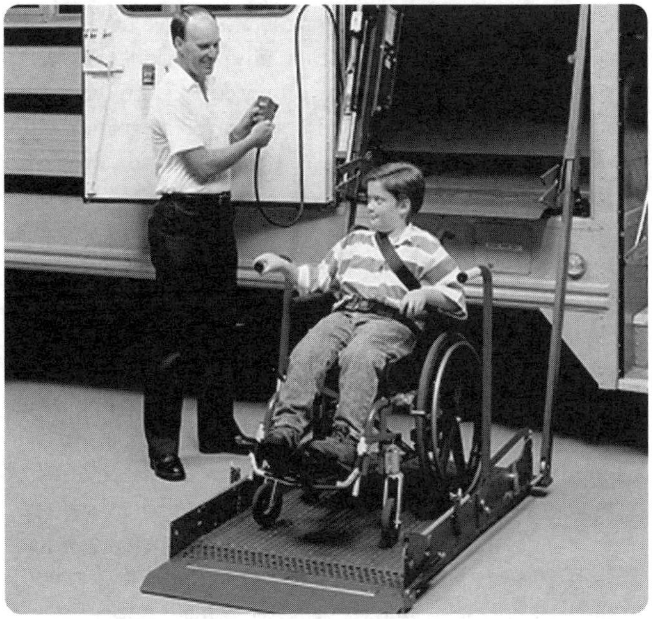

Figure 3.3. A student in a wheelchair can ride in a bus by using the lift.

Source: Braun Corporation, Winamac, IN. Used with permission.

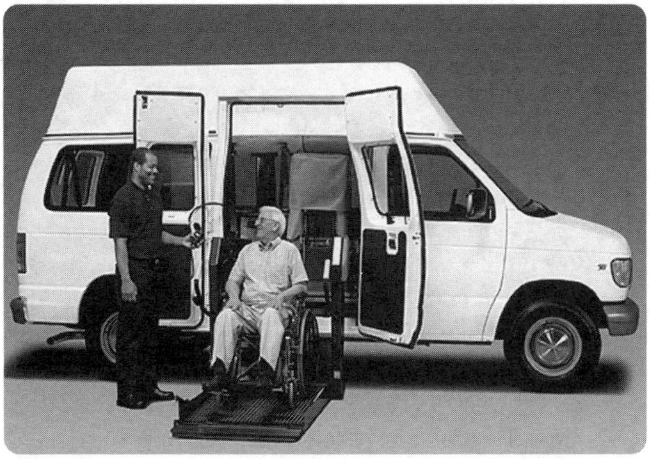

Figure 3.4. An alternative public transportation option for people with disabilities is a specially equipped van that can be made available for medical appointments and, on a fee-for-service basis, for other trips in the community. People with disabilities must apply for this service and obtain special identification to use it.

Source: Braun Corporation, Winamac, IN. Used with permission.

Personal Experience 3.2. Young Man With Brain Injury

Our team was treating a young man with brain injury that resulted from seizure-related anoxia. This client had long-term memory deficits for some information and short-term deficits for events that happened around the time of his seizures and for about 1 month after. (For example, at the time of the September 11, 2001, terrorist attacks, when everyone was talking about the event, this client had no concept of it at all.) The client could not drive because the seizures had occurred only 2 months prior, and state law required him to be 6 months seizure-free before driving.

The client wanted to get out more on his own because his wife worked during the day. He also wanted to return to college and his part-time job. He was only 26 years old, so time on his own and community mobility were important to him. His wife reported that he was doing extremely well when she was with him in the community. The speech therapist reported that his attention span, short-term memory, and problem-solving skills were functional if he used his strategies (a planner, memory book, and cell phone for safety backup). The physical therapist had worked with him on his walking skills and endurance and had determined that he was independent on all terrains and in a variety of weather conditions. I was his occupational therapist, and I worked with him on his community transportation options; the best option for him to try first was the bus, because his home was on a bus line.

The client was able to get bus schedules and demonstrated the ability to read them and plan routes to the places he needed to go. He was able to walk to and from the bus stop and get back home without help. It was decided that the occupational therapist should take him into the community to use the bus because it was a functional task.

As the occupational therapist, I gathered information from the speech therapist and physical therapist so that I would know his strategies and could reinforce them if necessary. The team all predicted that the client would be successful, but they were unsure how he would deal with the distraction and problem-solving challenges.

The first time the client tried using the bus, the goal was to go to his place of work for a visit and return home. It was estimated that the task would take 1.5 hours. I went with the client to observe and complete a preliminary worksite assessment. The client had planned which buses to take and determined which bus stops to use and the times at which the buses he needed stopped.

I arrived at 9:00 a.m., as agreed, but the client was not ready until 9:40 a.m. He was slow to get dressed, had trouble planning which medications to bring, and had trouble identifying how he would carry the supplies he needed to bring back to work. The time required was more than would be functional on a daily basis. His wife was surprised, because she did not realize how much she had been cueing him to get ready in a timely manner.

The client was able to locate his bus stop on his own and walk there independently. He did not have any trouble waiting for the bus or getting on it. He was able to push the button for the bus driver to let us off right in front of his place of work and exit the bus independently. Once at work, he had the skills to socialize with everyone, but he did get off topic at times and had trouble remembering specifics of some of the conversations. He left work on time; he found the correct bus stop and was able to make it home in 1.5 hours, not including preparation time for the task.

Because of the results of this task, the rehabilitation team worked with the client on planning and preparation for trips. Without cues, the client needed to develop his own planning mechanisms. With the therapists' help, he began making lists and using a timer.

On the next community outing, I wanted him to try a more complex task. The goal was for him to use the bus to go shopping and run errands. He planned to take the bus to the bank, the grocery store, and a friend's home.

This time the client was ready to go when I arrived. I reiterated that the goal was for him to act as though I were not there. If the client ran into problems, he was to solve them without my assistance, if possible.

The client again was able to get to his stop, get on the right bus, and navigate the trip independently. He had trouble with the distraction of people getting on and off the bus and talking while he was trying to pay attention to where he needed to get off. Because of the distraction, he missed one of his transfers, but he was able to solve the problem by getting off on the next major street, where he could get a connection on a different bus than he had planned.

The first destination was the bank, to get cash for the purchases he planned to make later that day. He ran into difficulty when the teller asked for his address, which he could not remember because he had just moved. She then

(continued)

Personal Experience 3.2. Young Man With Brain Injury, cont.

asked him for his last transaction, which he also could not remember because he had not done any banking since his injury. He dealt with the problem by explaining his impairment, then provided his Social Security number, date of birth, and wife's name and date of birth as alternative forms of identification. He was able to get the money he needed.

The client made it to all of his destinations and home safely, but on several occasions, he did not pick the quickest route, which delayed his travels. He had estimated that he would be able to do these activities safely and be home in 3 hours, but it ended up taking 5 hours.

This information gave the client areas he could work on with family and friends. The rehabilitation team consulted with the family on practice sessions, helping them set goals for each session.

If the client had not had time to try these skills in function, he may have returned to community mobility before it was safe for him to do so. If I had not taken him into the function, the areas in which he was having difficulty could not have been identified and worked on.

This story provides a good example of why rehabilitation professionals cannot overvalue the role of driving and undervalue the need for community mobility. Although the client still does not drive, it is not a big issue for him, because he is safe and successful in using the bus. He is working part-time, going to school, seeing friends, and running errands on his own. He plans to return to driving at some point but wants to wait until he feels ready to complete a driver's assessment. For this client, community mobility was of the utmost importance, and getting back to his life was achieved using alternative transportation.

may include small buses, vans, or taxicabs. Fees vary, depending on the option. Some churches, clubs, and service centers offer volunteer transportation options (transportation around the community provided by volunteers). Creative options include carpooling, hiring a college student or other young person as a driver, and creating a schedule for rides with family and friends.

Using volunteers or hiring a driver can be mutually beneficial to the driver and client. For example, a student who is interested in becoming an occupational therapist may want to earn some extra money by driving for a person with a disability. In this way, the driver can gain some occupational therapy–related experience and the client achieves community mobility goals.

In most cases, community-based training is essential to assessing the client's performance. The training can be completed by a home health professional who is working in the right type of model, which will allow him or her to work with clients who are no longer homebound—clients out in the community performing functional tasks as they normally would in daily life. It also may be completed by the clinical therapist if he or she has the ability to work in the community. The task may even be assigned to a responsible family member. Only the real function of the activity will reveal the client's ability to perform the task safely and independently. Performance is very different outside the clinical setting because things are more unpredictable (e.g., Who else will be on the bus? What problems will the client encounter? How will he or she handle them on the spur of the moment with people who are unfamiliar with his or her needs?). It is important to try to anticipate problems so that the client and family can be as prepared as possible.

Community mobility sometimes means that the family of the client owns an accessible vehicle for the client to ride in as a passenger. The occupational therapist generalist should be part of the team that plans the mobility device (e.g., scooter, wheelchair) the client will use to enter and remain secure in the vehicle. An important step in vehicle determination is deciding whether the option will meet the client's future needs. The vehicle should be safe and easy for the client to enter and exit.

I recently worked with a family, occupational therapist generalist, rehabilitation team, and vendor for a client who would be in a wheelchair long term. The family wanted to get out in the community together immediately, without seeing whether the client could drive again. The rehabilitation team had picked out the client's wheelchair several months earlier and had kept driving in mind. The client had the chair for 4 months, was comfortable with it, felt safe, and knew it worked for her. The vehicle needed to accommodate the client, her wheelchair, her husband and three children, and her 24-hour nurse. The client wanted a minivan, but many would not allow for the weight of the family and their belongings. As a team, we located two options with the needed weight capabilities.

The next dilemma was the space requirement. To provide room for a wheelchair, usually both of the middle seats in the minivan are removed. But because the client had

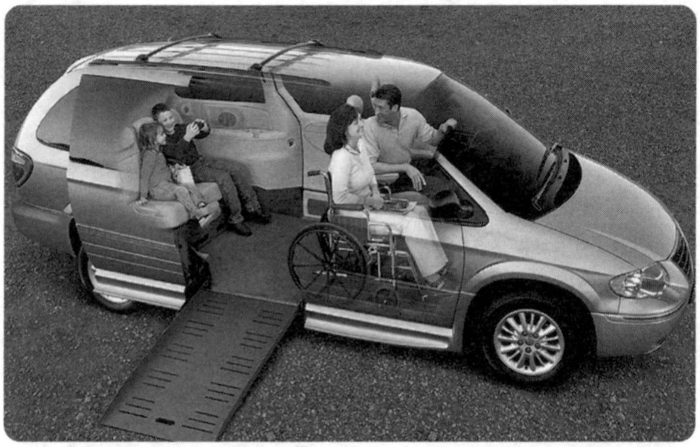

Figure 3.5. This minivan has been adapted for a passenger in a wheelchair, allowing the person to be mobile and independent in the community.

Source: Braun Corporation, Winamac, IN. Used with permission.

Figure 3.6. Having a vehicle adapted for riding or driving in a wheelchair can offer a person greater independence and mobility options.

Source: Braun Corporation, Winamac, IN. Used with permission.

three children and a nurse, the minivan required the back and middle seats for everyone to fit. The generalist, rehabilitation team, vendor, and family managed to find one minivan that met all the requirements; the resources of all involved were required. The minivan would fit her and her family, with room to get into the passenger front seat with her wheelchair. The minivan also has a removable front seat, which will allow her to be able to drive it later in her recovery. Getting the right modifications to be a passenger (Figure 3.5) or a driver (Figure 3.6) is a team effort.

Advocating for Community Mobility

Becoming involved in community mobility and advocating for alternative transportation options for people with disabilities and seniors are important new areas for rehabilitation professionals, particularly occupational therapists. It is important for therapists to work with the entities that will address these concerns in the future (e.g., local transportation companies, state and federal government, research committees). Therapists need to provide input now so that the services are simple to use, are cost-effective, have convenient operating hours, and are accessible. Occupational therapists can be critical in the development of these services.

Occupational therapists can work to get legislators to look at alternative transportation options to help people with disabilities and seniors. It is important that legislators hear now that this is an issue and be given concrete examples of what works, what does not work, and what is needed. When talking with legislators, therapists should be specific and be able to geographically define the areas of need. The needs in large cities are different from those of suburbs or smaller towns. There may be funding options on both local and federal levels to help address community mobility and alternative transportation. Occupational therapists can help by conducting research on needs for transportation, developing pilot programs, or conducting needs analyses. Entrepreneurs may have many opportunities to affect community mobility developments and create alternative transportation options.

Summary and Conclusion

All general rehabilitation therapists can and need to address community mobility. The occupational therapist can take the lead, but all areas of rehabilitation practice have a role to play. The family and the client frequently do not know where to start and are overwhelmed. They also are too close to the situation to really know what would work and what would be within the client's abilities. The occupational therapy driver rehabilitation specialist (OT/DRS) also can play a role in starting the process of looking at alternative transportation options. The OT/DRS can provide generalists with resources that can assist the rehabilitation team and the family.

Often, clients would not be so upset with the idea of giving up driving if they did not see it as giving up their ability to live life. In our culture, driving is the source of most people's transportation and is seen as a rite of independence. We have forgotten that driving is a privilege and that not everyone has the skills to drive. Everyone does, however, have the right to be an active member of society.

References

American Occupational Therapy Association. (2002). Occupational therapy practice framework: Domain and process. *American Journal of Occupational Therapy, 56,* 609–639.

Gourley, M. (2002, March 25). Driver rehabilitation: A growing practice area for OTs. *OT Practice,* pp. 15–16, 18–20.

Pellerito, J. M., Jr. (2005). *Driver rehabilitation and community mobility: Principles and practice.* Philadelphia: Mosby.

Pellerito, J. M., Jr., & Davis, E. S. (2005, March 21). Screening driving and community mobility status: A critical link to participation and productive living. *OT Practice,* pp. 9–14.

Stav, W. B. (2004). *Driving rehabilitation: A guide for assessment and intervention.* San Antonio, TX: PsychCorp.

History and Evolution of Driver Rehabilitation

ADED's Role

The Association for Driver Rehabilitation Specialists (ADED) was the first organization for professionals who work with people with disabilities to address driving skills. The organization was created in 1977 to support professionals working in the fields of driver education, driver training, and transportation equipment. The association first met in Detroit, Michigan. As of December 1, 2003, ADED's 540 members comprised occupational therapists, driver educators, licensed driving instructors, equipment dealers, equipment manufacturers, kinesiotherapists, physical therapists, rehabilitation engineers, rehabilitation specialists, rehabilitation technologists, and vocational rehabilitation specialists; 352 members are certified driver rehabilitation specialists (CDRSs).

ADED is the only organization that offers a certification in driver rehabilitation, which requires passing a certification test. The ADED definition of the CDRS and objectives of certification and eligibility are presented in Exhibit 4.1.

Those who pass the exam may call themselves certified driver rehabilitation specialists and use the initials CDRS behind their signature. The certification exam is offered one time per year at the ADED national conference. The test consists of medical and driving questions related to a client's ability to drive or be evaluated for driving. Understanding of the areas of driver evaluation and training, adaptive equipment, and knowledge of a variety of age groups as well as disabilities is needed to do well on this exam.

CDRSs have a variety of backgrounds. Many are occupational therapists, but some are driving instructors, driving evaluators, or other rehabilitation professionals. Choosing the CDRS who has the proper training and medical background and can offer the services appropriate for the client is important. If a client's impairment affects vision or cognition, is progressive, or is related to a physical disability, a CDRS who also is a medical professional would be the best choice for that person. Sometimes a team that includes a medical professional and driving educator or instructor who is a CDRS can be effective. The key is to work as a team, with the occupational therapist driver rehabilitation specialist (OT/DRS) as lead to analyze the client and his or her specific needs and then match that client with the professional that can best meet his or her needs.

ADED and the American Occupational Therapy Association (AOTA) are working together to identify the ways that they can influence the field of driver rehabilitation and develop potential collaborations for strengthening this important field. The bridging of ADED's efforts to train professionals in driver rehabilitation and AOTA's efforts to develop OT/DRSs is critical to ensuring that driver rehabilitation will meet the needs of clients in the future.

AOTA's Role

AOTA is new to the field of driver rehabilitation. The organization has begun focusing its efforts on the field because occupational therapists have the medical background and training for driver rehabilitation. This profession is predicted to grow, and AOTA wants to ensure that sufficient occupational therapy professionals are trained to meet the increasing demand for driver rehabilitation services. As a result, AOTA has worked over the past several years to raise awareness of occupational therapy's role in the practice area of driving. The organization has recognized driver rehabilitation as an instrumental activity of daily living (IADL) and identified how it fits into the occupational therapy framework. Also, AOTA offers online and in-person courses to educate occupational therapists in driver rehabilitation for older drivers.

AOTA's Older Driver Initiative and Expert Panel

An e-mail list is available on the AOTA Web site (www.aota.org) for OT/DRSs and occupational therapist generalists to share information about driving, to ask driving questions, and to get more involved in this specialty area. AOTA, in its Older Driver Initiative, also has devel-

Exhibit 4.1. Driver Rehabilitation Specialist Definition and Certification Objectives and Eligibility

Definition of a Driver Rehabilitation Specialist

The term *driver rehabilitation specialist (DRS)* signifies one who plans, develops, coordinates, and implements driver rehabilitation services for individuals with disabilities.

Objectives of Certification

The purpose of the certification process is to protect the public by

A. Providing measurement of a standard of current knowledge desirable for individuals practicing driver rehabilitation;

B. Encouraging individual growth and study, thereby promoting professionalism among driver rehabilitation specialists; and

C. Formally recognizing driver rehabilitation specialists who fulfill the requirement for certification.

Eligibility

Candidates may take the certification examination if they meet the education and/or experience requirements listed below.

A. An undergraduate degree or higher in a health-related** area of study with 1 year of full-time experience in degree area of study and an additional 1 year of full-time experience in the field of driver rehabilitation.*

B. Four-year undergraduate degree*** or higher with a major or minor in traffic safety and/or a driver and traffic safety endorsement with 1 year of full-time experience in traffic safety and an additional 2 years of full-time experience in the field of driver rehabilitation.*

C. Two-year degree in a health-related** area of study with 1 year of experience in degree area of study and an additional 3 years of full-time experience in the field of driver rehabilitation.*

D. Five years of full-time work experience in the field of driver rehabilitation.*

"Full-time" for ADED purposes means 32 hours per week.

*In the field of driver rehabilitation for ADED purposes means direct hands-on delivery of clinical (pre-driver evaluations) and/or behind-the-wheel evaluations and training with the client.

**Health-related degree means for ADED purposes occupational therapy, physical therapy, kiniesiotherapy, speech therapy, therapeutic recreational therapy, or other areas as approved by the Certification Committee.

***Undergraduate degree areas of study for ADED purposes means social work, vocational rehabilitation, health and physical education, counseling, psychology, or other areas as approved by the Certification Committee.

Note. From ADED, http://www.aded.net/i4a/pages/index.cfm?pageid=120.

oped handouts, promotional materials, and brochures about driver rehabilitation and occupational therapy practice, and the organization is finalizing a position statement on driver rehabilitation. The organization also is conducting an evidence-based review of literature on occupational therapy–based older driver rehabilitation therapies and is publishing clinical practice guidelines on driving (Stav, Hunt, & Arbesman, 2006).

To help define the occupational therapist's role in driving, AOTA has developed consistent terminology to align itself with other professions. AOTA also has initiated conversations regarding the role of occupational therapy in driver rehabilitation with ADED and the National Mobility Equipment Dealers Association; other organizations AOTA has developed relationships with include the National Highway Transportation Safety Administration (NHTSA), the Alzheimer's Association, the American Society on Aging, and the American Medical Association. These national organizations recognize occupational therapy as being a vital link to success in the performance of driving screens and evaluation. The main work of AOTA is on senior issues, as the funding for their efforts is from the Older Driver Initiative.

As the profession has evolved, so has the thinking about how driver rehabilitation is delivered and what each area of occupational therapy should provide. At first, it was thought that driving would be addressed at multiple levels within occupational therapy: the occupational therapist generalist, the occupational therapist with advanced training and skills, and the occupational therapy driving specialist. This approach, however, was confusing, because the many roles were not clearly defined. To address this confusion, in 2003 AOTA convened a panel of experts in the field of driving. The panel met over the course of a year to examine how to develop the driver rehabilitation profession and to determine the terminology that would best fit as the profession grew.

The panel concluded that two levels of driver rehabilitation exist. The occupational therapist generalist represents the occupational therapy profession as a whole, and the occupational therapist specialist has the expertise in driver rehabilitation; the latter category includes the OT/DRS. Both levels offer valuable tools.

Occupational therapists must understand the differences between the two skill levels and value what each has to offer to the profession of driver rehabilitation. Different tools are available at the different levels of practice (e.g., generalists may use predriving clinical screening tools, and specialists use specific assessments leading up to road evaluation). The generalist plays an important role in ensuring that driving is included on the general occupational therapist evaluation form. As described in Chapter 1, it is important to assess the client's baseline driving ability and gather information for dealing with driving-related rehabilitation goals.

AOTA is working to establish criteria for a specialist designation that acknowledges the occupational therapist's specialty skill in the area of driving, much as the association does now for certified hand therapists. The occupational therapist with specialized skill will be known as the OT/DRS.

Until the criteria are established, AOTA's panel agreed that an OT/DRS should be an occupational therapist or occupational therapy assistant who has approximately 3 years of practice and ideally has had a diverse rehabilitation caseload. The occupational therapist or occupational therapist assistant then could focus on developing the skills to specialize in driver rehabilitation. The OT/DRS will complete evaluations and training, and the occupational therapist assistant will be able to complete driving-related training and portions of clinical and road assessments under the supervision of the occupational therapist, consistent with practice guidelines. The determination of criteria is being addressed by the AOTA committee for working to address specialization of the occupational therapist as an OT/DRS. The committee's report will be available in 2006.

AOTA's Older Driver Initiative Activities

AOTA received a grant from NHTSA to encourage occupational therapists to address driving in their practices, to promote specialization in driver rehabilitation among occupational therapists, and to raise the occupational therapy community's awareness of this practice area. This grant is ongoing, with an annual renewal. There is no known end date. In 2003, AOTA used the grant to form an advisory panel of experts to address the Older Driver Initiative. The panel assists AOTA with projects, including developing the AOTA microsite (a smaller Web site, available at www.aota.org/olderdriver, for AOTA members and nonmembers), and editing the online course that AOTA released in 2004. The NHTSA grant also has funded a full-time AOTA position to address the Older Driver Initiative issues to keep the agenda moving and continue connecting AOTA with the key players in the driver rehabilitation field.

AOTA has formed a certification committee to develop AOTA's specialty certification in driving. As AOTA moves forward, it is important to promote occupational therapists as the correct fit for the field of driver rehabilitation while emphasizing the need for occupational therapists to have additional skills and training. To best serve clients, the occupational therapist must meet the right criteria, be trained properly, and work to develop the skills for the profession of driver rehabilitation.

Types of Driving Education Professionals

Several types of professionals educate drivers, as described below.

Driving Educator

Driving educators have a college degree in teaching driving. Some colleges offer driving education as a major or minor, although there are not many of these programs left. The department of motor vehicles (DMVs) for your state may be able to help you find a program in your area. Driving educators are experts in the teaching of driving and often get into the science of safe driving. They have learned the art of the classroom portion of teaching driving and on-the-road training for students without disabilities.

Driving Instructor

The requirements for becoming a driving instructor vary from state to state, but for the most part, a high school degree or the equivalent is the primary requirement. All states require that the person who wants to become a driving instructor must first be hired by a licensed driving school before they can become a driving instructor. Many states require that the instructor receive a set number of hours of training from the driving school that hired him or her. This training is provided by the school the instructor works for, usually by the school's owner. Before becoming licensed, the individual, after completing any training required, must pass state testing, which may include a regular road evaluation, a written exam for instructors, and an on-the-road evaluation with the state lead evaluator, who is usually a driving instructor working for the state DMV. Some states require that candidates have a certain number of hours of training before they can take the written and road test. Information on specific state statutes and requirements is available in *The Physician's Guide to Assessing and Counseling Older Drivers* (Wang, Kosinski, Schwartzberg, & Shanklin, 2003), available free from NHTSA.

Certified Driver Rehabilitation Specialist

A CDRS is an occupational therapist, driving educator, driving instructor, or other related professional (e.g., physical therapist) who has met ADED's criteria for hours of practice in the field and has passed the certification exam. See Exhibit 4.1 for details.

Occupational Therapist Specializing in Driver Rehabilitation

An occupational therapist specializing in driver rehabilitation has a college degree in occupational therapy, either as an occupational therapist or an occupational therapy assistant. He or she does not necessarily have occupational therapy experience before working in the field of driving. The occupational therapist also may be a licensed driving instructor, may work for a driving school, may be a CDRS, may have a degree in driving education, or may have other licenses that states grant in this practice area. Not all occupational therapists who practice in this field have any of the above driving-related qualifications; in many states, they are not required to as long as they are not teaching a new, unlicensed driver.

Although occupational therapists have the medical background to understand a client's disability or age-related health issues and how they affect driving, it is important that they obtain the appropriate training. Without a driving background and advanced clinical occupational therapy education (e.g., continuing education courses on vision; age-related health issues; and neurological disorders and treatment approaches for a wide range of disabilities, such as neurodevelopmental treatment, positioning, and wheelchair modifications), the occupational therapist will not have the right skills to perform the job. Acquiring skills over time in the clinical setting, developing specialties, and getting certified and trained to evaluate and teach driving are critical. This approach will keep the evaluation as safe as possible and generate the most reliable information and successful outcome for the client. In addition, occupational therapists who wish to specialize in driver rehabilitation should consider completing a mentorship with another OT/DRS, completing further education related to driver rehabilitation (see Appendix A), and completing advanced driving training, which is usually offered through the state DMV.

Need for Occupational Therapists as Driver Rehabilitation Specialists

The field of driver rehabilitation is emerging as an occupational therapy specialization for several reasons. People with disabilities, who years ago would have died, are being saved and living healthier and longer lives as a result of technological advances, and the general population is aging (Glomstad, 2005). Baby boomers are getting older and in the next 5 years will make up a large proportion of licensed drivers. In addition, as a result of medical advances, people who sustain a disability or injury have greater expectations of returning to an independent, productive lifestyle that includes driving. Driving is increasingly becoming a necessity because of poor city transportation, time constraints on disability transportation, ever-expanding suburbs, and the inability of families to shoulder the burden of transportation. People who cannot drive do not want to feel that they are a burden to others, but they need a way to get around in their community. NHTSA and other leaders in the field of older driver research, like AOTA, the American Association on Aging, and AARP, predict that the field of driver rehabilitation will experience a personnel shortage unless more occupational therapists undertake this specialization (Finn, 2004).

When a driving program does not specialize in the area of aging or disability, or if the evaluator does not understand the function of driving or purpose of a driver evaluation, generalizations as to who can and cannot drive often result. The driving evaluator or instructor who does not understand the client's unique medical issues and is unfamiliar with how age or disability may affect the client's driving also frequently make generalizations. Rarely should a person be deemed categorically unable to drive on the basis of a diagnosis; a thorough driver evaluation is required to rule out the possibility of driving. Even if the program uses an OT/DRS, if that person does not have the right practice skills and driving background, the client will not get the right service to meet his or her needs.

Necessary Skills for Becoming an OT/DRS

OT/DRSs constantly combine their clinical skills with their driving instructor skills. Their clinical expertise enables them to correctly assess their clients' skills and deficits and evaluate which skills are likely to be regained. They can select modifications to driving task components that are most appropriate for the client with regard to health and safety. OT/DRSs' driving training provides them with expertise in choosing various vehicle modifications and positioning the client properly to have the correct view of the road, allowing them to keep the evaluation or training safe. Their driver training background not only ensures thorough knowledge of the rules of the road but also enables them to maintain control of the vehicle at all times. Maintaining control includes correct use of the trainer brake.

These professionals also must be good drivers. Most states require a good driving record and safe driving habits for anyone who wants to work in this field. Some states require a certified copy of the applicant's driving record, only allow for minor infringements, and complete a criminal background check. Occupational therapists also must know how to teach the components of driving. They must learn what adaptations can be made to the client's vehicle, who installs the equipment, how to choose an equipment installer, how the equipment works, and how to teach someone to use it.

If the occupational therapist does not take these steps in becoming an OT/DRS, the program will not best serve the needs of the clients. Moreover, the program's liability may increase, because it will not be able to demonstrate expertise in the area of driving. If a case were brought to court, the OT/DRS's ability to prove his or her expertise would have to hold up in a court of law. Examples of proof include documentation of training completed in the area of driving, courses attended, books read, and hands-on training. Documentation should be specific as to when the training was completed, the number of hours that were completed, and who provided the training. Documentation also should include any courses the OT/DRS has given, any committees the OT/DRS has served on that demonstrate expertise in driving, and any credential obtained (e.g., CDRS).

In addition to having the right academic and practical skill sets before entering the field of driver rehabilitation, the OT/DRS should have the right personality for the profession. In evaluating driving and driver training, occupational therapists need to be calm, think and react quickly to an ever-changing environment, handle stressful situations with grace, stay two steps ahead of the client and of what is happening on the road, and remain objective. They also need to be able to work with the client and his or her family to clearly communicate the client's driving abilities. They need to be able to explain with compassion and directness that a person can no longer drive. They need to be organized and have good follow-through, so that the information gets communicated in a timely manner to the family, physician, and any other entity to which the state requires reporting. Occupational therapists need to have advocacy skills to assist their clients with state and local agency decision makers (e.g., DMV road testers) and to let others know of the helpful role of occupational therapists in driver rehabilitation.

Driver Rehabilitation Program Models for Incorporating an Occupational Therapist

Programs that use the skills of occupational therapists in driver rehabilitation come in many configurations. In the author's experience, the most effective approach involves the occupational therapist serving as the DRS. The occupational therapist can benefit from working with driving educators and licensed driving instructors that have expertise in driving, but the OT/DRS can take the lead for all clients with medical conditions or problems in the areas of vision or cognition.

The following sections describe several program models. Certainly, other models have evolved in the area of driving practice, but the models listed reflect some of the many approaches. When developing or working in a particular program model, it is important to continually reflect on whether the structure best meets the needs of clients.

Occupational Therapist Provides Clinical Evaluation, Driving Instructor Provides Road Evaluation

The relationship between and coordinated work of the occupational therapist and driving instructor are what make this model work. It is imperative that both professionals have some understanding of each other's area, communicate, and trust each other's skills and input. The ability of the driving instructor to use the occupational therapist's information to understand the client and then transfer the information into road evaluation is critical. The strength of this model is that the occupational therapist is involved in the driver evaluation and has input but does not have to be involved in on-the-road evaluation if he or she is not properly trained or has just started working in driver rehabilitation. The limitation is that the occupational therapist is not in the vehicle, so the driving instructor may miss critical information related to the medical aspect of the client that subtly affects driving, or the driving instructor may cue the client without knowing it.

Occupational Therapist Provides Clinical Evaluation and Rides Along With a Driving Instructor or Evaluator

As in all models involving more than one professional, communication between the two is critical. The occupational therapist and the driving instructor must develop a system for the occupational therapist to provide input

Personal Experience 4.1. Young Woman With Cerebral Palsy

A young woman with cerebral palsy from a small town had tried working with a school driving instructor. She wore a rigid ankle–foot orthosis on her right leg. The instructor had her use this foot for driving, but the client was not able to move smoothly from the accelerator to brake, had trouble with her foot catching under the accelerator, and did not feel the pressure that her foot was giving to the pedals. She also had trouble coordinating the movement of her hands, especially on turns. She was asked to drive on the road right away and was expected to learn to drive in 6 hours of training. Her instructor told her after 4 hours of training that she was not trying hard enough and that she was not smart enough to learn to drive. He recommended that she never drive and went so far as to tell the local department of motor vehicles (DMV) that she should not be allowed to have a license.

Fortunately, this woman had parents who were strong advocates for their daughter. The parents had their daughter start working through her school's department of vocational services; one of the goals was for her to learn to drive. I was a consultant to a contractor for the department, so I was asked to see the woman for a driver evaluation and, eventually, training.

In the clinical portion of the evaluation, I determined that this woman met the visual requirements for driving established by the state; that she was a bright woman able to problem solve and perform abstract reasoning; that she learned best by watching and doing rather than reading about something; that she had good use of her arms but had the best strength and coordination with her right arm; that she could walk functionally with her brace, but not without it; that she was of short stature; and that she was fearful of not being able to perform the task of driving.

Once the clinical portion was complete, the driving training followed. I used the clinical findings to start adapting the vehicle to meet her specific needs. I put a cushion on the seat so she could reach the pedals and see out the front window. I had her try driving with her right foot, but she was not smooth or coordinated in her movements. I switched her to a left-side hand control and had her try several styles of hand controls. She did best with the right-angle hand control. She could steer the vehicle using a spinner knob and could let go of the hand controls momentarily to safely use the blinkers, windshield wipers, and bright lights. She was able to drive on country roads near her house by the end of the evaluation.

After 10 hours of training, she was ready to drive and practice with her parents. After about 50 hours of driving practice with her parents, she scheduled her license test, but the DMV would not give her a full test because of what the previous instructor had told them. I intervened to educate the local DMV about the equipment she was using and the training she had received. She then took her test and passed.

My client and her family wrote me shortly thereafter thanking me. She said in the letter that I was the first person to really understand her and work with her within her skill level. Because I did not give up when others had, she was now driving, attending college, and living on her own. She appreciated my ability to adapt both the vehicle and my instruction style to her needs, something her previous instructor could not do.

during the ride-along without being a distraction or interfering with safe testing. The occupational therapist needs to have confidence in the skills of the instructor because he or she will have control of the vehicle. In addition, this approach requires equipment, such as a mirror the occupational therapist can use to see what the client is looking at while driving (see Figure 2.5). The strengths of this model are that both the occupational therapist and the driving instructor are a part of the whole process of the driver evaluation. If both parties value each other's roles and have good communication, the best of the two professions can be blended to serve the client. The limitations of this model are that the occupational therapist, although part of the road assessment, does not have control of the assessment. It is difficult to notice everything from the back seat, and if something is noted that needs to be tested more fully, it can be hard to communicate this to the driving instructor without distracting the client. This model also can be intimidating to the client.

Occupational Therapist Provides Clinical Evaluation and On-the-Road Evaluation, Driving Instructor Provides Driver Training

Many states have special criteria for training new drivers. If the driver rehabilitation program cannot meet those criteria, it may have the occupational therapist complete the full clinical evaluation and have the driving instructor provide the training. In those situations, it is important to establish a plan and provide ongoing feedback as to how the client is doing. The strength of this model is that the occupational therapist has full control of the driver evaluation clinic and road portions, which is less intimidating to the client and provides consistency. The limitations are that the client will need to have another person involved if training is needed, and if that instructor is not a part of the team or does not have training in the area of the client's needs, the client may not receive proper training.

Occupational Therapist Provides Clinical Evaluation, Road Evaluation, and Training

This is the OT/DRS model. Such models often rely on OT/DRSs who are state-licensed driving instructors. This type of occupational therapist is able to meet the evaluation needs of clients, as well as the driving instruction needs of new drivers or drivers with new equipment. The strength of this program is that one person does all aspects of the driver rehabilitation evaluation and training. The limitation is that, if that person is not properly skilled, the client will not get all the services needed to be safe and achieve his or her full potential.

Occupational Therapist Provides Full Driver Rehabilitation Services and Teams With Other Professionals as Needed

In this model, the occupational therapist provides the full range of driver rehabilitation and related services but teams with other professionals to meet clients' other needs. Such occupational therapists may refer clients to psychologists to help them with grief and other emotions related to cessation of driving and loss of abilities, or they may work with physicians to meet state reporting requirements. In addition, the team includes other driving resource areas as needed, such as working with a driving educator and an experienced driving instructor to meet the full driving needs of the client. This program's strength is that it can encompass all the areas needed for a complete, comprehensive driver evaluation and training program. The limitation is that it is hard to coordinate and may be time-consuming to manage.

Summary and Conclusion

A program should not be created for financial gain or simply because it is a trendy practice area. In occupational therapy organizations, if little demand exists for the program or if it would be cost-prohibitive for the sponsoring organization, a new driver rehabilitation program should perhaps not be implemented. Also, if an existing driver rehabilitation program does not meet the needs of the clients (e.g., if the client needs to use a minivan and is forced to use a car because the program cannot offer the minivan), then the program model should be questioned. Programs need to be clear about any areas they cannot address and should be able to provide resources and references to other programs that may help the client. The success of the clients and program depend on continual critical analysis. Adapting every program is essential as technologies and practice guidelines change and as the demands or needs of driving and drivers change. The programs that invest this time and effort will be the leaders in the field of driver rehabilitation and will thrive.

References

Finn, J. (2004). *Driving evaluation and retraining programs: A report of good practices.* Bethesda, MD: American Occupational Therapy Association.

Glomstad, J. (2005, June 27). Ready for the road? *OT Advance,* pp. 16–19.

Stav, W. B., Hunt, L. A., & Arbesman, M. (2006). *Occupational therapy practice guidelines for driving.* Bethesda, MD: American Occupational Therapy Association.

Wang, C. C., Kosinski, C. J., Schwartzberg, J. G., & Shanklin, A. V. (2003). *The physician's guide to assessing and counseling older drivers.* Chicago: American Medical Association & National Highway Traffic Safety Administration.

Considerations for Working With Specific Populations

Some clients require special consideration as a result of their membership in a specific demographic group. This is particularly true for elderly people, adolescents, new drivers, and people with congenital disabilities.

Elderly People

In working with elderly clients, occupational therapists should be aware not only of changes in vehicles that many younger people take for granted but also of specific changes in physical, visual, and cognitive capacity that occur as a result of aging. Occupational therapists must examine age-related issues affecting driving and community mobility (Pierce, 2003).

Changes in Vehicles

Elderly people need to stay updated on the changes that have taken place in vehicles. Airbags; antilock brakes; traction control; all-wheel drive; remote start, locking, and unlocking; and power seats, windows, steering, brakes, and doors are just some changes that may not have been installed in the driver's last vehicle. Drivers of all ages must be familiar with the operation of these advances and the risks associated with them (Sanders & McCormick, 1993).

Airbags can cause injury if the passenger or driver is too close to the steering wheel; at least 10 inches is a safe distance. They are particularly dangerous if the person driving is small or fragile or if the driver crosses his or her arm over the wheel in front of the airbag. The hand position now taught to new drivers is 9 o'clock and 3 o'clock instead of 10 o'clock and 2 o'clock, so that the arms do not cross the airbag. Drivers are now taught to "shuffle" or "push–pull" the wheel instead of using hand-over-hand maneuvers to make smooth turns, again to avoid having the arms cross the airbag (Mottola, 2004).

Antilock brakes are effective at helping the vehicle stop faster but only if the driver knows how to use them and does not panic when he or she feels the pulsing action that occurs when they are activated. Instead of pumping the brake pedal, the driver should maintain a firm and consistent pressure to activate the antilock brakes.

Traction control and all-wheel drive can allow the vehicle to handle better in certain conditions, but drivers need to remember that all vehicles will have trouble in heavy rainstorms and icy conditions; they should not think that these technologies will prevent any loss of vehicle control. It is important for them to learn how to appropriately control the vehicle when evasive maneuvers are needed.

All-power options can help elderly drivers quickly open and lock the vehicle. Drivers need to know that, with any computer system, things can go wrong, and they should have a backup plan should the electronics fail.

Sport utility vehicles (SUVs) are larger but not safer. Drivers of SUVs need to know how to drive them and how they differ from automobiles. SUVs have a higher center of gravity, require more planning before turning so as not to roll the vehicle, are at high risk of rollover during evasive maneuvers, and can make it harder for the driver to see all other traffic because the vehicles may have more blind spots and sit higher off the ground.

When an elderly driver purchases a new car, he or she should take time to thoroughly learn its features. It may have been a long time since the driver last drove a new car, and the new safety technologies will help keep the driver safe only if he or she knows how to use them (AAA, 2001).

"Well Elderly" People

The term *well elderly* is used to describe elderly people ages 65 and older who are aging healthy and free from disability. Changes in ability are related to the aging process (Eberhard, 1996). Many people in this age group are driving safely, but some are no longer safe and take a risk every time they get into a vehicle (Ball et al., 1998). Much research is needed in the area of these elderly drivers to determine the issues that most affect safety in driving (Owsley, 1997).

Personal Experience 5.1. Elderly Woman

One of my clients was a 93-year-old woman in for a driver evaluation. Her son wanted her to have the evaluation because he worked in the medical field and knew that the age-related changes she was experiencing may affect her driving. She completed clinical and road evaluations, and it was determined that she could continue to drive based on the results. She already restricted herself to driving during nonpeak times of the day, avoided the freeway, and did not drive long distances. She used the bus to get in and around her busy metropolitan area and drove only to places close by (running errands, attending community events). She knew that she could not drive forever and said that she had started using the bus to supplement her ability to drive with an increased comfort in her ability to use alternative transportation, which would become necessary later in life. In the meantime, she kept physically fit and exercised daily so that she would be able to stay active in her community and increase the number of years she could drive.

Many people of all ages make it a point to take care of themselves and their bodies. They eat right, exercise on a regular basis, get enough sleep, have ways to control stress, and are involved in leisure pursuits that keep them active. They go to the physician and optometrist for yearly checkups. As people age, these factors play a significant role in helping them age well (Fabiny, 2005). They are proactive about getting medical attention (and follow the recommendations of the medical professional in treating medical problems), keeping their skills sharp in all areas of life, and getting feedback on their performance of tasks that require high-level skills.

Numerous organizations have developed educational programs to promote safe driving practices among seniors, which have garnered widespread popularity (Owsley, McGwin, Phillips, McNeal, & Stalvey, 2004). Many safety programs are available to older drivers (ages 55 years or older) to regularly take refresher courses in the classroom, such as "55 Alive" (offered through AARP; www.aarp.org), AAA driving refresher courses (www.aaa.org), and "Coaching the Mature Driver" through the National Safety Council (www.nsc.org/chaptop/htm). These courses are offered locally by trained personnel; visit the organization's Web site or the local department of motor vehicles (DMV) for specific locations. These courses provide a way to brush up on the rules of the road and changes in road signs or rules, and they review issues related to older drivers. In addition, some older drivers may take a lesson or two from a driving instructor to improve and update their skills for safer driving. Many elderly drivers do exercises to maintain their reaction time, flexibility, and the physical skills required to get in and out of vehicles and operate their vehicle. They also may start self-restricting, which can be an appropriate way to stay safe (Ball et al., 1998). For example, people who self-restrict may no longer drive at night, avoid freeways, and cease long-distance driving. Family members ride along periodically to ensure safe skills and provide feedback on any areas that the driver could improve on for safety.

AAA has released a CD-ROM called "Road Wise Review," available for purchase from www.aaa.org. This program enables older drivers to assess their driving-related skills. The person using the program will need a computer and someone to assist him or her with the testing. The person assisting needs to have insight and skills to accurately measure the older driver as he or she follows the directions, sets up, and completes the testing.

AAA also is coming out with CarFit, a program designed to give elderly drivers a quick, comprehensive check of how well they fit in their car and how their car is set up. CarFit is similar to a health fair; elderly drivers come to CarFit in a nearby city with their vehicle and are seen by someone who is trained to look at how they fit in their vehicle. Both of these programs can be accessed at the AAA senior driver Web site (www.seniordrivers.org).

Another new program to raise awareness in the older driver community is the Drive Well program. This is a partnership between the American Society on Aging and the National Highway Traffic Safety Association to train professionals (e.g., occupational therapists, nurses, social workers, other allied health professionals) to give free community presentations to seniors, caregivers, and those who work with the older population in rehabilitation to raise awareness of issues of older driver safety and community mobility. This program also provides the health care professional with a tool kit to complete these presentations. To receive more information about this program or to register as a professional interested in obtaining training, visit www.asaging.org/drivewell.

Vision Changes. Although it is true that everyone can be proactive in aging gracefully, the aging process still affects everyone, and it is important to know how those changes may affect driving. The aging process affects several visual capabilities. Older people tend to have more difficulty dividing their attention between multiple stimuli or tasks and experience a narrowing of their useful field of view (Wheatley, 2001). The ability to see details in low contrast is affected, and the older driver will have more difficulty seeing at night, on rainy days, or in tunnels where there is less light (Decina & Staplin, 1993). This may, in turn, affect the ability to see everything from low-contrast signs (e.g., green sign with gray letters) to the dashboard and speedometer gauges. The field of vision typically narrows with age, so side-to-side movements of the driver's head become necessary to fully monitor what is going on around the vehicle (Owsley & McGwin, 1999). Contrast sensitivity can diminish, impeding the ability to see at night, in heavy rain or snow, or at dusk (Decina & Staplin, 1993). The eyes' ability to adjust from a dark tunnel to bright sun may become impaired, with increased glare sensitivity (Jennings, 1995). Some people notice the changes at a younger age than do others, but the aging process affects everyone's vision (Zoltan, 1996). It is important for occupational therapists and the general public to be aware of these changes so that people can be encouraged to be proactive in identifying this potential risk before it becomes a problem on the road.

The occupational therapist can help clients get proper referrals to evaluate and maintain healthy vision. It is important to know what tests optometrists use, what they evaluate, and what modifications can assist people's vision as they age. The occupational therapist can be proactive in letting the optometrist know how the concerns about the client's vision relate to driving skills. Optometrists too often focus on activities of daily living and do not always know how visual impairments affect the components of the driving task. They more often focus on state requirements for distance and peripheral vision. The input of the occupational therapist generalist or driver rehabilitation specialist (OT/DRS) can help ensure that the client receives optometric tests that enable a more thorough evaluation of how vision changes are affecting the client's driving.

Visual disorders that affect well elderly people include macular degeneration, glaucoma, and cataracts (Owsley, 2004). It is important that occupational therapists working with this age group learn about these vision disorders and make appropriate referrals for treatment. These disorders progress (Owsley, McGwin, & Ball, 1998), and clients eventually may not meet state requirements for driving or may otherwise be unable to drive safely. Although not all people with these conditions will have to quit driving, clients with these disorders should prepare for the eventuality of having to quit driving by learning about alternative transportation options in their area.

Some states have low vision programs for driving and regulations that permit bioptic driving; resources for bioptics are covered in Appendix A under "Low Vision." Older drivers need to be free from other disabilities to effectively learn to use bioptics and stay within the needed restrictions (bioptic drivers are restricted to areas they are familiar with and to certain speeds or types of roads).

Driver evaluations should examine visual skills in the task performance. If the client drives at night and during the day and in all areas, it is important that the driver evaluation look at how vision affects skill and safety under these conditions. Many people meet state vision requirements but are not safe drivers because of their vision. They do not see signs and often miss cues to slow down or stop because they need more time to see what is going on around them.

Many people realize this on their own, quit driving, and get medical attention (e.g., cataract surgery) to regain their vision for driving. Other drivers do not deal with their vision problems, for whatever reason; they may know that it interferes with driving but drive anyway. Often, family members are the first to voice safety concerns and no longer ride with them as a result, but they do not take action because they do not want to damage their relationship with the driver. In such cases, families often go to health professionals, the state DMV, or an optometrist to get assistance in evaluating whether their loved one still has the visual capacity for driving. Sometimes these needs are met successfully, depending on how aware these professionals are about the skills needed for driving, the state statutes and reporting structure, and the resources available for referral to an on-the-road evaluation. Families, health professionals, and state DMVs need information about age-related vision deficits to help ensure that elderly people have their vision and driving skills evaluated accurately.

Musculoskeletal Changes. Decreases in strength, range of motion, and reaction time occur with age, depending on how active a person remains (Owsley, 2004). Driving requires that a person have the physical skills to get to the vehicle in all types of weather, get in and out of the vehicle, steer the vehicle, operate the accessory controls (e.g., headlights, horn, wipers, turn signals), and operate the accelerator and brake. The controls need to be operated in a smooth, coordinated manner with good reaction time to whatever situations may arise.

Sometimes the reaction time from accelerator to brake becomes slow. Although the driver may mean to stop at the light, by the time it changes from yellow to red, he or she may be in the middle of the intersection before stopping. Some people have trouble maintaining lane position on quick turns, moving halfway out of their lane into the other lane or slightly over into oncoming traffic lane because they need more time to complete the motion.

These skills can be evaluated and sometimes improved if the driver works on the skills on a regular basis. If the skills cannot be improved, sometimes giving the person driving restrictions can be appropriate. For example, a driver might have trouble reacting as quickly as necessary to the fast traffic on a freeway; in this case, a restriction may allow the client to continue to drive safely. Such drivers may benefit from a radius restriction to driving only within 10 miles of their home, staying off roads with speed limits exceeding 45 mph, and avoiding freeways if the state in which the driver is licensed will recognize driving restrictions. These restrictions can be self-imposed, or an OT/DRS can have the restrictions placed on the client's driver's license so that it is an official restriction. Before considering a radius restriction, however, the OT/DRS should be sure that the client lives in an area that truly is familiar to them; people often move later in life. It also is important to ensure that the restrictions are safe for the driver, so he or she should have an on-the-road evaluation with the recommended restrictions, preferably by a trained professional (either the state DMV or an OT/DRS, depending on medical involvement).

Cognitive Changes. Cognitive changes in well elderly people include memory loss, particularly the ability to remember details; slower thinking or processing speed; difficulty learning new things; and decreased insight into themselves and their limitations (Owsley, 2004). These declines can be prevented or mitigated among people who continue to challenge themselves cognitively and stay active. Awareness of these declines among occupational therapist generalists can help this population find ways to continue to challenge their cognitive abilities. They can suggest activities or tasks that are meaningful to the client.

Cognitive declines can interfere with driving in a variety of ways. People with cognitive declines may forget where they are going or how to get there, particularly if they are driving to a new or unfamiliar place. Reduced processing speed impedes the ability to respond to situations in a timely manner. It also can interfere with the ability to "multitask": to listen to the radio, have a conversation, or even think about something else while driving. Having small children or a pet in the car can be too distracting and create safety problems.

Sometimes the driver will notice these changes and either self-limit or get a checkup to see what is going on. Often, the family or health professional first notices these declines and talks to the driver about them. If no disability is causing the declines, aging is likely the cause.

Whenever cognitive problems are noted, driving should be addressed to ensure that the driver is safe. A driver evaluation can make sure that the client is not getting lost, that he or she understands and reacts quickly enough to the information he or she needs to process, and that he or she can handle the distractions that occur with driving (limiting those over which they have control). It is important that whoever performs the driver evaluation has knowledge of cognitive deficits and how they affect driving, so that an accurate analysis is completed.

Personal Experience 5.2. Elderly Man

An elderly client limited his driving to only the 5-mile radius around his house and drove to medical appointments and short errands only. He lived in the middle of a large city on a main thoroughfare and had to exit without a light from his driveway. He did not have the physical skills to get onto the busy road fast enough and could not process all the information to be safe. Once he was out of the fast-paced traffic area, his skills for driving were safe. Using the driver evaluation results, the family, physician, and OT/DRS worked on a plan to move to a nearby apartment in the familiar neighborhood but on a more accessible road that would enable him to drive safely and provide long-term community mobility.

Driving has changed significantly since most elderly people originally learned how to drive. People often learned from another family member or friend, not a driving instructor. Rules of the road have changed. Speeds are faster; many four-lane roads and multilane freeways have been built; new tools for managing traffic have been instituted, such as reversible lanes and high-occupancy vehicle lanes; sprawl and associated construction are everywhere; and many more vehicles are on the road than there used to be. As a result, driving is a more difficult and challenging task than when the elderly population was younger. Keeping up with all of these changes is important to maintain safe driving. Driving to other states for trips or vacations or living seasonally in two different areas also complicates the function of driving.

Often a driver evaluation is key to determining a person's understanding of current road safety and ability to drive under the conditions they face. Sometimes living in a less busy area or updating skills enables driving for a longer period. Without such changes, though, the client's skills may not match the demands of driving.

Adolescents and Adults With Special Needs

When they reach the age of driving, adolescents of all abilities want to pursue the task, just as their friends are doing. Adolescents with learning disabilities, attention deficit hyperactivity disorder, mental health disorders, autism, Asperger's syndrome, or mental retardation want to drive, too. They often start off like any other teenager, working with their school driving program or a licensed driving instructor. For all adolescents, driving is a dangerous task because of their lack of experience and immature judgment; adding a cognitive disorder to the mix certainly complicates matters.

This approach will work for some students if it is provided in combination with structure, practice, and patience from their parents. Many adolescents, however, are not ready to drive. Even with adolescents who are ready to drive, their parents may feel unable to keep them safe during practice or may notice that their child does not learn things as quickly as other teens. Some teenagers often do not accept feedback at all from their parents.

Understanding the impact of various diagnoses on driving is critical to deciding whether and how to teach a teenager to drive. Some students may complete lessons with a driving instructor but still be unsafe on the road. Other students may not be able to pass the permit test because they cannot read the questions, do not do well with written tests, or have poor study skills.

As with adult clients, the teaching method and the skills of the driving instructor need to match the individual teenager. Teen clients with learning disabilities or mental health issues often benefit from a teaching style that breaks information down into its smallest discrete parts, then builds to the task as a whole. These adolescents often do best with hands-on activities rather than a lecture or pen-and-paper tasks. They are often concrete, linear thinkers and have trouble with abstraction. These traits can interfere with the ability to learn to drive if they are not identified and compensated for.

Adolescents may have areas of deficit in addition to the learning disability or low IQ scores. As with all clients, vision, cognition, and physical capabilities need to be evaluated for their possible effects on driving. Understanding the client's learning style is particularly important in working with adolescents.

Adults with these disabilities have the same risks and needs in the area of driving, but they may have fewer problems, because they are not also dealing with the angst of adolescence along with their disability. Adolescents have hormonal changes, fewer life experiences, and a not fully formed frontal lobe, which add to the problems they face.

Breaking Down Driving for People With Learning and Congenital Disabilities

Driving and learning to drive are complex. Both require that the person be able to learn about safe driving and rules of the road to take the state written test. This includes classroom training for new drivers of a certain age (usually younger than 18), studying the state's driving manual, and passing an exam. Clients with whom I worked who had learning disabilities and congenital disabilities often had particular trouble focusing during the classroom training hours. They often benefit from additional private tutoring and using multiple methods to learn the information (e.g., reading, seeing, doing). It may take them several attempts before they pass the written test. The written test is usually given on computer, but it can be read to the person orally by a state DMV instructor if needed; accommodations need to be scheduled in advance with proper reasoning given.

Training of clients with disabilities usually includes repeating instructions until the person grasps the ideas or concepts and can incorporate them into the driving routine. Training will take longer than for the average driver, but there should always be progress and carryover from session to session to ensure that the person has the potential to be a successful, safe driver. The client also may need restrictions, which may be lifted over time if his or her mastery and skill level increase. Restrictions may be on speed or radius. The client also may keep his or her permit longer and practice with a parent or caregiver longer before he or she has the skill to road test and drive alone.

A way to help clients with disabilities learn to drive is to break each driving task into smaller pieces of information and allot time for the learning and repetition of each piece. An example of this is breaking down the use of side mirrors and the overhead panel mirror in the vehicle. Once the client has control of the car, can steer, and can use the blinkers, he or she should be introduced to using the mirrors. While practicing in a parking lot, the client can begin to occasionally monitor the overhead panel mirror before turning or pretending to change a lane, letting the OT/DRS know what he or she sees. Learning smaller amounts of information at a time with repetition can be the key for this population to learn and be safe drivers. If too much information is taught at once or out of sequence, the client may not learn the information or may not use it to be safe in driving.

The number of lessons, amount of repetition needed, and grading of the activity will depend on the individual and the effects of their disability. Clinical testing can be helpful to determine the client's abilities, limitations, and learning style—all information the OT/DRS can use to determine the client's ability to drive, as well as the approximate number of lessons that will be required.

Clients in this population should not practice with their parents prior to starting in vehicle evaluation or training. This is not a safe situation for the parent or the client because often it leads to the parent never wanting to practice with the client, or it scares the client from driving. When the client is ready, he or she should first go to the OT/DRS, who will be the initial lead in safe practice sessions. These clients will often be considered new drivers longer than people of their age without disability. People with disabilities will keep their learner's or provisional permits longer and need supervision longer to develop safe independent driving habits.

The road test can be intimidating for these clients, even more so than for other populations or disability groups. They may become nervous testing with someone who is unfamiliar, and they may have more trouble calming their nerves for best performance. They may need to become familiar with the road test so that they can feel more comfortable and do their best. It is not uncommon for these clients to road test more than one or two times before passing.

Working With People With Learning Disabilities

In working with people with learning disabilities, it is important to know what type of learning disability they have and how much it affects their daily life. The occupational therapist should find out from the clients' physician what medications they are on, how long they have been taking them, and what the side effects are.

People with learning disabilities often have a difficult time attending to a task or shifting attention correctly. They may veer off the road while looking at scenery because their hands follow where they are looking. They may need a correction from the driving instructor to get safely back into their lane. Adolescents with learning disabilities may appear to do well with driving on quiet roads or in less-demanding situations, but their skills may deteriorate when the demands increase and the stimuli in the environment become more distracting. It is critical that these adolescents develop attention skills to stay safe.

In addition, students with learning disabilities may be concrete thinkers. These youths oversimplify rules and have a decreased ability to generalize. They have trouble dealing with exceptions to a rule; that is, they generally apply rules in their most concrete form to all situations. The reality is that rules always need to be analyzed, reviewed, and sometimes applied differently or not at all in light of a given situation and the demands of the task at the moment. Adolescents with a learning disability do best when they have insight into their areas of deficit and learning style; unfortunately, they often do not, partly because of their age and partly because of concrete thinking.

People with a learning disability often can pay attention for a short while, but if they become tired or drive for a long time, their skills may decline. It is important to keep lessons short and lengthen them as the adolescent learns the skills. It is helpful to incorporate lots of repetition into the lessons. Clients need to learn their limits under the supervision of the instructor. They ultimately may need restrictions on the duration of their driving and driving radius.

> ***Personal Experience 5.3. Male Teenage Driver***
>
> One of my teen clients was a concrete learner; he had obtained his license and begun driving on his own. On one occasion, he could not remember where he was going. He drifted slightly in the lane and then changed lanes. A police officer was concerned that the driver was lost, so he decided to pull him over. As the officer followed him with his lights on, the driver switched lanes to the right to get out of the policeman's way. The officer had to put on the siren and motion for the teen to pull over. When the driver finally pulled over, the officer asked him why he had not done so right away. The teen's reply was, "I would only have pulled over had I done something wrong. I did not do anything wrong, so you could not have had your lights on for me, so I did not need to pull over." This is one example of concrete learning, the oversimplification of rules, and decreased ability to generalize.

People With Congenital Disabilities

The effects of congenital disabilities vary according to the type of disability and the person. The important thing to remember when working with a client with a congenital disability is that he or she has had the disability since birth, and the body and brain have learned to use other avenues to adapt to situations. Such clients have not known the world another way. As a result, they need to be screened differently. For instance, depth perception is often affected in children with certain types of disabilities; they have learned to judge distances differently than people with full use of both eyes. They still lack depth perception per se, but they have found a different way to gauge distances. The occupational therapist needs to understand this distinction.

The generalist has an important role with this population because these clients often have received occupational therapy intervention long before the task of driving is even thought of or needs to be addressed. Parents often are overwhelmed with trying to understand what the future will hold for their child while balancing their other work and childrearing responsibilities. The occupational therapist can help the parents with early planning for higher level tasks. Knowing that the client aspires to higher level tasks will ensure that therapy or intervention is not stopped too early and that the right areas are addressed when the opportunity exists to make the most difference.

For example, learning to use both hands from day 1, even if one is weaker than the other, or learning to do different things with each hand, is critical when evaluating the ability to control a car. Involving a child in any type of physical play or interaction to teach cause and effect is important to everyday function and critical to high-level tasks, because such games improve response time. Sports or activities that require eye–hand coordination teach spatial relationships that can help prepare for the driving task. These concepts are harder to learn when a person is older. Most people have interactions that have taught them these skills all their lives before they try using them in driving.

Even as recently as 10 years ago, people born with disabilities were treated with a different set of expectations. They were not seen as able to function on their own, and fewer recreational, sports, and other opportunities existed for them. Parents, the rehabilitation team, and the client need to be aware of these opportunities to build skills. Education can help reinforce the importance of functional involvement.

Skills needed for the driving task can be reinforced passively. For example, in vehicles, it is important for children to be able to see out the windows. The more often they can look straight out the front window, the more normal their perception of the driving task will be. Children grow up watching their parents drive, noticing the lights, signs, other vehicles, and their parents' responses to those vehicles. They often ask questions or comment on what they see others doing on the road. If a child always faces backward or sideways in a vehicle because of a chair or assistive device, such experiences will not be available to them. Keeping this fact in mind in deciding on equipment and transportation options can help ensure as normal an interaction with the driving environment as possible.

Adolescents with congenital disabilities often are no longer seen for medical therapy services and may only qualify for consultation services in school. Some adolescents interested in driving may not have had any therapy interventions since they were small children and may lack important skills needed for driving. Pediatric therapists and occupational therapist generalists should be encouraged to include exercises geared toward higher level skill development as early as possible.

The OT/DRS's clinical evaluation, as always, will look closely at the client's physical skills, vision, cognition, and reaction time as they relate to the task of driving. Reflex patterns and their causes will be determined, along with the extent to which they interfere with function. The OT/DRS also will ask many questions about the client's physical activities (e.g., sports) and use of mobility devices; success with those devices may affect the success and skills the person may already have learned in relation to driving.

The driving portion of the evaluation needs to be broken down into components, and the abilities of the client need to be taken into account to determine his or her true potential for driving. Many people are given misinformation because the professional who is trying to help them does not understand their medical condition and how to best work with them to elicit the best outcome for them. Sometimes a driving instructor without medical background will progress the client too quickly, and sometimes the correct equipment is not chosen because of a lack of understanding of what the client needs to function properly. The OT/DRS is able to provide the best analysis of the client's driving abilities.

If the client has never used both hands to do separate activities, he or she will have great difficulty with driving at first. If the OT/DRS breaks down the task and suggests therapy interventions and home programs to develop these skills, the outcome to driving may be successful.

It is important not to underestimate the skills of the OT/DRS in understanding the learning style of the client. His or her ability to break down the task and convey information successfully can make a huge difference in the outcome. Progressing the client incrementally and providing repetition and feedback are essential in teaching the activity.

Dwarfism and Short Stature

People who have dwarfism or are short of stature should receive a driver evaluation to ensure that the most appropriate adaptive equipment is selected and the correct training is received. The OT/DRS will measure the client's height and limb length to best determine his or her adaptive equipment needs. With dwarfism, other congenital disabilities may need to be evaluated to determine the client's ability to drive. Adaptive equipment that may be helpful includes extended pedals (Figure 5.1), hand controls, spinner knobs, seat cushions (Figure 5.2), adapted mirrors, accessory controls, mini-steering wheels, electronic accelerator and brake, and reduced or no-effort steering.

Autism and Asperger's Syndrome

Different varieties and degrees of autism exist (Asperger's syndrome is a form of high-functioning autism). Autistic behaviors include difficulty interacting in or interpreting social situations, difficulty shifting attention to meet the demands of the activity, and overly concrete thinking. Teens with autism often have trouble with transitions from one activity to the next or from one situation to another.

Figure 5.1. Seat cushions for people with dwarfism or who are short of stature.

Source: Delta Integration, Inc., Lancaster, PA. Used with permission.

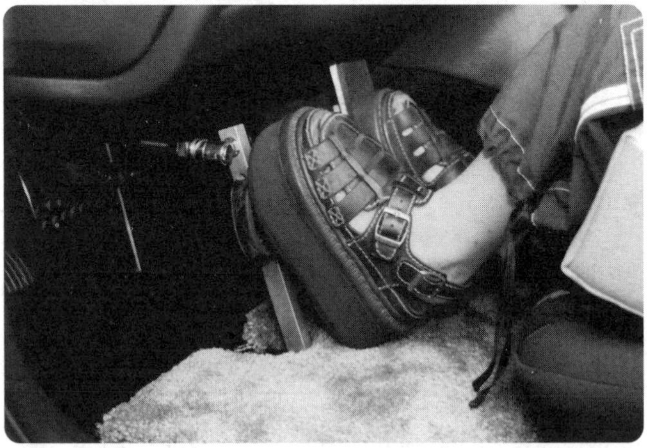

Figure 5.2. Extended pedals for people with dwarfism or who are short of stature.

Source: Adaptive Mobility, Inc., Lancaster, PA. Used with permission.

Having a bad day can affect our driving abilities in a negative way; on some days, we are more distracted than others. Imagine if those distracted days occurred all the time and each time we drove, we risked not paying sufficient attention to be safe. This is the case for many people with autism.

In working with people who have autism, it is important to know how they interact in social situations, what their attention span is, and whether they need an aide to help them accomplish their activities of daily living. In addition, the occupational therapist should understand how each client learns best. If the client has any behavioral issues, it is important to know whether he or she can control those behaviors. Medications to increase attention or to help with mood can affect driving.

The clinical assessment should include the usual tests of cognition, vision, and physical abilities along with questions about the rules of the road, signage, and social aspects of driving. Social situations often are uncomfortable to people with autism, and they may not understand how to interpret social situations or nonverbal communication. Safe driving, however, requires social skills, and clients with autism must have sufficient social skills to ensure their safety on the road. Clients who pass the clinical assessment should understand that they still may not be safe on the road.

If the occupational therapist thinks it is appropriate to move to the on-the-road assessment, he or she should assess how the client learns new information and coordinates physical, cognitive, and visual skills to control the vehicle. Distracting the client with the radio or talking will help demonstrate how the client filters information that is not relevant to driving. Most clients with autism will need to limit distractions: no radio, no cell phone, no eating, and no large groups in the car.

Mental Retardation

When working with clients with mental retardation, it is important to know their IQ and how they functionally use their level of intelligence. These clients also need to be able to understand the responsibility involved in driving and the risks involved with operating a motor vehicle. The more they do independently for themselves at home and at school, the better chance they have of being able to drive. Regardless of IQ, a driver needs to be able to generalize information and quickly process and react to information.

People with this disability are generally hands-on learners and require significant repetition. They need the activity of driving broken down into its components, and benefit from learning one component at a time before integrating them.

Once a client with mental retardation learns to perform components of driving, he or she must be able to put the pieces together and integrate them into performing the task as a whole. Clients need to make progress at each lesson, and each lesson needs to be broken down into a purpose, plan, and expected outcome. It is not fair to overtrain such clients and then tell them they cannot drive. The OT/DRS as trainer must set expectations and draw the line when expectations are not met in a timely manner.

Cerebral Palsy

The occupational therapist should know about the different types of cerebral palsy (e.g., athetoid, spastic) and how they affect people. Cerebral palsy can affect all extremities or primarily be on one side. It is important to know what movements the client is capable of, what movements he or she can control, and whether the client has primitive reflexes that may interfere with driving. Clients' abilities

Personal Experience 5.4. Woman With Cerebral Palsy

I had a client with cerebral palsy that affected primarily her legs and left arm. Her first driving instructor had no medical background. He had her drive using a left-side hand control and use a steering wheel but no adapted steering device. He took her out onto the road right away, even into traffic. The client was unable to drive safely; she had trouble staying in her lane, did not know rules of the road as they related to safe driving, and was not able to pass her road test after 6 hours of training. The driving instructor felt she was not trying hard enough and did not practice enough.

I evaluated the woman in my vehicle in a parking lot using the same controls she used with the previous driving instructor. She struggled with movement between the accelerator and brake and did not have the strength to steer. I had her try a right-hand control and left spinner knob.

Her skills improved, and she had better strength and control steering with her left arm. Her right arm was stronger but had less range of motion for larger movements. Because she still had some trouble with quick steering, we tried reduced-effort steering, which improved her control of the vehicle.

The next problem area involved parking, stopping, and navigating between obstacles. My client had trouble understanding position in space and how her movement affected the environment at different speeds; she had trouble gauging how much time she needed to slow down and stop. She also did not fully scan her environment and missed information, especially on the left side. To work on these problems, my client received occupational therapy from a generalist and was given a home exercise program and visual tasks. She progressed with her driving skills after about 3 months.

This client needed more training than someone without a disability of her age because she needed information to be broken down along with considerable repetition to learn new skills. It took her about a year to learn how to drive; with a combination of OT/DRS intervention along with parents practicing once she was safe with the driving task; and she eventually got her license. She is currently independent in all driving except freeway and night driving.

can be assessed throughout their lifetime to help them learn to compensate and integrate any reflexes that they possibly can. The client's will and persistence play a role. Given two individuals with the same condition and similar obstacles to driving, the one with the strong will to drive generally will work harder and have better functional results than the other.

If a client has a startle reflex, associated response of other extremities when doing a hard task, or spasticity or increased tone, he or she may be able to diminish their effects through adaptive equipment, medication, or positioning. The therapy must begin early, however. The client may first learn to crawl, then walk, then ride a bike and play sports, and then move to harder tasks such as driving, community mobility, and work. The activity demands increase over time.

Vision disorders seen with cerebral palsy include lack of depth perception, double vision (which may be corrected surgically or treated with vision exercises when the child is young), and nystagmus. The strategies and approaches for addressing vision problems are different for children because their eyes, brains, and bodies are not yet fully developed. It is more difficult for adults to compensate for vision problems if they have never received therapy for them.

When the person with cerebral palsy is ready to be evaluated for driving, he or she should be seen by an OT/DRS, not just a regular driving instructor. The need for specialized training and equipment must be determined, and the client's abilities as they relate to driving must be correctly assessed. If the evaluation determines that the client is not capable of driving, the OT/DRS will understand whether the client's capabilities can change with further therapy. Most clients with cerebral palsy will be able to attempt an on-the-road assessment, unless state regulations exclude them from driving for a particular reason.

Spina Bifida

Like clients with cerebral palsy, clients with spina bifida benefit from having life experiences to draw from that involve movement and higher level of function. It is important that clients with spina bifida—and all clients, whether living with a disability or not—have life experiences that enable them to achieve a developmentally mature level, because driving

Personal Experience 5.5. Man With Spina Bifida

A client with spina bifida had graduated from high school when he turned 21. He lived at home with his parents and had no responsibilities. He came to the driver evaluation with dirty clothes, dirty hair, and body odor of urine and sweat. He did not have life experiences with sports or other physical activities, and he propelled his chair only when forced to do so. He watched TV and played video games most of the time. He did not have many friends and found social situations awkward.

This client was bright and did well on the cognitive and visual clinical assessments. He did not do well, however, with abstract reasoning, spatial relationships, or divided attention. The client used a manual wheelchair and was able to transfer independently into the car and stow his wheelchair on his own. He had the strength and coordination to use the hand control and spinner knob but could not figure out how to control the vehicle or understand how what he did affected the vehicle. He could not react quickly and had trouble knowing what to pay attention to. He could not get used to doing more than one thing at a time and became frustrated any time another car came into the parking lot.

This client would have done much better if driving had been planned for earlier in his life and if he had had normal life experiences. The skill of driving was not within his current reach, and he had never been taught how to work hard to learn something new or gain skills. He was given home program ideas, and his parents were given feedback on building responsibilities at home so that he would learn needed skills to be in the community, live more independently, get a job, and possibly drive in the future.

requires a level of maturity to ensure safety. Clients who have been sheltered, have had everything done for them, have not had to deal with the consequences of their actions, or have not had to meet others' expectations tend to be emotionally immature. It is important that clients be exposed to challenging environments and required to meet everyday expectations so that they can mature like anyone else in their age category does.

New Drivers

Driving requires a level of responsibility to do it safely. New drivers must have developed a sense of responsibility in their day-to-day environment so that they can comprehend the seriousness of driving and what could occur as a result of their actions. Otherwise, driving will be tackled as though it were a game or fun activity. New drivers are most commonly adolescents, but anyone who has not had responsibilities or consequences in other aspects of life may have difficulty understanding how serious the business of driving is and the serious consequences of errors.

With new drivers with disabilities, the OT/DRS will assess their potential for safe driving, the amount of training that will be needed, and whether that training needs to be specialized or performed by a driving instructor. A full report of the skill level, restrictions, and other related findings will be reviewed with the new driver and his or her family and sent to the physician. Some states require the physician to send in a statement or form related to the ability of the client to drive.

New drivers with disabilities may need help studying for the written test required to get a learners' permit. State drivers' manuals are often written at too high a level or have too many details that are not critical to know right away. Such students often benefit from commentary driving (generally done with their parents), which involves the student sitting in the passenger seat and commenting on what they see related to what they are learning. This approach can be effective with teaching hands-on learners.

Once the learners' permit is obtained, lessons can begin. It is important to go at the pace of the student. With adolescents with disabilities, the instructor should let the student and parents know that the number of lessons and practice will be more than the average adolescent would require. The instructor also should provide plenty of opportunity for the new driver to learn to generalize information. The new driver may not graduate to driving independently for some time and will likely do so incrementally. He or she may keep a learners' permit much longer than most new drivers and may not pass the road test on the first try.

Summary and Conclusion

The field of occupational therapy is diverse, addressing issues for a variety of age groups, cultures, and abilities—physical, cognitive, visual, or mental health. Occupational therapists in all areas of practice work with a wide range of populations who need to have driving analyzed or evaluated. Occupational therapists see this diversity in population and are in the unique situation to take the lead in addressing this growing area of practice.

The way driving is addressed will vary by population, but the importance of addressing it is the same. It is critical that driving is not forgotten or overlooked. Knowing what type of questions or concerns may arise with each population is an important step in assisting the client to get the right services to meet his or her needs. Be it a physical, mental health, or age-related concern, getting the right information to the client at the right time will make all the difference. It is important that occupational therapists in all areas of practice with all populations be able to break down the task of driving and appropriately address it for each client.

References

AAA. (2001). *How to help an older driver: A guide for planning safe transportation.* Washington, DC: Author.

Ball, K., Owsley, C., Stalvey, B., Roenker, D. L., Sloane, M. E., & Graves, M. (1998). Driving avoidance and functional impairment in older drivers. *Accident Analysis and Prevention, 30,* 313–322.

Decina, L. E., & Staplin, L. (1993). Retrospective evaluation of alternative vision screening: Criteria for older and younger drivers. *Accident Analysis and Prevention, 25,* 267–275.

Eberhard, J. W. (1996). Safe mobility for senior citizens. *IATSS Research, 20,* 29–37.

Fabiny, A. (2005). *Living better, living longer: The secrets of healthy aging.* Cambridge, MA: Harvard Health Publications.

Jennings, L. A. (1995). Performance components predictive of errors resulting in motor vehicle crashes in older drivers. *Work: A Journal of Prevention, Assessment, and Rehabilitation, 5,* 277–290.

Mottola, F. R. (2004). *Partnership for driver excellence: Teen, parent, teacher* (5th ed.). Cheshire, CT: Frederik R. Mottola Publications.

Owsley, C. (1997). Clinical and research issues on older drivers: Future directions. *Alzheimer's Disease and Associated Disorders, 11* (Suppl. 1), 3–7.

Owsley, C. (2004). Driver capabilities. In *Transportation in an aging society: A decade of experience* (pp. 44–55). Washington, DC: Transportation Research Board, National Research Council, National Academies of Science.

Owsley, C., & McGwin, G. (1999). Vision impairment and driving. *Survey of Ophthalmology, 43,* 535–550.

Owsley, C., McGwin, D., & Ball, K. (1998). Vision impairment, eye disease, and injurious motor vehicle crashes in the elderly. *Ophthalmic Epidemiology, 5,* 101–113.

Owsley, C., McGwin, D., Phillips, J. M., McNeal, S. F., & Stalvey, B.T. (2004). Impact of an educational program on the safety of high-risk, visually impaired, older drivers. *American Journal of Preventative Medicine, 26,* 222–229.

Pierce, S. (2003). The occupational therapist's roadmap to safety for seniors. *Gerontology Special Interest Section Quarterly, 26*(3), 1–2.

Sanders, M. S., & McCormick, E. J. (1993). *Human factors in engineering and design* (7th ed.). New York: McGraw/Hill.

Wheatley, C. J. (2001). Visual perceptual aspects of driving. *Physical Disabilities Special Interest Section Quarterly, 24*(3), 1–3.

Zoltan, B. (1996). Factors that influence the patient's vision, perception, and cognition. In B. Zoltan (Ed.), *Vision, perception, and cognition: A manual for the evaluation and treatment of the neurologically impaired adult* (3rd ed., pp. 185–190). Thorofare, NJ: Slack.

Considerations for Working With Specific Disabilities

Working With People With Physical Disabilities and Conditions

Many physical conditions can affect driving and the nature of the driver evaluation. In all cases, the occupational therapist driver rehabilitation specialist (OT/DRS) providing a driver evaluation should evaluate the client's medications; whether the condition is stable, progressive, or improving; the impact of fatigue; and the likelihood of physical, cognitive, and visual deficits. This chapter focuses on factors specific to clients who have particular disabilities and conditions. For information on driver evaluations in general, see Chapter 2.

When choosing the driving device, the therapist needs to consider the client's needs, physical ability to use the control, need for the assistance that the control provides, and cognitive understanding of how to use the device safely and to consider which device will fit into the client's vehicle. For example, numerous types of hand controls are on the market. The basic right-angle style pushes in to brake and pulls down at a right angle to accelerate. The push/pull style of hand control pushes in to brake and pulls out to accelerate. The sure-grip style pushes in to brake and tips toward the person to accelerate, requiring small movements and little force to use. Each hand control has a purpose; an individual may use one type of control better than others. It takes a trained person, such as an OT/DRS, to match the client and his or her needs to the right equipment. Vendors are helpful in this process, but they do not understand the medical components of the disability and need to work in conjunction with the OT/DRS (see Chapter 8).

Total Hip or Knee Replacement

It is important to address driving during the occupational therapist generalist's initial evaluation after a person has had a total hip or total knee replacement because these clients often do not spend much time in acute care or rehabilitation. They need to know when they can drive. If a client should not be driving for a certain period, this expectation needs to be made clear. Before a client begins driving again, he or she should not be taking pain medication, should be able to ambulate safely, and needs to be at least 2 weeks' postsurgery. The client needs to have a plan for driving once these criteria are met. Involving the physician in this is critical to developing the right criteria for the client and ensuring that the plan is monitored with the physician's agreement. What intervention and services are needed will depend on which leg is affected, the state of the client's general health and mobility, and any secondary conditions that affect driving ability. Depending on the age of the person and the level of recovery, driving with the leg that had the surgery may be an option. If the client has too much pain or does not have adequate range of motion or coordination for driving with the affected limb, then the occupational therapist should focus on transportation alternatives or adaptive equipment.

It is important to work with the client on how to safely enter and exit their home; how to get around in the community; and how to safely get in and out of vehicles, whether as a driver or passenger. A client who needs a cane, walker, or other assistive devices needs to be able to stow it in the vehicle independently. These areas can be worked on in therapy in addition to the client's other goals for activities of daily living.

Many people need to learn how to get into vehicles safely, especially as they are healing, so that they do not reinjure the hip or knee. Some people need adaptive equipment, such as a leg lifter, a doorjamb handle (Figure 6.1), or a pivot disc on the seat. These options all can help with safety and are not too expensive.

It also is important to have the physician tell the client how long he or she must wait before returning to driving; otherwise, people often try driving again right away, even if

Figure 6.1. Doorjamb handle.

Source: Occupational Therapy Solutions, Inc., Minneapolis, MN. Used with permission.

Figure 6.2. People with total knee or hip replacement may need to use hand controls, such as (A) the basic right-angle control or (B) the sure grip control.

Source: Courage Center, Minneapolis, MN. Used with permission.

doing so is painful (Ganz, Levin, Peterson, & Ranawat, 2003). The client also needs to know if his or her pain medication is contraindicated for driving; a nurse, physician, or pharmacist will usually provide this information. Before the client drives again, recovery should be assessed at the anticipated healing point to ensure that he or she has the strength and is sufficiently healed to drive pain-free.

Some people with total hip or knee replacement need to learn to use hand controls (Figure 6.2), because the strength of their affected leg decreases so significantly, because driving causes pain, or because the leg is not healing properly. It is important to show clients options for equipment (e.g., cane, walker, or scooter) and to review the proper ways to stow equipment (e.g., do not stow equipment in front of an airbag; secure equipment in such a way that it will not move in case of an accident), making sure that they have the skills to do so safely. Options for equipment storage include cartop carriers (Figure 6.3), a lift to load a chair or scooter into the back of a minivan or car (Figure 6.4), and lifts for side and back entry (Figures 6.5 and 6.6). Back entry makes parking easier, as the client will not need space next to the car for the lift.

Once a person is in the vehicle, there are options for transferring from the wheelchair or scooter to the driver's seat. Options include a three-way power seat with electronic or manual control options (Figure 6.7) or a power lift seat (Figure 6.8), or the client can use a truck, so that the wheelchair can act as the driver's seat (Figure 6.9). The OT/DRS must assess the choices and train the client carefully to ensure his or her safety (Figure 6.10).

If the client has decreased strength or if his or her coordination or reaction time seems to have been affected, a driver evaluation is indicated. The occupational therapist, physical therapist, physician, or nurse can provide the client with options for driver rehabilitation; as always, using a

Figure 6.3. Cartop carriers.

Source: Braun Corporation, Winamac, IN. Used with permission.

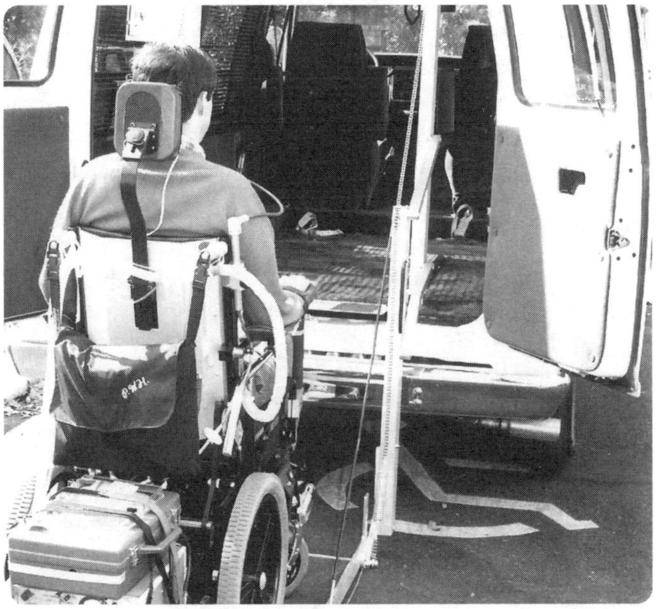

Figure 6.4. Lift for stowing a wheelchair in the rear of a vehicle.

Source: Adaptive Mobility, Inc., Orlando, FL. Used with permission.

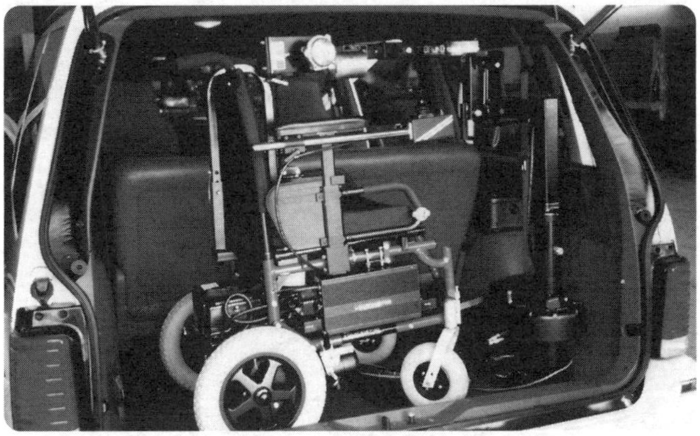

Figure 6.6. Rear-entry lift.

Source: Adaptive Mobility, Inc., Orlando, FL. Used with permission.

Figure 6.5. Side-entry lift.

Source: Adaptive Mobility, Inc., Orlando, FL. Used with permission.

Figure 6.7. A three-way power seat with electronic or manual control options.

Source: Adaptive Mobility, Inc., Orlando, FL. Used with permission.

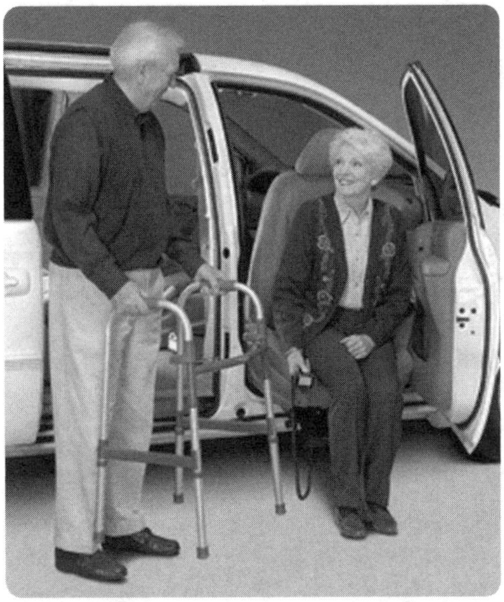

Figure 6.8. A power lift seat.

Source: Braun Corporation, Winamac, IN. Used with permission.

driver rehabilitation specialist who is an occupational therapist is beneficial.

In the driver evaluation, the evaluator will clinically assess the client's physical skills and any secondary disabilities. Reaction time, speed, and coordination of response will be tested, usually in the vehicle but sometimes in the clinic first. The clinical assessment should include an analysis of how the client gets into and out of his or her vehicle; the evaluator will determine whether any adaptations will be necessary do this safely. The OT/DRS also should make sure that the driver does not fatigue and that driving does not cause pain that decreases performance skills. Some people with total hip or total knee replacement surgery need to learn to use hand controls because the strength of their affected leg decreases so significantly, because driving causes pain, or because the leg is not healing properly. It is important to show clients options for stowing community mobility equipment and to make sure that they have the skills to do so safely.

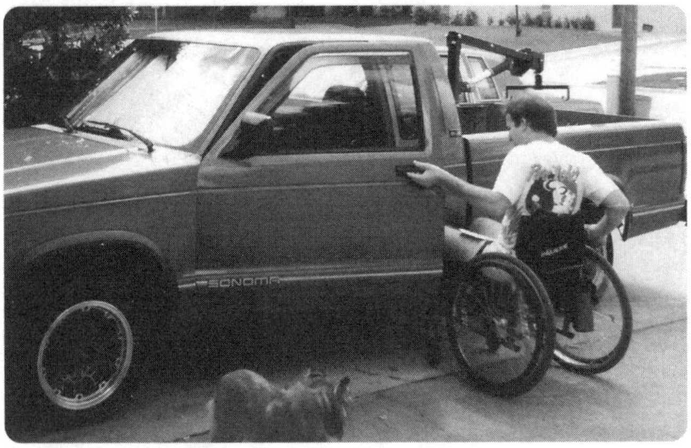

Figure 6.9. A truck in which the wheelchair acts as the driver's seat.

Source: Adaptive Mobility, Inc., Orlando, FL. Used with permission.

Ankle–Foot Orthosis or Full Leg Brace

If the client has an ankle–foot orthosis (AFO) on the driving leg, the physical therapist or occupational therapist generalist should explain the risks of driving with that leg. If the client cannot bend the ankle and the device covers the entire foot, his or her ability to move the foot from the accelerator to the brake accurately and quickly will most likely be affected. The client also may have impaired strength and coordination in the leg on which the brace is worn. Sensation on that foot will be impaired because of the plastic AFO. Removing the AFO for driving is not an option unless the client has full use and function of that leg or foot for driving, including operation of the pedals, smooth movements, functional range of motion and strength, and good sensation. For many, using the other foot for a left-foot accelerator adaptation (Figure 6.11) or hand controls (Figure 6.2) becomes the safest option for them.

Prosthetic Leg

There are currently no restrictions on driving for people with prosthetic legs. However, state departments of motor

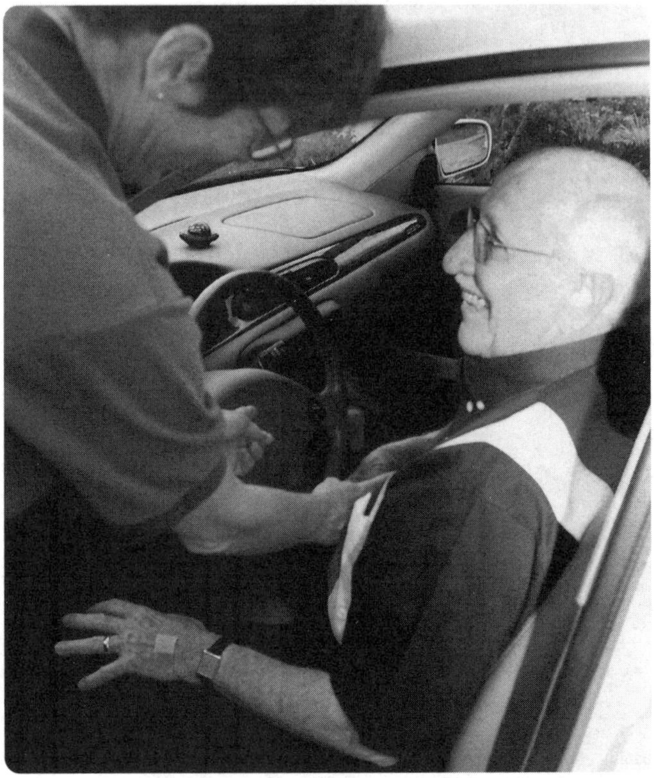

Figure 6.10. The OT/DRS must assess the choices and train the client carefully to ensure his or her safety.

Source: Adaptive Mobility, Inc., Orlando, FL. Used with permission.

Figure 6.11. Left-foot accelerator adaptation.
Source: Courage Center, Minneapolis, MN. Used with permission.

vehicles (DMVs) frequently require that a person with a prosthetic leg perform a road test to demonstrate control of the vehicle and ability to drive. Limitations of driving with a prosthetic leg include decreased sensation; limited movement patterns in the foot, ankle, and knee; and slower ability to move the foot from the gas to the brake in an emergency. These areas need to be identified so they do not become risk factors for the client.

It would be beneficial for the client with a prosthetic leg to have at least one session with the OT/DRS to learn these areas of concern and learn safe techniques, along with trying out the other options (e.g., left-foot accelerator, hand controls), so that the client can make an informed decision. The OT/DRS can evaluate whether driving with the prosthetic leg is the safest method for the person. In addition, the client must be careful not to look down to see what the prosthetic leg is doing. Situations become harder to interpret when using a prosthetic leg to drive. The OT/DRS should discuss transportation alternatives and vehicle modifications with clients who have prosthetic limbs. Clients often pursue such alternatives once they learn about them.

Prosthetic Arm

To drive safely, clients with a prosthetic arm need to have feeling in the shoulder to feel the amount of pressure they are placing on the gas and brake with the hand controls and feel the resistance of the steering wheel. Again, the key requirements are sensation, range of motion, and strength in the prosthetic limb. Such clients require a driver evaluation from an OT/DRS to ensure that they have the skills and can use adaptive equipment safely.

The type of prosthetic arm plays a role in selecting adaptive equipment. Most adaptive devices are made for prosthesis that are a clamp style (a metal hook at the end of the prosthesis operated to open and close using shoulder movements and muscles). Spinner knobs can be adapted for use with a prosthetic arm. Depending on the level of amputation, other prosthetic options exist for hand controls.

Arthritis

Arthritis can affect many aspects of the body, causing pain, loss of movement, and sometimes swelling. The most common form of arthiritis are

- *Osteoarthritis:* A degenerative joint disease in which the cartilage that covers the ends of the bones in the joint deteriorates, causing pain and loss of movement as the bone begins to rub against bone. It is the most prevalent form of arthritis.
- *Rheumatoid arthritis:* An autoimmune disease in which the joint lining becomes inflamed as part of the body's immune system activity. Rheumatoid arthritis is one of the most serious and disabling types, affecting mostly women.
- *Gout:* Affects mostly men. It is usually the result of a defect in body chemistry. This painful condition most often attacks small joints, especially the big toe. Fortunately, gout can be almost completely controlled with medication.
- *Ankylosing sponsylitis:* A type of arthritis that affects the spine. As a result of inflammation, the bones of the spine grow together.
- *Juvenile arthritis:* A general term for all types of arthritis that occur in children.
- *Systemic lupus erythematosus (lupus):* A serious disorder that can inflame and damage joints and other connective tissues throughout the body.
- *Scleroderma:* A disease of the body's connective tissue that causes a thickening and hardening of the skin. This disease can affect body functions, breathing, swallowing, and range of motion in all extremities.
- *Fibromyalgia:* A condition in which a widespread pain affects the muscles and attachments to the bone; it affects mainly women (Arthritis Foundation, 2005).

Osteoarthritis affects many people as they age. The effects can be mild to severe and can change from day to day or get worse with activity. Osteoarthritis primarily affects the hands, upper extremities, back, legs, and neck and can increase the likelihood of falls due to weakened joints or decreased gross motor coordination. The medications taken to decrease the pain and inflammation can interfere with driving and with the ability to get in and out of a vehicle.

Figure 6.12. T-bar spinner knob.
Source: Courage Center, Minneapolis, MN. Used with permission.

Figure 6.13. Smart–view mirrors.
Source: National Institute for Driver Behavior, Cheshire, CT. Used with permission.

Osteoarthritis also can interfere with safe use of alternative transportation options.

Arthritis can affect strength, range of motion, and concentration for driving (if the driver is in pain or on medications that are contraindicated for driving). Many types of arthritis are progressive; the type of arthritis needs to be considered in evaluating a driver's long-term safety options. Rehabilitation professionals involved with people with arthritis should assess their functional range of motion, strength, positioning, walking or mobility device, and pain level; the physician should evaluate the client's medication regime as it relates to driving. A driver evaluation can evaluate the client's short- and long-term equipment needs, training requirements, and safety with the task of driving at that time and into the future. As with other driver evaluations, the OT/DRS will conduct a clinical evaluation; if successful, it will be followed with an on-the-road assessment.

Some of the basic adaptations that can be used to protect small joints and overuse are spinner knobs; T-bar steering (Figure 6.12); straight-bar steering; keys or holders that are larger and easier to hold; and adapted mirrors such as the smart–view mirrors (Figure 6.13) that enable the client to check the blind spot even if he or she is unable to turn his or her head. There also are seat belt extenders available from vehicle manufactures if the client has limited range of motion and is unable to properly buckle the seat belt.

Occupational therapist generalists, rheumatologists, and families—and the professionals and team members who work with them—need to be aware of how arthritis can affect driving skills. Medical professionals can be proactive in asking about driving as they are addressing other functional skill areas for patients with osteoarthritis. The primary care physician should inventory all the patient's medications, even if some medications are used only during painful exacerbations of the condition, to make sure that no medications contraindicate driving. The physical therapist can work on transfer skills into and out of the car and in the community. The occupational therapist can work on energy conservation techniques and joint protection so that the client can maintain a healthy lifestyle. Identifying how the client is able to move, what motions are affected, and what the client's endurance and energy level are offers insight into the person's mobility options. The occupational therapist should review this and other information to determine whether the patient has range-of-motion limitations, pain, medication issues, decreased coordination, decreased strength and endurance, or balance and mobility issues that may interfere with safe driving. A referral to an OT/DRS for a driver evaluation then needs to be generated.

The OT/DRS's clinical assessment will focus on joint range of motion issues, strength, coordination, balance, use of mobility devices, progression of the arthritis, and history of falls and injuries related to the arthritis. If the client has no other secondary diagnosis, vision and cognition will still need to be assessed because aging does affect these. In the driver evaluation, the OT/DRS will focus on how the client gets into and out of the car and whether he or she is using a safe technique. The OT/DRS also will teach the client how to stow equipment safely in either the trunk or the back seat. If the client cannot walk safely or has trouble with walking long distances, the OT/DRS can recommend that the client be fitted for an electric wheelchair or scooter. It is important to make sure that the client has the neck range of motion to scan the environment in and around the vehicle and use the mirrors; if range of motion is limited, a larger panel mirror or blind-spot check (smart–view) mirrors may be needed. Some clients require adaptations such as large buttons for accessory controls; a spinner knob to provide more control and strength over steering the car; accessory controls on the spinner knob; a doorjamb handle to assist with getting into and out of the car (see Figure 6.1); a built-up key; remote start; or electric windows, door locks, and trunk.

The client should be able to operate the accessory controls on the vehicle and have the range of motion and strength to shift gears and buckle his or her seat belt. Many people with arthritis benefit from having an extender for the seat belt so that they do not have to reach so far to buckle. Not using the seat belt is unsafe; even a small accident can cause major injury when a person's joints are already impaired.

Once the fit of the car is addressed, the client should demonstrate his or her ability to use the accelerator and brake; the OT/DRS should measure the client's accelerator-to-brake reaction time and smoothness of movements. As with driver evaluations for elderly clients with other conditions, if the client is able to move smoothly from accelerator to brake, the assessment can move onto the road, progressing to situations requiring more complex driving skills. Parking can sometimes be difficult for people with arthritis because of joint pain, decreased upper-extremity coordination, and decreased neck range of motion; other areas of difficulty include driving in parking lots; operating accessory controls; and making larger motions, such as left turns. If the client can drive, but only with state-mandated restriction, it is important to see the client drive under those restrictions to ensure that he or she has the appropriate skills.

People who have arthritis have good days and bad days. Clients need to have insight into that fact so that they know to avoid driving on bad days, if necessary. Some clients must give up driving as their arthritis progresses, so it is important for the occupational therapist to examine alternative transportation options with clients who have arthritis.

Issues in Working With People With SCI

People who sustain a spinal cord injury (SCI) at any level have some type of physical impairment. The occupational therapist should ask about any secondary conditions, either diagnosed or undiagnosed. Some people had medical conditions before they sustained their SCI (e.g., mental health issues, diabetes, seizure history); others sustained additional injuries at the time of the SCI (e.g., head injury, fractures). All diagnoses may affect driving.

Many people who sustain an SCI are young and have a long life ahead of them. Community activity, school, work, and relationships are important functional life skills for their age group. Alternative transportation options or driving will allow them to live independent, active lives. Some funding sources will help this age group if alternative transportation options or equipment for driving will allow them to attend school and work. The state division of vocational rehabilitation is an option. When evaluating the expense of driver rehabilitation for young people with an SCI, it is important to keep in mind the number of years that they will need to use the equipment, the avenues that will be opened up to them because of improved mobility, and their increased earning potential because of this ability.

The level of a person's SCI affects his or her ability to drive and the type of equipment and vehicle that he or she will need. A person with paraplegia will most likely need less technical equipment than a person with quadriplegia. Mobility devices also affect a person's ability to get out in the community and the type of vehicle he or she drives.

Mobility is a person's ability to get from one place to another safely and independently. The mode of mobility can change, depending on whether the person is at home, on a short or long community outing, or dealing with weather conditions. Occupational therapists should be familiar with all of a client's mobility options so that they can be planned for in relation to driving (Table 6.1).

Mobility aids affect what type of vehicle people with SCI drive, the equipment that they need to stow in the vehicle, and how they are going to secure that equipment. Often the mobility device is ordered early in rehabilitation to allow the person to get around in the facility or hospital. It is important to look at a client's long-term needs. If it is hard to predict what a client will ultimately need, renting equipment can be a good alternative.

It is important to determine what the client with SCI needs for seating, pressure relief, trunk support, and ease in maneuvering and to see which devices will work under the conditions of actual use. School and work demands, home accessibility, transportation needs and, eventually, driving are all factors to consider in selecting mobility devices for the long term.

Once the mobility devices have been picked and the client is functioning to his or her maximum potential with regard to driving-related skills, it is time to refer the person to the OT/DRS. It is important that occupational therapist

Table 6.1. Mobility Options and Effects on Driving

Mobility Device	Impact on Driving
Manual wheelchair	The person will need to make sure that he or she can get to and from the car independently. Will the client be able to use the wheelchair for all community mobility function, even long distances? *Rigid frame:* Needs to be stowed in the trunk or in a large vehicle (e.g., truck or van). *Folding frame:* Chair can be stowed in the passenger seat, back seat, or car top carrier.
Transfer equipment	Transfers need to be possible in all weather conditions that the client may encounter. Equipment such as transfer boards, transfer discs, and overhead handles need to be stowed safely in the vehicle.
Scooters	A plan should be made for scooter use, even if it is not used all the time. With use of a lift, scooters can be stowed in a car trunk or in the back of a truck or van. They also can be driven into a van with a ramp.
Electric wheelchair	An electric wheelchair can be stowed in a car trunk or in the back of a truck or van. It also can be driven into a van with a ramp. The person can then drive from the electric wheelchair or transfer into the driver seat. *Control device:* Control devices such as joysticks, T-bars, and head array and their location may affect where the driving equipment needs to be placed. Driving devices should be placed so as to ensure full safe function. *Arm rest:* Arm rest type (e.g., swinging, stationary, removable) may affect transfer into the seat of a vehicle. It also can affect what size the chair is once it is folded down.
Canes or other walking devices	Be sure the client's walking device will work in all weather circumstances. He or she may need an additional grip on the end of the cane or device when using in snow and ice. The equipment should be able to be stowed independently and safely.
Ability to tie down or secure the mobility device	Mobility equipment should be stored safely so that it does not become a moving object in case of an accident or sudden maneuver. Chairs need tie-downs in a van, even if no one is sitting in them. Equipment should not be placed in front of an airbag device. Seat belts can be used to secure equipment, or equipment can be placed in a tight spot.

generalists cultivate relationships with DRSs so that they know how the driver rehabilitation program can meet their clients' needs. For example, some driver rehabilitation programs focus only on cars and clients with low technological needs; others specialize in vans and high-technology equipment. Knowing what different companies provide will help the generalist make the most appropriate referrals.

Likewise, OT/DRSs should develop relationships with the vendors who install adaptive equipment. Vendors need to value the OT/DRS's recommendations for particular equipment. The OT/DRS should write out specific recommendations for the equipment, ensure that vendors are qualified to install the needed equipment, and either be there for the final fitting or evaluate the installation shortly thereafter to ensure that the equipment meets the client's needs.

Once the client with an SCI has been referred to an OT/DRS, the usual evaluation process will take place. The OT/DRS will complete a clinical assessment that focuses on evaluating the client's physical skills for driving, examining the impact of any secondary diagnoses on driving, and determining whether any medications could affect safe driving. The clinical focus will be on trunk strength, upper-arm strength and function, coordination, and lower-extremity spasticity and tone. The OT/DRS also will consider the client's mobility device and vehicle. The goal is to obtain an accurate picture of the client and his or her strengths and limitations for driving. The clinical evaluation will be used to ensure that the client meets all state statutes and plan the on-the-road assessment.

The main objective in evaluating clients who need adaptations only to drive is to ensure that the right equipment is installed and to estimate the number of hours of training needed before a client can drive on his or her own. Some clients need additional time in the parking lot, either for additional training or to ensure vehicle fit, before the on-the-road evaluation. It is important that the training be completed both in the trainer vehicle as well as in the client's adapted vehicle.

Clients who use a wheelchair should try transferring to the driver's seat to find out whether they need to drive from their wheelchair. If they are going to drive from the car seat, they will most likely need a six-way power seat to safely transfer. Wheelchairs will need locking devices to stay stable while the vehicle is in motion; drivers should be able to operate locking devices themselves.

After the client's vehicle had been adapted, the OT/DRS should inspect it to ensure that the correct equipment was properly installed and placed. Every vehicle has a different feel to it once adapted, so making sure the client is safe in a variety of driving circumstances is important. The length of time required for the client to feel comfortable with the adapted vehicle varies. The driver evaluation should include an estimate of the hours of training that will be required. Using a checklist of expectations or a lesson plan throughout training can help organize feedback for the client and guide their expectations of the training process. Such tools also can provide a framework for documentation of the client's progress.

Clients with paraplegia or quadriplegia have specific needs, which are discussed in the following sections.

Paraplegia. Most people with paraplegia have decreased sensation in their legs and do not have full use of them; as a result, they often cannot use standard floor pedals. Their options for driving depend on their size, their mobility devices, and their preferences. A simple hand control, along with a spinner knob, may be all that they need. Occupational therapists should be aware of the available equipment options to pick the best match for the client. As with all equipment, it is important to consider whether the client can learn to use it with ease, function in the community, and be safe.

In working with clients with paraplegia, it is helpful to have a variety of equipment options at hand; they can be mounted on a quick-release mechanism in the vehicle. Numerous hand control and accessory control options are available, although some are not options for certain types of vehicles. Leg room is an important consideration, particularly for tall drivers and vehicles that lack good leg room to begin with; some hand controls allow for more leg room than others. When measuring clients for hand controls, they should sit in the chair in which they will be driving. Some people with paraplegia will drive from the driver's seat; others will drive from their wheelchair. In addition to leg room, the view through the windshield also is affected by the size and placement of the driver's chair.

Because of the requirements of the task, the stronger arm is usually used for steering and the weaker for the hand controls. If the client uses both arms approximately equally, it is best to pick the side that the primary accessory controls are on to minimize need for other equipment. If the client has leg spasms or lower-extremity tone, it is strongly recommended that an accelerator guard be installed so that the client does not accidentally accelerate the vehicle during spasm.

It is important to look at the client's seating and positioning in the car. If the client does not have good trunk balance, especially when making turns, he or she will need a chest strap in addition to the seat belt. It is important that such clients use the seat belt, too, and not just rely on the chest strap, because it is the seat belt that has been crash tested with the vehicle for safety. The client should be able to set and see out of all mirrors and check the blind spot, either by turning or with blind-spot check mirrors. The client's view out the windshield should let him or her see the road; a cushion may be needed for additional height.

If the driver with paraplegia is going to use hand controls, he or she should have a spinner knob. Spinner knobs fit in the palm of the hand and come in a variety of styles and should be chosen according to the client's physical needs and preference. T-bar (Figure 6.12), pin, and tri-pin (Figure 6.14) are among the most popular types. They are not required in all states, but they are strongly recommended for controlling the vehicle in evasive maneuvers, parking in

Figure 6.14. Tri-pin spinner knob.

Source: Courage Center, Minneapolis, MN. Used with permission.

tight spots, or controlling the vehicle after hitting a pothole in the road. Clients who do not want a spinner knob or who have difficulty using one can try driving without one, but it is important to be sure that doing so is a safe option for them. People with a large hand span and strong hands generally have the best outcome with spinner knobs. After selecting the knob model, the DRS will write a prescription that tells the vendor where on the steering wheel to attach it.

Clients who use hand controls must be able to use secondary controls such as turn signals, headlights, windshield wipers, and the horn. They often do this by momentarily letting go of the hand control (the vehicle will start to slow down slightly) to activate those controls. Clients who can best do this have good arm and hand function, have the hand control on the same side as the secondary controls, and have had time to practice the maneuver. As with all equipment, they should practice in a parking lot before driving on the road. If the hand control is not on the same side as the secondary controls or if the driver cannot accomplish the maneuver in a timely manner, then the secondary controls can be placed on a switch on the spinner knob or hand control, or a touch switch can be mounted in an easily accessible location.

Quadriplegia. People with quadriplegia vary in their level of disability, depending on their SCI level, recovery complications, and the nature of their injury. Their ability to use their arms, their trunk strength, and any mobility devices will directly affect the equipment and vehicle they use for driving. The medical stability of the client and ability to drive in all weather conditions also are important factors. Many people with quadriplegia have impaired sensation; respond negatively to hot or cold temperatures; and have other medical complications, such as spasticity, autonomic dysreflexia, or orthostatic hypertension.

People with quadriplegia usually use some type of power wheelchair unless they have spared functions, in which case they may use manual wheelchairs. They need to be able to transfer and stow their equipment to be able to drive a car. This is usually quite difficult unless they have an incomplete injury. Considerations for power wheelchair users include the type of vehicle, ramp, and lift. It may be necessary to drop the floor or raise the roof of the vehicle, depending on the height of the person in the chair. The weight of the person in the chair and whether he or she will drive from the chair or the seat of the vehicle also should be considered.

The clinical assessment again helps the DRS select the equipment and vehicle most appropriate for this person. The equipment and vehicle needs for people with quadriplegia vary greatly, depending on the SCI and remaining function. Some people can use hand controls, but most will need a tri-pin mount that they push forward for acceleration and pull back for braking. Many people with quadriplegia need equipment such as an electronic accelerator and brake (Figure 6.15), which are operated with a forward-and-back motion, or a mini-steering wheel (Figure 6.16), which can be mounted in a variety of locations. The primary and secondary accessories can be either on a scanner operated by a switch or plate or voice activated. Joystick controls to operate the accelerator, brake, and steering are an option. This type of equipment is available from many manufacturers; information can be obtained from the National Mobility Equipment Dealers Association. To properly select and fit this highly specialized equipment, the OT/DRS must be highly trained and qualified in its use, be able to teach clients how to use it, and work with vendors who are certified in the installation. People who drive with this equipment cannot have any vision or cognitive deficits and require many hours of training to use it safely.

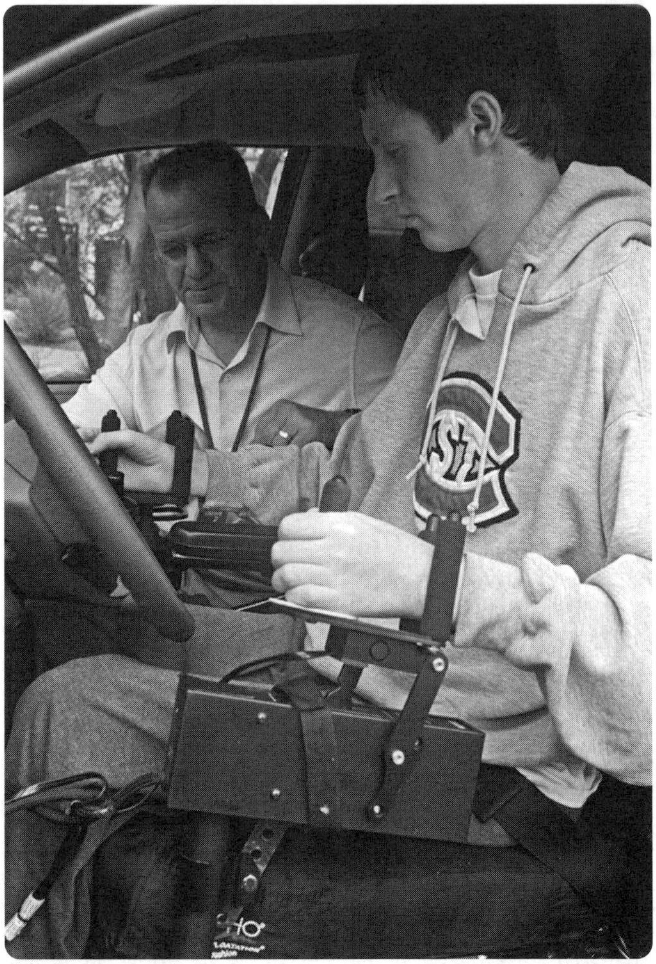

Figure 6.15. An electronic accelerator and brake.

Source: Courage Center, Minneapolis, MN. Used with permission.

Figure 6.16. Mini-steering wheel.

Source: Adaptive Mobility, Inc., Orlando, FL. Used with permission.

Working With People With Common Health Problems

Many health problems can affect the ability to drive safely. This section highlights some common health problems that occupational therapists may encounter in giving driver evaluations.

Low Vision and BiOptic Lenses

A strategy to compensate for low vision while driving is called BiOptic driving, which uses a bioptic telescope for driving. Before recommending BiOptic lenses, though, be sure that the state allows it and that the client is a good candidate for that type of device.

The BiOptic telescope is a useful driving aid for people with conditions that reduce resolution or visual acuity while substantially maintaining peripheral vision. Such conditions include albinism, nystagmus, cataracts, and corneal diseases, as well as macular degeneration, diabetic retinopathy, and other conditions that affect the central macular area (see Figure 6.17).

A BiOptic is a lens system with a telescope attached to a pair of glasses above one's normal line of sight. This allows a trained user the opportunity to detect objects or movement using the wide field of view available through the regular spectacle lens and to resolve fine details such as road signs and traffic lights by glancing briefly and intermittently into and out of the miniature telescopic unit. BiOptic lens systems used for visual assistance in the driving task are available in a number of different styles, sizes, and powers. The most common power ranges from

Figure 6.17. A variety of reasons and disabilities may cause low vision. In states where it is allowed, BiOptic driving can assist a person with low vision to continue to drive.

Source: Crossroads Easter Seals, Indianapolis, IN. Used with permission.

2X–5.5X ("X" refers to the strength or power of magnification of the telescopic unit).

A driving program designed to work with BiOptics should have an optometrist with training in fitting of the BiOptic lens and an OT/DRS who, through mentoring with an existing program in BiOptics, specializes in the training of clients in the use of BiOptics. The training is detailed and takes time and repetition. The candidate for BiOptics needs to live in a state that allows BiOptic driving and must have intact cognitive and physical skills for driving.

A good book that covers low vision and BiOptic driving that can provide background on this specialized skill in driver's rehabilitation and has information on the states that allow it along with their requirements for training (e.g., how many hours of on-the-road training that need to occur) is *Driving with Confidence: A Practical Guide to Driving with Low Vision,* by Eli Peli and Doron Pely (2002).

Diabetes

The effects of diabetes over time mean that elderly people with this disease often are experiencing its most serious effects. If diabetes is not well managed, it can affect circulation, sensation in extremities, vision, and cognition, all of which are areas that can affect driving. In addition, diabetic shock, in which the person loses consciousness, could occur while the person is driving if the diabetes is not managed effectively. Occupational therapist generalists should know how to screen clients with diabetes for physical, cognitive, and visual effects during evaluation and treatment. Anyone who wants to drive and has deficits in these areas, regardless of cause, needs an on-the-road driving assessment.

Many states have regulations that require people with insulin-dependent diabetes to provide a letter from a physician stating that they still possess the skills to drive. These skills need to be evaluated when the occupational therapist generalist sees them to rule out any difficultes or concerns. Many physicians will not write such letters until the client has had an on-the-road driving evaluation. In these cases, it is best for the person to be seen by an OT/DRS because of his or her medical background and understanding of how diabetes can affect driving.

Many people who have lost sensation in their legs or lost coordination as a result of diabetes will go to great measures to continue to drive, even lifting their leg with their hand to move it from accelerator to brake. This is not safe. If such drivers need to react quickly, they cannot respond in time. They also cannot maneuver smoothly because they cannot feel how much pressure they apply. Even if they limit their driving, they are an accident waiting to happen. Such drivers often do not raise their concerns with their physician out of fear that they will no longer be able to drive. They do not know that options such as hand controls may enable them to continue to drive.

In completing a driver evaluation for clients with diabetes who had physical impairment, the OT/DRS should clinically test their sensation (usually with deep-pressure touch to their feet and legs); have them walk on a straight line, toe-to-toe, and backward; and have them show the accelerator-to-brake motion with their foot without help from their upper extremities. In the vehicle, before the road test, drivers should again show the leg movement from accelerator to brake and press the pedals with varying pressure to assess how well they monitor control and pressure. A Vericom

Personal Experience 6.1. Woman With Amputation

I once had a client who, during the clinical evaluation, revealed that she had been driving with her left leg because her right leg had been amputated 3 years previously. The only adaptation for driving that she had tried was a left-foot accelerator. The site where she was first evaluated for driving did not discuss the hand control option with her because it was more expensive and required more training, even though the option could have fit her needs farther into the future.

The client needed to have her left leg amputated; fortunately, her physician was aware of our program and referred her to us to try hand controls. My client was able to learn those and maintain her driving abilities. She said that the hand controls were easier for her to learn and felt safer for her than the left-foot accelerator, and she noted that she would have saved money if she had had the hand controls installed from the start.

When we saw her we wanted to be sure to think about her long-term driving needs, including the possibility of not driving. Because of increasing difficulty with walking, she planned to order a scooter. Consequently, she purchased a minivan with a ramp so that she could pull into it with her scooter independently. She also had six-way power seats installed on the driver and passenger sides so that she could safely transfer from the scooter to the driver's seat and transfer as a passenger so that her husband could drive when she could not.

in-car reaction time tester can be used to measure the speed of the accelerator-to-brake movement. It is important to observe how smooth the motion is and whether the foot is getting caught on the pedals. It often is possible to determine in the parking lot that the driver is not safe, at which point he or she should be given concrete information as to why. The evaluation can be an awakening for the client and his or her family. If the client does not have sensation in the legs or even shows declines, hand controls may be an appropriate option. Decreases in sensation and coordination will progress, so planning ahead and learning the hand controls can help minimize the risk of future accidents.

If a driver does well on the clinical tests and reaction time test, the on-the-road test can proceed. As with all on-the-road tests, it should start on side streets with little traffic and slow speeds and then progress to situations requiring greater demands of the driver's skills.

Poor circulation is a physical effect of diabetes that sometimes leads to amputation due to infection or pressure sores that do not heal. If the right leg has been amputated or if the left leg is significantly stronger than the right leg, another option for drivers is a left-foot accelerator (Figure 6.11). Many drivers, however, find it more difficult to learn this application than to learn hand controls and eventually progress to hand controls anyway; consequently, the occupational therapist should consider recommending hand controls (Figure 6.2) if right-leg driving is not possible.

Vision changes, including low vision and diabetic retinopathy, can occur if diabetes is not controlled well. People with diabetes should have regular eye checkups to monitor any vision changes. If they are still driving, they should tell their vision care specialist so that he or she can screen for peripheral vision, contrast sensitivity, distance and near vision, and superior or inferior visual fields. It is helpful for occupational therapists to cultivate good relationships with eye care specialists in their area; doing so can help get the word out about occupational therapist services for visual problems as well as driving.

Occupational therapist DRSs should complete a clinical assessment of visual skills for all clients with diabetes because this disability often affects vision. Distance vision, peripheral vision, depth perception, sign recognition, color vision, and contrast sensitivity should all be examined. Asking the client to track a pencil with a large eraser is one approach to looking for smooth, coordinated eye muscle movements, accommodation, and convergence skills. The results of the vision assessment help guide how to plan the on-the-road assessment.

On the road, a student eye-check mirror positioned on the dashboard of the vehicle enables the evaluator to see the driver's eyes. It is important to determine whether the driver is scanning properly, with quick, smooth movements. The driver should also use all mirrors and perform regular blind-spot checks (e.g., checking over the shoulder before switching lanes). Drivers should be able to go through dark areas, such as tunnels, and cope with the bright light as they emerge from the dark area. They also should be able to read road signs and respond appropriately. The test should show that drivers had the ability to scan intersections as they approached and continued to do so as they proceeded through. It is important to know the visual deficits that are present as a result of the diabetes to first know if they can drive in accordance with the state statute and then if they can compensate safely for any deficit that they may have in the driving task.

History of Falls

A history of falls can significantly affect driving. The falls may have caused physical injuries, leading to cognitive deficits, or they could be a sign of a disease process, decline in physical skills, or judgment.

The occupational therapist generalist should get a history of the client's falls. How many has the client had, and over what period of time? Can the falls be attributed to environmental factors that can be changed so that the client can avoid the fall in the future? Did the client start taking any new medications that could cause vertigo or lightheadedness and contribute to the falls? Are vision changes a contributing factor? Would increasing physical strength and endurance help prevent falling? Does the client need assistive devices, such as a cane, walker, or scooter? Do the falls occur mainly on ice or in bad weather? If falls have affected the client's physical, cognitive, or visual skills, then a driver evaluation is recommended.

Heart Attack

A person who had a heart attack should not immediately return to driving. Heart attacks and their effects vary widely from person to person. Some people just need a short recovery before driving again; others are on medication that is contraindicated for driving. Heart attacks can cause oxygen deprivation to the brain (anoxia); therefore, vision, cognition, and physical function must be evaluated in relation to driving. Anoxia related to the time the person was without oxygen can severely impair cognition; the person may retain some skills but still have damage to cognitive function. Even

Personal Experience 6.2. Woman With Heart Attack

A woman who had had a heart attack 3 months earlier came in for a driver evaluation. She had returned to performing basic tasks around the house and visited the community with her husband. She was referred to me because her husband felt that she seemed slightly confused at times, and he was afraid that she may get lost if she drove. I conducted the clinical and road assessment driver evaluation. She did well on clinical testing of basic memory but had moderate problems with problem solving, sequencing, and visual processing speed and had trouble remembering the details of the instructions. Her physical skills and vision scored within functional limits. On the road, she was able to perform in the parking lot and quickly transitioned to residential streets. Once she left the non-busy side streets, she had significant trouble with processing information to make quick decisions and act on them. She needed to pull over almost immediately.

The client was in the hospital for only a short period, had virtually no rehabilitation after her heart attack, and was functioning well at home with her husband. It was not until she started more challenging tasks that her deficits were noticed. As the driver evaluation was reviewed, her husband was able to identify other high-level activities that his wife was having trouble with at home (e.g., using her computer, managing their overall calendar, multitasking). She did not pass her driver evaluation, but the driver evaluation got her back into therapy to work on these higher-level skills to improve her functioning in daily life.

At only 60 years, the client had just retired and wanted the freedom of her previous activity levels. If she improves in other areas, driving is something she can look forward to in the future. For the moment, her husband would have to continue to meet her transportation needs, and her family was glad she was getting the therapy she needed.

people with mild cardiac disorders that have the potential to affect driving should be evaluated.

Stroke

Stroke is a major cause of disability that strikes approximately 500,000 people every year in the United States (Fisk, Owsley, & Pulley, 1997). Strokes affect the body according to the side of the brain in which the stroke took place. The severity and duration of the effects of the stroke vary from person to person. Physical difficulties usually are seen immediately after the stroke occurs; they may clear up quickly, linger, or become permanent. Following stroke, it is important to check for vision, communication, and cognitive deficits. The occupational therapist generalist will focus on stabilization in the initial period following the stroke and gain an understanding of the skills the client had before the stroke.

People who experience stroke can be young. They may be raising children and often are working and active in their community before the stroke. Getting clients back to as normal function as possible is important for their mental and physical recovery as well as for their livelihood.

The generalist's understanding of the different functions that each side of the brain governs will help them in understanding stroke's effects on clients. Generalists can evaluate clients' balance and walking skills, vision, cognition, speech, and declines in physical ability. They also can gain an understanding of what driving means for the client. If the client has small children, can the client get them in and out of the car alone? Can the client handle distractions? These skills can be analyzed and problem solved to some extent before referral to the OT/DRS.

Strokes sometimes result in aphasia (a speech problem in which people cognitively know what they want to say but cannot get the words out) or receptive aphasis (when a person does not understand or cannot make sense of what others are saying). If the client has aphasia, it is important to know whether it is expressive, receptive, or both. People with expressive aphasia will do poorly on tests that involve language, but they often have intact cognitive skills for performance of the driving activity. The occupational therapist should use tests that are adapted to test a specific function (e.g., driving) and not use language-based tests that may show false negatives regarding a client's skill. The OT/DRS should have clinical tests available that are adapted for use with aphasia, such as using hand signals for response to questions and the Motor-Free Visual Perception Test (Korner-Bitensky et al., 2000). The speech therapist is an important link to understanding what mode of expression is most accurate for the client.

The generalist can work with clients on language skills for safety; some clients carry a card in their billfold that explains their speaking difficulties so that people they encounter in the community have a clearer understanding. Developing emergency plans related to community and home skills is an important first step toward getting ready to pursue driving skills. It is important to complete an on-the-

Personal Experience 6.3. Man With Heart Attack

Several years ago I saw a 60-year-old man who had had a heart attack and a period of anoxia. He had returned to work and was living with his wife at home. Six months after his experiences, he wanted to pursue driving. The occupational therapist generalist completed a screening of his skills and did not determine any deficits that would impair driving. His distance and peripheral vision met the state requirements. He was able to remember long-term information and did fairly well with short-term memory. He had good reaction time, was walking functionally with slight decrease in his balance, and had good motor coordination and strength in his upper and lower extremities. His executive skills were not screened. Because this client had significant deficits initially and mild deficits that showed up on the screening, the generalist recommended that the client have an OT/DRS do the driver evaluation.

The generalist, physician, and client were fairly sure that he would pass the driving evaluation but thought that he might need restrictions. I completed a clinical evaluation and on-the-road evaluation. He did well on the physical assessments (e.g., range of motion, coordination while seated, strength, sensation) but had trouble with dynamic standing and walking. He had good peripheral and distance vision, but his depth perception was mildly impaired, and he reported double vision when he was tired. He had not told anyone else of those episodes because they did not interfere with function and no one had asked him. He demonstrated fairly good short-term and long-term memory but did poorly on assessments of divided attention, problem solving, and sequencing. He and his wife both reported that his functional skills at home were fine, but at work he had problems getting things done, and the quality of his work had diminished since the heart attack. They thought it was because he was just still tired.

The road assessment started in the parking lot; I started by reviewing the location and setup of everything in the vehicle. The client was not able to get the vehicle out of the parking lot. He could not coordinate his upper extremity motions for steering with the response of his foot to the gas and brake. He was able to focus on only one thing at a time (e.g., when asked to stop the car, he stopped, but he could not hold his lane position). When he needed to concentrate on lane position or parking in the parking spot, he could not control the speed of the vehicle. After the evaluation, when I asked how he thought he had done, he replied that he felt it had gone well. It was not until I went over all areas of concern that he began to understand how his deficits interfered with function and safety.

This illustrates the helpfulness of the generalist's test and the need for caution even when deficits appear mild. Putting all the skills together and responding to multiple stimuli in a timely manner projected his deficits. The client could successfully overcome the deficits in a slower-paced activity, but driving was too fast for the client's abilities. He started to realize this after the driver evaluation, but I knew that he still did not fully understand and was not ready to move on.

I referred him back to the occupational therapist generalist he was working with to address community mobility and evaluate his skills at work. He also was referred to a neuropsychologist for neuropsychiatric testing to better determine his areas of deficit and his ability to recover. He was referred to a psychologist to deal with his feelings about giving up driving and to deal with deficits that resulted from the anoxia after his heart attack. This collaborative effort addressed all of the client's areas of function. It is important that all rehabilitation professionals value each others' roles and have resources to get the correct referrals. The OT/DRS needs to have these resources and relationships to ensure that the people who no longer can drive or need more therapy will have these needs met.

road evaluation with people with aphasia so that their functional skills can be fully assessed; often the client's performance skills will exceed clinical predictions.

The OT/DRS will assess the stroke's effects and the adaptations the client may need for the vehicle. As with other clients, the driver evaluation will start in the parking lot and progress to the road; if equipment training is involved, it may take more than one session before the client can practice on streets. The focus of the evaluation is on potential for safe driving with use of equipment.

Working With People With Neurological Disorders

A variety of neurological conditions may affect driving. If the client is not able to communicate clearly or has short-term memory deficits, anger management issues, or fatigue, those

Personal Experience 6.4. Man With Brain Injury

I saw one of my clients 5 years after he experienced a brain injury as a result of a motor vehicle accident. An OT/DRS in a rehabilitation facility in the area had evaluated him the year before; the client had failed that test. The client was persistent with his desire to drive, telling his physician that he had failed because the evaluation had not taken place where he normally drove. Because I worked for a community-based facility, we received the referral. With the client's permission, I checked the information from his first evaluation. It was unclear whether the client failed because of the type of assessment, but the information did give me areas on which to focus (e.g., insight, attention span, problem solving). He scored within functional limits on the vision and physical tests when I tested him, but he had mild to moderate impairments in visual processing speed and appeared to have moderate difficulty with planning and problem solving.

He completed the road assessment immediately following the clinical testing. He did well in the parking lot and on side roads. Once he was on four-lane road with traffic, his skills started to deteriorate. He had trouble maintaining focus with the distraction of the environment (i.e., scanning what other vehicles were doing while maintaining lane position, waiting for the OT/DRS's instructions on where to turn). At one point, he had to go to the bathroom and started to move a lot without identifying the problem (I had to cue him to stop at a restroom in a gas station). He did not visually search intersections ahead of time or before proceeding (he only scanned forward, not searching for what was going on around the vehicle).

At the end of the assessment, the client was asked how he felt that he did. He said that he felt he did great and identified no areas of problem or concern. Even after I went over the results of the evaluation, the client could not see that he was lacking any skills for safe driving. The client did not pass the driver evaluation; it was determined that the reason for failure was the client's lack of skills, not an unfamiliarity with the environment. This provided closure for the family and physician, and steps were taken to cancel the client's driver's license. With the results of the driver evaluation, these steps are easier to validate.

issues will need to be addressed. Sometimes the client needs to attempt a task in the community (e.g., a shopping trip) to realize his or her level of impairment. Doing this in a safe, supportive manner is key to helping them move on in their rehabilitation process. Many people with neurological conditions also have visual impairments; it is important that the rehabilitation professional understand the client's visual deficits and any corrections that can be made. Many clients with neurological disorders take medications to improve cognitive function or to manage depression, behavior, or pain; as always, medications should be assessed to see how they might affect community mobility and driving.

Brain Injury

It is important to know what caused a client's brain injury, whether he or she is stable, and what secondary conditions may affect driving. Brain injury can affect the client's level of insight as to the effects of his or her disability. Physical skills that may be affected by the client's brain injury include the ability to get into and out of a vehicle, stow mobility devices, operate the pedals, and react in a timely fashion. It is important to understand the client's cognitive level: How is the client's short-term memory? Long-term memory? Does the client's memory decline with fatigue? Executive skills of problem solving, sequencing, planning ahead, dividing attention, and alternating attention are critical to driving. Individuals with brain damage often have deficits in visual, cognitive, or motor processes that may cause difficulties in maintaining lane position, assessing speed, merging with traffic, and attending to more than one driving task at a time (Fisk et al., 1997). Neuropsychological testing can be helpful in assessing the level of damage and the likelihood that skills will return.

The client's social skills, anger management, ability to interact with people in a variety of settings, and insight are important because driving is a social activity that involves being in the community. Driving is highly social in that the driver needs to be aware of what other drivers are doing and stay calm when other drivers do not do what they are supposed to do. It is important to be able to interpret the mannerisms of other vehicles: Are they stopping? Switching direction? In addition, it is important to be able to interpret the expressions on other drivers' faces in some situations (e.g., when trying to change lanes in heavy traffic). Driving is highly complicated and social even though most people do not think of it as such.

With brain injury, rehabilitation requires working in distracting, physically demanding, and time-sensitive situations, unlike many other rehabilitation situations. Personality measures, particularly of aggression, substance abuse, depression, psychosis, and character disorder, also should be included in screening tools for driving for people with

Personal Experience 6.5. Man With Head Injury

A young adult male client had sustained a head injury as the result of an assault. He was receiving occupational therapy at home and was able to care for himself, cook, and clean. He wanted to focus on community skills and driving.

He used a manual wheelchair for long distances and a cane for walking because of decreased ability to use his left leg. He had no function in his left arm and moderate left neglect. He could walk in and around his house with his cane most of the day and could compensate for his vision loss in his familiar home environment. Little activity at home challenged his weaknesses, and he did not understand why he could not drive yet.

The physical therapist and I scheduled an outing with the client to a grocery store. Our main focus was to determine his function in the community and assess whether he could use alternative transportation. Our secondary goal was to assess his visual neglect and challenge his ability to get around and interact with other people. We wanted to see whether he could remain calm and get items in a timely manner.

Our client scheduled a ride with a transportation service for people with disabilities to get to the grocery store. He was able to get from his house to the van and from the van to the store with his cane (needing moderate assistance for balance on the ice). Once at the grocery store, he could push a cart, putting the cane into the cart, but he had trouble seeing to the left in this large, unfamiliar environment. As a result, he often ran into items on his left side or people to the left of him. He had considerable difficulty maintaining his position to the right side of the aisle and needed to slow down considerably.

Our client did not realize his deficits on his own at first; he needed moderate cues from me before he started to integrate this skill. When he got tired, his skills deteriorated. He had a hard time driving the cart, turning it, and responding to others driving their carts. He had a hard time staying calm when it became busier in the store and other people were not being careful with their carts. (He mumbled some inappropriate words to people a couple of times before he decided to pull aside and take a break!) He eventually found all the items that he needed, but it took him 1 hour to locate and buy 10 items.

Once the client was home, we analyzed the experience and how it would translate to driving. Had the store experience been a driving task, he would have had several accidents. He would have had to stop in the middle of the road to process information, would have had to slow down well below the speed limit to see items to the left side, and would not have seen many items at all that could have been critical to safety on the road. The experience helped the client understand why he was not ready to drive and gave him insight into why it was important to work on those skills. The experience increased his motivation to work on his deficits.

brain injuries (Hopewell, 2002). Initially, the focus is on teaching compensation techniques, using planners and adaptive equipment, allowing more time to do things, decreasing the level of distraction, and minimizing the things that cause frustration. With brain injury, clients' ability to compensate for deficits is limited. For example, one can limit distraction in the vehicle (e.g., no radio or eating while driving) and avoid busy intersections and freeways, but it is not possible to control most factors in the driving environment, such as weather, traffic patterns, road construction, and emergency situations. It is important to know this so that in rehabilitation the team does not just focus on compensation strategies.

In rehabilitation with clients who have brain injury who wish to return to driving, the occupational therapist should choose therapies that challenge the client's physical skills, vision, and cognition once they are ready. The therapy should take place in increasingly distracting environments. The client should work on multiple tasks at once so that he or she sets priorities and reevaluates them as the tasks are accomplished. To recreate what happens during driving, situations should be created that require clients to move while performing a task, then move while other objects move, and then stay still and react to moving objects. Clients also need to work on timed tasks and speed. If they have neglect issues, they need to learn to compensate for them. They also need to work on scanning large areas for information, again while they are moving and being timed, so that they know they can do it quickly enough for the skill of driving.

Getting clients to understand their strengths and limitations will help them develop insight, which is critical to safe driving. Lack of insight is a red flag for the ability to drive.

The driver evaluation will focus clinically on the client's physical skills, vision, cognition, speed of response (both physically and cognitively), and the level of insight into his or her deficits. It also is important to ask the client and his or her family about the client's ability to remain calm under stress. Managing distractions, shifting attention, identifying primary information over secondary background information, and remembering information all are important to driving. Deficits in vision and compensation techniques should be assessed to determine whether the client is functioning within state regulations for driving. Some appropriate tests that may be helpful are range of motion, manual muscle strength, sensation measures of arms and legs, Optec 2000 vision tester, confrontation vision testing (to check alignment of the eyes, accommodation, convergence, and tracking skills), Trials A and B, and the Cognitive Linguistics Quick Test.

Brain Tumors

Although the rehabilitation professional will focus on many of the same strategies and areas for clients who have a brain tumor as for clients with brain injury, some differences are important to acknowledge. It is important to know where the brain tumor was located (if it has been removed) to have a better understanding of which physical, visual, and cognitive functions may be affected. It also is important to know whether a surgical intervention took place, whether any infection occurred related to the surgery, and whether radiation or chemotherapy were needed. Brain tumors and their treatment can affect a client's skills, level of endurance, and strength. It is important to know whether the treatments have been completed and whether they were successful. If the tumor will continue to grow, the client should be worked with similarly to clients with progressive neurological disorders, as described later in this chapter.

As with brain injury, it can be difficult to determine the full effects of the brain tumor in the clinical setting. The impairment is sometimes not evident until the client must cope with a distracting environment or high-demand activity. Any client who has had a tumor that has caused vision, cognitive, or physical deficits should have a driver evaluation.

Personal Experience 6.6. Man With Brain Tumor and His Wife

A woman called me in tears after her husband had a tumor removed and his physician gave him the approval to return to driving. He drove home from the appointment and did fine until they were on the freeway and came to road construction. The cones, cars, and lane changes affected his vision, and he could not see clearly to navigate through the site. There was no place to pull over, so the woman had to help with the wheel and talk him through until he could safely pull over. The situation was terrifying to them. They had not known that there was such a thing as a driver evaluation. They were glad to know of the service and wished it had been recommended in the first place.

Fibromyalgia

Fibromyalgia affects physical skills, endurance, movement, and reaction time; during exacerbations ("flare-ups"), it can be completely debilitating. The key is to know the areas that are affected and what triggers the client's flare-ups. The client needs to have keen insight into the fibromyalgia and how it affects him or her. On bad days, clients may not be able to drive because of pain or fatigue, and it is possible that they may reach a point at which they do not drive at all. As a

Personal Experience 6.7. Man With Brain Tumor

A young man whom I evaluated after he had a brain tumor removed presented a good example of how challenging it is to fully evaluate brain injury. A preclinical screen in the hospital found no physical deficits or vision deficits; he had mild cognitive impairment. He decided on his own to take the driving evaluation for his own piece of mind.

His clinical assessment revealed a mild deficit with divided attention. As the on-the-road assessment progressed to busier streets with more traffic and distraction, he started to have difficulty focusing and maintaining lane position. He became distracted by areas that he had not seen for a few months while he was in the hospital and how they had changed. He could not figure out what to do when a road construction site came up suddenly, and he needed to pull over. I talked him through the process of getting safely to an area where we could switch places so that he did not have to drive home.

My client was amazed at how hard driving was. He was functioning well at home and had taken the bus in the community without noticing any difficulties. Fortunately, he found out in a safe way that driving was beyond his skills. He was referred to occupational therapy to work on high-level cognitive skills.

Personal Experience 6.8. Woman With Fibromyalgia

A client with fibromyalgia was returning to work after an exacerbation. Her employer was concerned about her ability to work a full day once she returned and her ability to drive home safely. The employer hired me to perform a worksite evaluation and a driver evaluation on the same day to assess her skills.

My client lived in the city and drove 45 miles into a rural area to get to work. She needed to be able to drive in varied weather conditions, at night, and at various times of the day. She did not really have to deal with rush hour because she went the opposite direction. The clinical analysis determined that she would not need adaptive equipment, so the on-the-road assessment focused on her ability to drive while she tired. The worksite evaluation would focus on her ability to pace herself during the day so as not to cause an exacerbation.

At work, we set up her workstation so it was ergonomically correct. Nevertheless, working a full 8 hours took a toll on my client, and her driving abilities were not as good on the way home as on the way to work. A follow-up call the next day determined that she had some negative effects from the full day she put in, and her supervisor felt her work quality was lacking in the last 2 hours that she was at work.

In light of the evaluation results, it was determined that my client needed revisions to her workload and the length of her day. For several months, she worked 4-hour days, with one rest, and drove herself safely to work and back. At 3 months, another evaluation of work and driving was performed, and her tolerance had increased to a 6-hour workday. It was determined that this would probably be her maximum workday length to stay healthy and avoid another exacerbation of her fibromyalgia. After a year, she was still working and driving and had not experienced any exacerbations. She also was attending a fibromyalgia support group, which she felt helped her with coping and lifestyle adjustments.

result, the occupational therapist should help the client plan for long-term community mobility. Pacing is important to safe driving with this disability.

Clients who have fibromyalgia may need adaptive equipment, such as panoramic mirrors, if they cannot turn to check their blind spot or see what is behind them. If the fibromyalgia primarily affects the client's legs, hand controls can be a good option.

The on-the-road assessment should emphasize the impact of pain and fatigue; reaction time and speed with which the client moves between the pedals; positioning; and need for mirrors if the client lacks neck or back range of motion or has pain in those areas. The road evaluation needs to be long enough for the client to see what happens when he or she becomes tired. The client should be challenged when tired to assess whether distance or time limits on driving are necessary.

Epilepsy and Seizures

Before a person with epilepsy or other seizure disorder can drive, the condition must be controlled. Each state has its own regulations for how long epilepsy must be under control before a person can drive in that state; the range is from 3 months to 1 year. In some states, if a seizure can be related to a specific incident and is not likely to recur, a physician can provide a letter attesting to that fact and the person can return to driving. The occupational therapist should screen for any cognitive, visual, or physical changes that may affect driving, although many people with epilepsy have no such deficits. In addition, the occupational therapist should find out if the client knows when a seizure episode is imminent.

Guillain-Barré Syndrome

Guillain-Barré syndrome is a self-limiting condition that affects each person differently. The residual effects following the client's recovery may affect driving. Many people who have the syndrome must learn to pace themselves, or they will experience some decline in cognitive, physical, or visual function. A driver evaluation can help clients determine their skill level and balance the demands of driving with the propensity for fatigue.

In the clinical testing, the occupational therapist will focus on determining the full effects of the Guillain-Barré syndrome by assessing the client's condition previous to the syndrome. It is important to know how severe the case was and how quickly the client recovered. As in all driver evaluations, the clinical findings will be used to determine the need for any adaptive equipment. The road evaluation will focus on safe driving, with consideration of the impact of fatigue on the client's driving. If the client's abilities do vary throughout the day, the occupational therapist may suggest restricting the client's driving to certain times or conditions.

Progressive Neurological Disorders

The key to working with clients who have a progressive disorder is remembering that their level of function will change. Progression differs for everyone and depends on the type of disability. Some medications can slow deterioration but have side effects that can worsen function. Occupational therapists can draw on various techniques to help clients with progressive disorders cope. It is important to help clients understand what having a progressive illness means for their future, both in relation to driving and in relation to other important life skills. This approach can help clients and their families adjust proactively to the changes instead of just reacting to them.

When addressing the skill of driving the task is twofold. First, the OT/DRS must ensure that the client can drive safely. Second, the occupational therapist must help the client plan for the future. The client will need to consider equipment and community mobility options that will work for him or her over the long term. The occupational therapist should help the client transition to the adaptations when he or she can no longer drive.

Talking about the high-level demands of driving early on will help identify the risks of this activity to the client. Too often, driving is not discussed until clients are having so much trouble that they have been a safety hazard for quite some time. Clients themselves may not be the best people to judge their skill, especially as their disease progresses. If they do not know that other transportation options are available, they often will hide their driving difficulties out of fear of losing their ability to participate in the community. The family, physician, and therapy team will play a vital role in watching for these signs and taking action. If everyone involved knows ahead of time the options and resources, they will be more likely to ask questions and identify concerns.

Clients with progressive disorders generally need frequent reevaluation; once every 6 months is the recommended minimum. If the family will not ride in the car with the client, it is a sign that driving is no longer within the client's level of function. The occupational therapist can review with the family some of the more subtle warning signs that the client's driving skills have become seriously impaired.

Alzheimer's Disease and Dementia. Alzheimer's disease and dementia are progressive and will affect a person's ability to drive at some point (Duchek, Hunt, Ball, Buckels, & Morris, 1998). The nature of these disabilities is such that a person's physical skills are often better for longer than their mental or cognitive skills, especially for inherently difficult tasks such as driving. Clients with Alzheimer's disease or dementia often are able to pass a physical fitness test for driving or a rules-of-the-road performance test even after they are no longer safe to drive because driving is an overlearned skill; if the client gets help from others to find his or her way or alert him or her to upcoming hazards (or are simply told what to do), the client physically can still drive. These strategies are not safe, however; no state allows a person to have assistance to drive safely. Adding a restriction that a person cannot drive alone is not a safe driving adaptation. Even a driver who has a learner's permit needs to be the one in control of the vehicle and eventually learn the skills to drive on his or her own.

> ### *Personal Experience 6.9. Woman With Dementia*
>
> I met with a woman recently diagnosed with dementia for a driver evaluation in her area. Her physician had some concerns about her ability to drive, but the client and her daughter felt that her driving was functional. The woman had problems with short-term memory and divided attention on the clinical testing. She did well on the part of the road assessment that involved the instructor giving her directions and performing driving tasks. The assessment switched to testing her driving abilities without instruction. She identified several places that she would drive regularly. Once she was in full control of the vehicle, her driving skills deteriorated. She went out of her way to get to her destination, could not locate one of the places that she needed to go, and three times performed unsafe maneuvers because she was confused about where she was. If she had done a state road test or an instructor-led test, she probably would have passed, as they don't assess path finding in most cases. However, on her own, in the challenge of driving environment, she was not safe. It was recommended that she not continue driving.

People with Alzheimer's disease and dementia eventually lose their driving skills. Much controversy exists as to whether people with either of these diagnoses are safe to drive in early stages of illness (Eberhard, 1996). This population presents unique challenges in driver evaluation. Because of the progressive nature of their illness, it is important to perform regular reevaluations of driving skills (Hesman, 2004).

Once Alzheimer's disease and dementia progress to a certain point, people who have either condition have extreme difficulty learning new information, generalizing,

Personal Experience 6.10. Woman With Likely Alzheimer's Disease

One of my clients was a woman who lived just outside a large city. She had not been diagnosed yet, but it appeared that she had early symptoms of Alzheimer's disease. She had been pulled over by a police officer on her way home from church because she appeared confused, and her driving patterns were erratic (she had turned around twice). She could not tell the officer where she was going or where she came from. Her husband was located and drove her home. The police officer turned in documentation to the state DMV, and the client's physician was requested to provide a statement about her ability to continue to drive. The physician wanted the woman to have an OT/DRS evaluation before submitting the form.

The woman did all right on the clinical testing, but she had moderate difficulty with memory testing and divided attention. She drove functionally for the first part of the road assessment, when physical skills were examined and the instructor gave directions. Once the woman needed to drive to areas in her neighborhood, her skills decreased. She got lost for 30 minutes when driving to a grocery store in her town, 10 miles from her house. She wound up downtown before realizing that she was not heading toward the grocery store. She needed help to find her way back and remain safe in the dense traffic. She did not pass the driver evaluation; the part of the evaluation in which she needed to perform all functions of driving was the path finding, which she could not complete safely. She probably would have had the skills to pass a state road assessment, but she was not a safe driver.

path finding even in familiar areas, and multitasking (Duchek et al., 1998). Getting through intersections, especially uncontrolled ones (i.e., those that have no stop sign or stop light), making left turns, judging vehicle speed without looking at the speedometer, and assessing the speed of other traffic are difficult for them. Remembering where they are, the purpose of the trip, and getting efficiently and safely back to the task at hand following distraction can be issues for clients with Alzheimer's disease or dementia. People with these conditions talk as if they are functioning well but cannot perform the skills in a functional, safe way (e.g., they will take 1 hour to make a 5-minute trip). It is vital to remember to test not only these clients' physical skills but also their visual and cognitive skills.

In the initial evaluation, the occupational therapist generalist should perform cognitive tests to determine the client's current level of function. Assessment tools that many facilities use include the Allen leather lacing evaluation and the Cognitive Performance Tests (Allen, Earhart, & Blue, 1992). These tools do not say whether a person can drive, but they give information as to the need for further testing. A neurologist should rate the client as to stage of disease.

People with Alzheimer's disease or dementia demonstrate wide and varied skills at each level. Much about their functioning seems to depend on how quickly they were diagnosed, how well they responded to medication, what their diet and exercise habits were before the disease, and whether they retain their insight into themselves and how the disability affects them (Duchek et al., 1998). At some point insight is affected. Some clients do not have the insight that it is time to stop driving, even if they have been in several accidents, have become lost for long periods of time, or have failed a driver evaluation. They often explain why an incident happened in such a way that it appears that their skills are preserved.

The OT/DRS should clinically evaluate all skills before the road assessment, being aware that some clients in this population will sometimes have the ability to talk around

Personal Experience 6.11. Man With Likely Alzheimer's Disease

I had a client in for a driver evaluation whom I suspected had Alzheimer's disease. The first time I saw this man, he demonstrated safe performance on the clinical and on-the-road evaluations. He was seen 6 months after being diagnosed and demonstrated the skills and insight to drive in his area; however, he could no longer drive in unfamiliar areas or during rush hour. Six months later, his skills had deteriorated to the point that he could no longer drive safely. He accepted this, helped by the fact that the driver evaluations had allowed him to drive for a full year, and he had had time to plan for alternatives to driving to maintain community mobility.

their areas of deficit and try to get information from the evaluator to help them do better on the testing. Alzheimer's disease and dementia can affect vision, cognition, and physical skills. Special attention should be given to the accuracy of the client's insight and the ability to multitask, prioritize information, and make quick decisions. Path finding, orientation, and ability to shift attention are other important skills.

It is important to challenge clients and have them try to figure out problems on their own while looking for consistency between what they say and what they are able to do. It is important to not cue the client during the clinical assessment. Clients often are extremely clever at asking questions or covering their decreased skill with the strength of their verbal skills and will try creative ways to get the assessor to help. They also will offer many reasons for why they were not able to do a particular activity or why the inability to do a task was an anomaly.

The family's input is essential in these cases. They often can provide the best information about the client's driving and function at home. It is important to use this information in conjunction with the information gathered in the clinical evaluation and the road evaluation. This is a difficult population to evaluate properly, and no information about these clients can be overlooked. It is difficult for caregivers to judge when these clients should stop driving (Eberhard, 1996).

In completing the road assessment for people with Alzheimer's disease or dementia, it is essential to see them in their home driving environment to evaluate their physical and cognitive skills for driving. It is important to observe the client's ability to get to and from destinations in the safest manner and in good time. If the client becomes lost, can he or she recover in a timely fashion and get to the destination in a smooth, safe fashion? Such clients often do well when they are evaluated because they can hold their skills together for short periods of time and know it is important to do so during this road evaluation. If the client is allowed to relax a bit and drive the instructor around in the home area, the skills often decline. The client's normal driving skills and habits may not be as safe as those demonstrated when being formally evaluated. The client may not have the skills to both drive safely and navigate on his or her own—that is, without explicit instruction from the evaluator—because of difficulty with decision making.

Parkinson's Disease. Parkinson's disease affects the ability to control body movements. It begins with small twitches that people hardly notice at first. The twitches eventually build to tremors and then large, all-body movements. The extraneous movements are fatiguing and can interrupt sleep. Medications that can help calm the movements have side effects, including periods of rigidity and the inability to move. The medications can slow down reaction speed and thinking, thereby affecting driving. As the disease progresses, clients should be evaluated for their driving skills. It is important not to wait until the movements or frozen patterns are so bad that the client puts himself or herself at risk while driving.

Parkinson's disease progressively weakens patients' motor skills and also can impair thought processes. Patients often have trouble focusing their attention and may have slower reaction times (Heikkila, Turkka, Korpelainen, Kallanranta & Summala, 1998). The ability of patients with Parkinson's disease to drive may be overestimated by both the patients and their neurologist (Heikkila et al., 1998).

When working with clients who have Parkinson's disease, it is important to know how the disease progresses and affects driving. Many people who are in the early stages of the illness or who have good treatment are safe to drive. Occupational therapists should ascertain how quick the client's progression has been. Some people have a fast progression and notice declines every month, whereas others will go for months or even years without much of a

Personal Experience 6.12. Man With Parkinson's Disease

I once had a client with Parkinson's disease who was referred to me by his physician. The client would have periods during the day in which he could not move for several minutes. The physician would not authorize the client to continue to drive until an evaluation was completed. The client did not feel that his skills were affected; he could tell when he was about to lock up and could get off the road before it happened.

The evaluation consisted of 1 hour of clinical testing and 2 hours of on-the-road testing. I observed the client in a variety of driving situations. He was able to drive safely for the first half hour, but he then started to have trouble with lane position and coordination of movements. At one point, he pulled over safely because he felt that he might lock up. When it happened again, he needed assistance to pull over safely and was not able to resume driving. I recommended that he not drive because it was too risky; my client disagreed, but his physician and family agreed with the evaluation results. The physician then cancelled his license.

change. The physician and rehabilitation team need to monitor this and provide feedback on areas of concern related to progression.

The OT/DRS should monitor the client's ability to make quick, coordinated movements, to use upper and lower extremities as the motions relate to driving, to concentrate, and to pay attention to multiple stimuli and use appropriate speed of thinking. Some people can learn to drive more safely by deciding to drive only when their medications interfere least with their abilities or when they are not fatigued. Other suggestions include keeping driving trips short or sharing driving with another person. If the client has problems with neck range of motion or cannot turn the head without the whole body following, adaptive mirrors can help.

The on-the-road assessment will focus on the ability to coordinate leg movements in a way that is safe for driving. The client should be able to steer the vehicle and maintain solid hand position during turns, at different speeds, and in areas such road construction. It is important to observe whether extraneous movements or rigidity interfere with safe driving ability. It is important to stay on the road long enough to see how changes occur when the client becomes tired at the end of the evaluation.

Multiple Sclerosis. Multiple sclerosis affects each person in different ways and progresses at different rates. The disease affects physical skills and can affect vision and, sometimes, cognition. These changes can happen quickly or slowly. By the time someone receives a diagnosis, he or she often has had the disease for years. It is important with this population to remember that the disease is progressive; the client's future needs must be considered, not simply his or her current needs. Monitoring this type of client is important; the physician and family must be involved to ensure that the client is reassessed should there be any changes in the client's health. The client may not need a reassessment every 6 months, as with other progressive diseases, but his or her health needs to be monitored as part of a long-term plan for driving safety.

Occupational therapists and other rehabilitation professionals can assist clients who have multiple sclerosis in a variety of ways. As with all clients with progressive illnesses, they should discuss long-term community mobility options. The clinical evaluation will focus on physical skills, current and potential future mobility devices, and screening for any cognitive and or visual changes. Adaptive equipment that may be beneficial for people with multiple sclerosis includes hand controls, panoramic and smart-view mirrors, and accessory controls.

Amyotrophic Lateral Sclerosis. Because of the quick and devastating progression of amyotrophic lateral sclerosis (ALS), adaptive equipment for driving is usually helpful only for a short period of time. The OT/DRS should assess the

Personal Experience 6.13. Woman With Multiple Sclerosis

I recently worked with a client who had had multiple sclerosis for 10 years. She had been only a secondary driver until her husband lost his sight due to macular degeneration. As she started to drive more she noticed that it was not safe for her. She could not always feel the pedals, and her legs would get tired after about 20 minutes. She mentioned the difficulties she was having to her physician, and the physician wrote a prescription for hand controls.

She and her husband found a vendor that would install hand controls in her car. She had never used hand controls before; her husband had her drive with her feet to a parking lot, where he showed her how the hand controls activated the accelerator and brake. She then tried the controls while he sat in the passenger's seat trying to talk her through the process, even though he could not really see what she was doing. She got the accelerator and brake mixed up and overaccelerated. She then panicked and started to go in circles very fast; her husband described it as "doing donuts." Her husband was able to talk her out of it and had her drive home with her feet. She did not use the hand controls again for several months.

One day she was driving with her feet, and her foot became so fatigued that she could not make it home safely. She and her husband were on the highway; he reached over her and used the hand controls while she steered. Fortunately, a police officer passed them and pulled them over. He ordered my client to be tested by the state DMV for driving and gave her information on our services for driver's training.

After 6 hours of training, my client could drive safely, and she passed her DMV road test. She told me that no one had ever told her that such evaluation services existed or that lessons were recommended for the hand controls. She was also fortunate that the equipment the vendor installed actually was the correct equipment.

physical effects of the disease, screen for secondary diseases that may affect vision or cognition, and determine how fast the disease is progressing. This information will be used to determine whether it is safe for the client to drive with his or her feet, whether the client will be able to get into and out of the vehicle in all weather conditions, and whether the client's arms are strong enough to steer. The on-the-road test should focus on endurance. Adaptive equipment that can be helpful includes hand controls, electronic accelerator and brake, mini-steering wheel, adaptive mirrors, and accessory controls. High-tech equipment (Figure 6.18) can help a person drive for a longer period of time, but it is costly and requires much training. By the time a client with ALS finishes the training, he or she may not be able to drive for much longer even with the equipment. This population may require reevaluations even sooner than the usual 6-month minimum; a 2- or 3-month interval is most likely going to be the case.

If the client wants to use adaptive equipment, borrowing equipment generally makes more sense than purchasing it. Some national loan programs that help ALS patients obtain other adaptive equipment may be able to help with adaptive equipment for driving.

Working With People With Mental Health Disorders

A wide variety of mental health issues or disorders may affect driving (Hopewell, 2002). Many mental health providers overlook driving when they are working with their clients. They either assume the client does not drive or they do not see a clear relationship between the diagnosis and driving. It is sometimes easy to see how a physical disability can affect driving; however, some mental health problems have a greater impact on driving than certain physical disabilities. Discerning the effects of a mental health disorder can be difficult. Drivers who are not emotionally stable are a risk to themselves and the public. People who cannot control their moods are at higher risk for a road rage incident. Other mental health disorders increase the risk for distraction, falling asleep at the wheel, inattention, inability to solve problems or sequence, and inability to see abstractly.

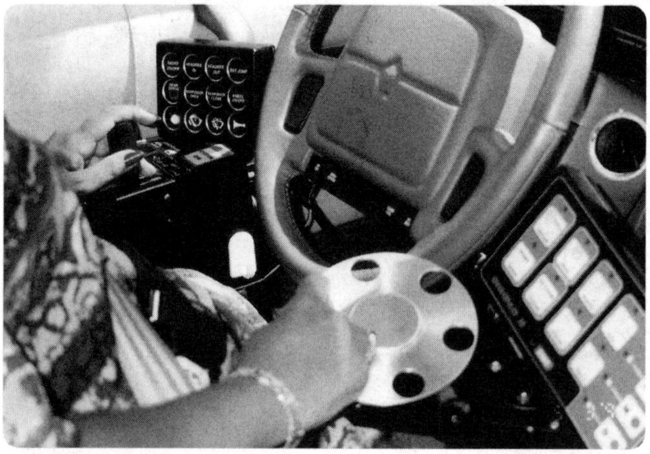

Figure 6.18. High-tech equipment that can help a person to drive for a longer time.

Source: Adaptive Mobility, Inc., Orlando, FL. Used with permission.

Medications to control mental illness may affect driving skills. Many such medications come with warnings to not operate motor vehicles. Some medications have additive or synergistic effects with other medications and together can have a negative impact on driving. Many medications will make people tired or slow down their responses. It is important that the physician review all medications a client takes in light of their impact on driving and, if possible, prescribe alternative medications that do not interfere with driving. Some clients with mental health disorders self-medicate with alcohol or over-the-counter drugs; it is important to ask the client and the caregiver about these possibilities (Spearing, 1999).

State laws require that a person be mentally stable to drive. The state is unaware of such people unless the mental health professional, family, or law enforcement agency identifies them according to state policy. State DMVs will request information from a driver's physician concerning a driver's fitness to drive if they receive information concerning his or her mental health. Physicians who are asked to verify whether a patient is safe to drive often refer them for driver evaluations.

The OT/DRS should gather information about the client's mental health and mental health history, success with treatment, and insight into the areas of concern. As always, the family's perspective is important. It is important for the occupational therapist working with clients with mental health disorders to have clinical mental health experience, coursework in psychology, or continuing education in various mental health disorders.

Depression

Depression is a common, treatable disorder. People who have depression and want to pursue driving must be able to function in everyday life. Some people who have not been treated for depression or who have not been treated successfully should not drive. During acute depression, a driver may not have the focus or awareness to drive safely. Depression is treated with medications that can interfere with driving skills. Getting out and being social can help improve depression, but being unable to drive may add to the depression.

Mental health professionals need to be aware of the impact that depression can have on driving and should screen for the client's driving needs and abilities. An occupational therapist mental health professional will have the right tools to complete such a screen. Clients with depression need to be screened for emotional stability, cognition, and reaction time. During acute depression, clients may not have the emotional ability to handle the stresses associated with driving; difficult road situations could cause anxiety or even road rage. Depression can affect problem solving, attention span, multitasking, and decision making. The client's mental and physical reaction time also can be delayed.

During the on-the-road assessment, the amount of stress and distraction needs to be closely monitored. The client needs to be able to drive on all types of roads and handle stressful driving situations, such as left turns, intersections with traffic, unmarked intersections, freeway merges, lane changes, and busy parking lots. Under stress, the client should demonstrate safe technique while remaining calm. The client should not overreact or become angry or aggressive toward other drivers. It is important to know whether the client has better times of the day than others. It may be necessary to schedule additional sessions to ensure that the client can perform the driving task when fatigued.

Bipolar Disorder

Bipolar disorder involves states of mania and depression. Mania involves impulsivity, poor planning, inability to focus, and difficulty controlling temper. These are all areas of concern with regard to safe driving skill. It is important to know how the client is affected in the manic and depressed states and whether he or she has warning signs of mood changes. People with bipolar disorder often manage well with medication.

It is important for the occupational therapist to know how long the client has been stable. Information should be gathered from family and friends because they often have better insight as to how the client's bipolar disorder might affect his or her driving. Has the client had many tickets,

Personal Experience 6.14. Woman With Bipolar Disorder

One of my clients was a woman in her 20s who had bipolar disorder and wanted to learn to drive. She had started lessons with a driving instructor, but her vocational counselor was worried about road rage and referred her to me for a driver evaluation.

She did well on all clinical testing but had mild impairment with divided attention. Even though she did well on the testing, she was angry that the tests were being done. She kept saying, "I just want to drive; let's get on with this." Her skills in the parking lot and on side streets were safe, but I decided that she needed two or three lessons to ensure that she could learn safe driving with emotional composure.

In traffic she was able to focus enough to drive, but she was not always safe. She had a hard time dealing with people who did not follow driving rules. She stayed calm but would mutter profanities under her breath at them as she continued to drive. I had her pull over, and I reminded her that not everyone follows safe driving rules. The driver needs to watch out for those errors and respond correctly and safely. She accepted the feedback and continued with the driving lesson.

During the third lesson, my client attempted freeway driving. It was stressful, and as she came off the freeway, she suddenly became angry about some feedback about road rage given to her during the previous lesson. She became angry, and her driving skills were not safe. I asked her to pull over, but she would not because she thought she was being safe. I had to help her steer and slow down so that she would be driving safely. Because I could not get her to pull over, I asked her to turn into a parking lot to "work on parking skills." My client calmed down, and we did two parking maneuvers before I drove back to her apartment. I did not review her performance at that time because were alone in the car together and she was still angry.

The next day, we scheduled an appointment with my client's vocational counselor, and I recommended that she not drive due to her inability to control her emotions. This feedback was provided in a safe atmosphere with support. My client became angry and required intervention from her psychologist to process the results and move on.

Occupational therapists in the role of DRS need to understand how to test and intervene with clients who may not be in good control of their emotions. People who have mental disorders may find that stressful situations challenge their ability to manage their emotions. The OT/DRS needs to be prepared for this possibility and make the appropriate adjustments to his or her approach.

accidents, or road rage situations? If the client has been a driver in the past, getting a copy of his or her driving record also can be of value.

For bipolar clients, the driver evaluation should examine the client's ability to drive, manage stressful situations, concentrate, remain calm, and deal with multiple distractions in a variety of driving situations. It is important to note any mood changes. In traffic or busy intersections, does the client take the time to analyze information to make an appropriate response? Can the client process information quickly enough to stay with the flow of traffic and to remain safe? When other drivers do not do what they are supposed to do, does the client remain calm or overreact? The ability to keep emotions under control in all aspects of driving is vital.

Anxiety

Anxiety disorders can affect a person's ability to stay calm, focus, and react appropriately in driving situations. High-level, challenging tasks often increase anxiety and may cause a panic attack. People with an anxiety disorder can be safe drivers if they manage their condition with relaxation techniques, lifestyle changes, or medication. People who have good driving skills when they are not experiencing anxiety may benefit from driving lessons and relaxation techniques.

People with anxiety often benefit from an approach that is supportive and progresses in slow, concrete stages. It is important to build skills, but it should be done incrementally, so that the client gains confidence before a new skill is added. When this approach is used in conjunction with relaxation and coping strategies, success can be achieved.

Paranoia

Clients who have paranoia may not be safe to drive because they may perceive other drivers' driving behavior or habits as a personal attack. People with paranoia also may have delusional thoughts that distract them from task performance. They may miss or misinterpret information, leading to inappropriate responses. Paranoid thoughts or delusions can be managed with medications, but some medications interfere with driving skills. People with paranoia should not drive unless they are stable and have insight into their condition. The occupational therapist should obtain information about the cause of the paranoia, if known; how the paranoia is managed; and the support of the client's family.

Posttraumatic Stress Disorder

Some clients who have anxiety or other difficulties with driving have posttraumatic stress disorder as a result of being in vehicle crashes, either as a driver or passenger. Such clients should demonstrate emotional control and the ability to learn and incorporate relaxation techniques. Because they do not react until they are in the task, they often need some training time and clinical work before it can be determined whether they will be able to drive. Driving skills should be taught incrementally, adding components as the client gains comfort with each new skill. The occupational therapist can help the client identify why driving is important to him or her and what about the task creates anxiety. Deep breathing and relaxation techniques can help these clients cope with stressful road situations.

> ***Personal Experience 6.15. Woman With Anxiety Disorder***
>
> I provided a driver evaluation for a 30-year-old woman who had had an anxiety disorder all her life. She was on several medications, but her physician had determined that they did not interfere with driving skills. She had learned to manage the anxiety, but it had gotten in the way with her learning to drive. My client had worked with two previous driving instructors, but the stress of traffic was more than she could handle.
>
> After completing the clinical assessment, we practiced driving in a parking lot and progressed to side streets in her area. My client needed to feel comfortable with the vehicle and needed the information presented slowly, in steps. With this approach, she was able to progress to being safe with rural driving on all types of roads. She practiced with her husband and 6 months later became a licensed driver.

Schizophrenia

Schizophrenia is a chronic disease that can be severe and disabling to the brain (Spearing, 1999). Onset is usually when a person is in his or her late teens to early 30s. Schizophrenia can be managed with medications, but it is important, as with all medications, that these not be contraindicated for driving. The person with schizophrenia may have periods of time when he or she should not drive. Driving may be problematic for people with schizophrenia because of the cognitive impairments associated with the disorder (Pellerito, 2005). The client may experience disordered thinking or inability to "think straight." Thoughts may come and go rapidly; the person may not be able to concentrate on one thought for a very long time and may be easily distracted and unable to focus attention (Spearing, 1999).

People with schizophrenia often show blunted or "flat" affect. Their ability to show emotion and their emotional

Personal Experience 6.16. Woman With Posttraumatic Stress Disorder

One of my clients had posttraumatic stress disorder as the result of a truck hitting her mother's car while she was the passenger. She had no trouble being a passenger, but she could not drive without having a panic attack. She worked with me for 10 hours of in-car training, and she worked with her psychologist on relaxation and imaging techniques. The first time she drove with me, she could not drive on any streets on which there were other vehicles. By the end of her training and therapy, however, she could drive on all roads up to 55 mph except for the freeway.

expressiveness decrease. They may withdraw socially because they feel and act different. There is a high rate of suicide among people with this diagnosis because of these feelings of being different and the inability to adequately express themselves. Approximately 10% of people with schizophrenia (particularly young adult men) commit suicide (Spearing, 1999).

It is important with this diagnosis to evaluate attention, visual perception, problem solving, and reasoning (Pellerito, 2005). Schizophrenia can lead to serious cognitive impairment, and it will be important to see how the client handles the stress of traffic, with distractions. The OT/DRS doing the evaluation should note whether the client can remain calm, attend to driving, and make safe decisions in a timely manner.

Summary and Conclusion

It is important that all occupational therapists feel comfortable addressing driving within their scope of practice and experience with the disability groups they serve. It is essential for therapists to understand how the client's disability, areas of strength, and limitations will affect the task of driving.

The occupational therapy generalist needs to understand what the OT/DRS does to address driving in general and what modifications may be available for the client so that a client who could potentially drive is not dismissed. The generalist must value the extent of what is provided during the OT/DRS evaluation (clinically and on the road) and the expertise it takes to assess equipment needs and provide proper training.

Knowledge of what the OT/DRS does lends credibility to the generalist's referral, not only for the client and his or her family, but also for the rehabilitation team and physician. The client and family must also be prepared for the expense to be able to make good financial decisions about the cost of returning to driving or finding possible funding sources.

The generalist's basic knowledge and planning in working with a variety of disabilities assist in the process of screening, planning for appropriate referrals, and smooth transition to the specialist. Knowledge of the client's particular needs will greatly benefit the OT/DRS in providing best services.

The disability the person has, primary and secondary conditions, past driving record, the license status, and driving needs are all important considerations. This chapter has given an overview to begin this process and assist the generalist in increasing his or her comfort level in addressing driving and working as part of a team to obtain information and address driving with the OT/DRS.

References

Allen, C. K., Earhart, C. A., & Blue, T. (1992). *Occupational therapy treatment goals for the physically and cognitively disabled.* Rockville, MD: American Occupational Therapy Association.

Arthritis Foundation. (2005). *The facts about arthritis.* Retrieved December 1, 2005, from http://www.arthritis.org/resources/gettingstarted/default.asp.

Duchek, J. M., Hunt, L., Ball, K., Buckels, V., & Morris, J. C. (1998). Attention and driving performance in Alzheimer's disease. *Journal of Gerontology and Psychological Sciences, 53B,* 130–141.

Eberhard, J. W. (1996). Safe mobility for senior citizens. *ATSS Research, 20,* 29–37.

Fisk, G. D., Owsley, C., & Pulley, L. V. (1997). Driving after stroke: Driving exposure, advice, and evaluations. *Archives of Physical Medicine and Rehabilitation, 78,* 1338–1345.

Ganz, S. B., Levin, Z. A., Peterson, G. M., & Ranawat, S. C. (2003). Improvement in driving reaction time after total hip arthroplasty. *Clinical Orthopaedics and Related Research, 413,* 192–200.

Heikkila, V. M., Turkka, J., Korpelainen, J., Kallanranta, T., & Summala, H. (1998). Decreased driving ability in people with Parkinson's disease. *Journal of Neurology and Neurosurgical Psychiatry, 64,* 325–330.

Hesman, T. (2004, October 3). Study tracks Alzheimer's effect on driving. *St. Louis Post-Dispatch,* p. A1.

Hopewell, C. A. (2002). Driving assessment issues for practicing clinicians. *Journal of Head Trauma Rehabilitation, 17,* 48–61.

Korner-Bitensky, N. A., Mazure, B. L., Sofer, S., Gelina, I., Meyer, M. B., Morrison, C., et al. (2000). Visual testing for readiness to drive after stroke: A multicenter study. *American Journal of Physical Medicine and Rehabilitation, 79,* 253–259.

Peli, E., & Pely, D. (2002). *Driving with confidence: A practical guide to driving with low vision.* River Edge, NJ: World Scientific.

Pellerito, J. M., Jr. (2005). *Driver rehabilitation and community mobility: Principles and practice.* Philadelphia: Elsevier Mosby.

Spearing, M. K. (1999). *Overview of schizophrenia* (NIH Publication No. 02-3517). Washington, DC: US Department of Health and Human Services.

Selected Therapeutic Interventions

Occupational therapists who are driver rehabilitation specialists (OT/DRSs) benefit from collaborating with other medical professionals who work with those clients who have the potential to become drivers. Occupational therapists can consult with other medical professionals to determine whether the deficits identified in the driver evaluation can be treated and what approaches could be used.

The OT/DRS and occupational therapist generalist need a good working relationship. Each professional will gather information that should be shared with the other to best serve the client. Following the driver evaluation, it is important for the generalist to make the appropriate referrals to help the client overcome any deficits that are identified. For example, referral to a physical therapist may be most appropriate for certain mobility issues; vision problems may be best handled by an optometrist, ophthalmologist, or behavioral optometrist, depending on the issue. Some clients have previously received occupational therapy but are at a point at which they will benefit from addressing higher level functions; in those cases, the OT/DRS must be able to convey sufficient information to the client's physician so that he or she can write the referral or prescription for therapy. It is important to determine which activities of daily living (ADLs) in addition to driving are affected by the client's deficits, because most medical payers will not pay for occupational therapy for the sole purpose of driver rehabilitation.

Many occupational therapist generalists may not be used to addressing higher level skills. An OT/DRS can explain to the generalist how to work on driving skills in the therapy setting and help identify appropriate specialists for referral. Teaming with other professionals can help people achieve either community mobility or safe driving. It also helps clients to realize their limits if they are unable to gain the skills needed for either task. If the client is not a candidate for driving, it is important to give closure to this task in a supportive manner and work with the generalist to reinforce the situation. Only with this professional collaboration can clients receive the best service possible.

Ideas for Therapy Interventions

Occupational therapy intervention has two levels (Pellerito & Davis, 2005). The first addresses the client's ADLs, which are the critical tasks a person needs to perform for daily life function; the second focuses on the client's instrumental activities of daily living (IADLs). IADLs are complex tasks that involve a high level of skill, insight, and integration to perform safely. Driving, work, aspects of community mobility, and parenting are examples of IADLs.

To address IADL skills, the occupational therapist needs to shift his or her thinking. Some compensation techniques taught initially in rehabilitation are effective for ADLs but not IADLs. Instead of compensation, the focus with IADLs is on insight, speed of response, work in distracting and challenging environments, use of the affected and unaffected side, and integration of skills for smooth movements and responses.

The generalist will want to work in a busy, noisy clinic and have the client attempt a difficult task that requires a high level of concentration, with interruption for other tasks, so that the analysis of higher level cognitive skills can be determined. For example, the client could begin work on a three-part cooking task, be interrupted with a phone call that asks him or her to get another task started, and then return to the cooking task. To make the exercise more challenging, the therapist could time the activity or ask the client to finish all parts of the meal at the same time.

Computerized games can provide a safe way to simultaneously practice many driving skills: eye–hand coordination, problem solving, sequencing, processing speed, and attention span. Some games come with a steering wheel, accelerator, and brake pedals, like a real car. These games are not exactly like driving, but they require use of some of the similar concepts.

Automobile simulators are helpful but not required (Figure 7.1). They enable clients to practice driving in a simulated session to see their abilities and where they lack skills.

Personal Experience 7.1. Man With Brain Injury

A client with brain injury was unable to drive because of decreased attention span and visual impairment. He was functioning in his home, so he did not notice the impact of his deficits. Driving, having community mobility, managing money, and making safe decisions were still issues for him. He was motivated to improve these skills so that he could be on his own and return to work. The occupational therapist generalist initially did not see the need to address these IADL skills, but once we sat down and reviewed a plan for the client, she was able to see the importance of those skills to his function.

The client received outpatient occupational therapy and then at-home treatment for a year. The generalist and I would talk periodically to review his goals and increase the complexity of the task and level of expectations.

Ultimately, the client needed 6 hours of driver's training to incorporate what he had learned in therapy into the driving activity. He also learned to use adaptive mirrors to check his blind spots fully and watch behind him as he backed up. He was able to return to driving with restrictions, was independent in the community, and returned to work part-time.

This feedback can be motivating. Simulators can help with skills such as steering smoothly and maintaining lane position. Some simulators allow the therapist to grade the activity and allow the client to work on driving tasks that are progressively more complex. Interactive simulators allow the user's actions to affect the simulated driving environment.

Vision

Understanding how vision works, along with the vision requirements for driving, is important to address vision appropriately. Some clinic activities work on visual skills. It is important to work on these skills in a hierarchical system. (Mary Warren, OTR/L, has this type of method mapped out in a pyramid form; see Appendix A.) The foundation for visual skill is oculomotor control, visual fields, and then visual acuity. The next step is attention, followed by scanning, pattern recognition, visual memory, and visuocognition. The highest level is adaptation through vision (Warren, 2005a, 2005b, 2005c). In building on vision skills, the occupational therapist generalist needs to evaluate what skills the client does and does not have. Work on areas with deficits needs be done, and these skills must be mastered before a difference can affect the higher levels. For instance, work on the area of visual scanning, if the levels lower are intact, will involve this hierarchical process. Static–static vision tasks are those in which both the client and the objects they are tracking are still (e.g., reading). Static–dynamic tasks are those in which the client is still, and the objects they are tracking are moving. Dynamic–static tasks are those in which the client is moving, but the objects are stationary. Dynamic–dynamic tasks, the highest level task, are those in which both the client and the objects are moving. Driving requires use of all these skills and the constant shifting among them. It is highly complex from a visual perspective.

Figure 7.1. Driving computer activity with wheel and pedals.
Source: Courage Center, Minneapolis, MN. Used with permission.

Driving can involve any combination of these visual tasks. It is difficult to do and not fully possible if the driver has any visual deficits, attentional difficulties, or processing-speed problems. The environment changes each second on the road. No drive is ever the same. Some ideas to work on these components are mentioned below.

The Dynavision is a large board with many lights that is mounted on a wall; the client pushes a corresponding button when a light comes on (see Figure 2.1). The task is timed and can be done with full or partial quadrants to work on general or specific reaching and vision. The tool has several modes ranging from beginner to advanced. Working on the Dynavision in a busy area with the device on a higher setting can help the client address visual deficits. Asking the client questions while he or she is working on the task can address divided and selective attention skills.

To work on dynamic–static skills, the client can walk down a busy hallway while locating information in a quick, systematic manner. The occupational therapist can set up the task ahead of time by placing sticky notes with numbers or pictures at various heights along the hallway. The client can then be asked to find the numbers in numerical order while walking—no stopping allowed. The task should be timed, and the goal should be to reduce the time required to complete the task. To work on dynamic–dynamic skills, the client could go outside and scan for people wearing certain colors or certain types of cars while walking or scan for certain types of cars while driving in a parking lot.

Working with clients to raise insight and awareness of any vision deficits will help them learn to scan to the areas of their deficit in an efficient, fast manner. Teaching scanning patterns can help clients not miss important information in their environment.

Physical Skills

The client may need to improve the use of both extremities to drive. Doing so also may help the client in other functional tasks. Focusing on the more heavily affected or weaker upper extremity is important. Some occupational therapists use induced therapy programs whereby the client is forced to use the affected extremity while the "good" extremity is kept from helping. Some research projects currently under way (including one at the Sister Kenny Institute at Abbott Northwestern Hospital in Minnesota; see www.allina.com/ahs/ski.nsf/) are working to show that, for some people, this method is successful in regaining function of the arm after sustaining a stroke. This forced use will at times improve the person's functions, so that he or she can help with that arm in tasks like driving and will need less equipment or increase safety. It also can help in driving so that the person can steer with two hands and can use the accessory controls safely.

To maintain independent mobility in the community, clients must be able to carry out tasks that require dynamic movements. It is not useful to have a client up and walking if he or she cannot balance while walking up a ramp, stepping over a curb cut, or reaching for something while walking. If the client has deficits in these areas that cannot be overcome, he or she may not be safe with unsupervised walking in the community and may need to instead use a scooter, chair, cane, or walker.

To steer and use hand controls, bilateral use of the extremities is needed to perform the task in a traditional manner. The more skills the person has to perform the function of driving, the fewer the number of adaptations he or she may need, saving the person money and training and possibly simplifying the task. Many people with diagnoses such as cerebral palsy will need to develop this skill to drive if they have the potential to do so in the traditional manner. Typing and playing games on the computer can foster this skill. Simulators can help clients practice the needed movements and coordination. Throwing, catching, and playing other athletic games are also good therapy interventions.

Sports also can help with eye–hand coordination, information-processing speed, the client's perceptions of the relationship between himself or herself and moving objects, and other aspects of spatial relations. Sports can teach a person much about cause and effect and relationships of things to others. This can help with keeping a vehicle in a lane, turning it, and gauging space required for the vehicle (e.g., parking spaces).

Riding a bike, with or without adaptations, will give a client a sense of movement and reaction at various speeds. This task has two purposes: One goal is to get clients mobile; the other is to teach them how to do this safely in different environments. Bicycling teaches the skills needed for driving but at a slower pace, so clients can process the information easier. It is a good precursor to evaluating whether the skill of driving is a possibility. Graduating the client to use of a go-cart, golf cart, scooter, or moped can also help reveal whether the skill sets are there.

Cognition

Divided and selective attention are important driving skills. A driver must continually choose what information needs to be attended to at a given time and cope with multiple demands on his or her attention. Again, a noisy clinic can be an effective place in which to address these issues. Clients can work on tasks that require a high level of attention while a TV is on, people are talking, and phones are ringing. The quality of the work and time required to complete it should be analyzed. The task can be varied and its complexity increased to challenge the client. If the clinic has the Useful Field of Vision tool, it can be used to assess a client's divided visual attention and selected attention (see Figure 2.2).

Distractibility can be worked on in therapy. First, it is important for the client to be aware that he or she has problems with distractibility and will need to compensate for it. Ways to compensate during driving include keeping the radio off, limiting who else is in the car, and driving during non–rush hour times. The client still needs to be able to concentrate in the face of distractions, however.

A busy, noisy clinic is a perfect place to work on concentration and attention skills. For example, the client should be asked to work on a complex task during the busiest time in the clinic. Possible tasks include following written directions to put together a small engine in the midst of visual and auditory distraction while being timed and interrupted, or playing a game on a computer. Activity ideas are endless and should be personalized for the client, focusing on areas of weakness and, ideally, interest. He or she will have to be able to focus to successfully complete the task. Such tasks will be hard at first, but through this practice, skill and awareness can be developed.

Memory skills are important for driving. In one memory exercise, the client is given 5 minutes to look over a room; he or she must then leave the room and list or say everything that he or she remembers seeing. The amount of time and information present can be varied to make the task even more challenging. Scavenger hunts are a fun way to work on these skills, too. The client can be given a map or clues for finding a set of items in the clinic or even outside the clinic. Clients are allowed to read the clues when they are outside the clinic area, but must leave the clues in the clinic and remember the clues once they are outside the clinic. Once outside, they have a set amount of time to find the objects.

Other Skills

Before driving, clients need to learn to manage stress and learn as much as possible about the task of safe driving as it relates to their disability or condition. These skill areas can be simulated in occupational therapy to gain insight without endangering the client or the community. Activity ideas about how to practice these skills in a safe, nonthreatening manner can be given to the client's family.

Stress Management

Visualization and relaxation techniques can help prepare clients—particularly those who are anxious about driving—for the stresses of driving. If traffic bothers the driver, concentrating on ways to relax in those situations can help him or her transition back to the driving task. If the driver has trouble remaining calm because others are not considerate or are not following the rules of the road, the DRS can help him or her work on staying calm. The client needs to develop insight into his or her stress management problems and into ways to avoid becoming upset about driving situations. Role-playing a variety of scenarios—in the clinic, not on the road—can help the client develop healthy coping skills.

Commentary Driving

Commentary driving can be quite helpful for clients who are trying to develop driving skills. In commentary driving, the client is an active passenger. He or she is given assignments to pay attention to certain tasks the driver is doing, such as scanning the intersection. As a passenger, the client is asked to do the same task, analyze what he or she sees and determine the proper response. The passenger also can comment aloud on the driver's activities while in the car, letting the driver know if he or she missed any information or what might be done differently. These tasks need to be set up to work on specific areas and should be done in such a way as to not distract the driver.

Another version of commentary driving assists memory by giving the driver directions to a familiar location. This task can be made more difficult by having the passenger read a map and navigate to an unfamiliar location.

Clients can work on visual skills by scanning for information and telling the driver what catches their attention and what they would do if they were driving. They can work on scanning intersections, looking ahead on the road, or looking for specific situations discussed in advance. Constructive feedback on the client's performance can be given once the drive is complete.

The occupational therapist generalist and DRS can work together to give the client ways to use commentary driving to work on a variety of driving skills. It is important for the occupational therapist to break down the tasks and give guidance on how to process the sessions for the client to gain the most information in a learning process. Commentary driving activities, in conjunction with driver evaluations and driving training sessions, are helpful for reinforcing new skills or practicing new skills before using them on the road. The DRS should be involved in the design of commentary driving exercises to ensure that the skills are addressed in a graded, safe manner and that the driver understands the purpose of the exercise.

Summary and Conclusion

If the occupational therapist generalist is aware of addressing driving and community mobility as part of the IADL plan for the client, therapy interventions that work toward restoring function in these areas can be a part of the client's long-term goals. It is important to know what is covered by the source paying for the occupational therapy intervention, but if the goals help on a variety of ADL and IADL goals in addition to driving, clinical coverage usually is not a problem. The occupational therapist's ability to break down the task of driving and community mobility and to have a working relationship with the OT/DRS can help the the client develop the skills for safe, independent community mobility or driving in the future. Occupational therapy treatment intervention can help prepare the client to do his or her best on the driver evaluation and to address goals that the client needs.

References

Pellerito, J. M., Jr., & Davis, E. S. (2005, March 21). Screening driving and community mobility status: A critical link to participation and productive living. *OT Practice,* pp. 9–14.

Warren, M. (2005a). *Evaluation and treatment of visual perceptual dysfunction in adult brain injury, part I.* Seminar available from visABILITIES Rehab Services, Inc., www.visabilities.com.

Warren, M. (2005b). *Evaluation and treatment of visual perceptual dysfunction in adult brain injury, part II.* Seminar available from visABILITIES Rehab Services, Inc., www.visabilities.com.

Warren, M. (2005c). *Postural and motor control following adult brain injury.* Seminar available from visABILITIES Rehab Services, Inc., www.visabilities.com.

Working With Vendors and Manufacturers of Adaptive Equipment

Installing adaptive equipment in a vehicle requires working with one or more equipment vendors. Vendors are certified by manufacturers to install their equipment. Vendors who are not certified for a particular type of equipment have not received the proper training to know how to install that equipment. To ensure that equipment is installed correctly, it is best to use a certified vendor. Too many errors can occur when a vendor does not understand the equipment and is not trained in the installation, and some errors can cause injury or death.

Equipment manufacturers work with vendors to sell their equipment. Some will sell their equipment only to certified vendors; some will sell it to any vendor in need of the equipment. Both vendors and manufacturers can belong to the National Mobility Equipment Dealers Association (NMEDA), a national organization. NMEDA sponsors meetings, training, and seminars related to driving and people with disabilities, and it promotes certification.

Occupational therapist driver rehabilitation specialists (OT/DRSs) should establish a working relationship with the vendors in their area. They should know what equipment each vendor is certified to install, how to refer a client to the vendor, and how much time is needed to install the equipment. Some vendors will let customers come to their shop, pick out their own equipment, get it installed, and drive away; they do not promote the idea of driver evaluation or go over the risks of using adaptive equipment without training. It is best to work with vendors who understand the DRS's role in driver rehabilitation and the importance of the driver evaluation. Doing so can avoid the problem of installing equipment that does not work for or endangers clients, whether because of fit or because of improper training. (In one case that I know of, a man who had not been properly trained in using a left-foot accelerator drove his truck through the garage of his house, killing his wife, who was in the living room.)

Good working relationships with vendors help promote the role of the OT/DRS, but they also help clients get what they need for independence and safety. Once vendors value this relationship, they feel more comfortable referring customers to OT/DRSs for driver evaluations, even though doing so increases customers' costs. Some vendors will not install equipment without an OT/DRS playing a role in intervention and training. Vendors may even have an occupational therapist on staff who can help customers find an OT/DRS for a driver evaluation, secure prescriptions for equipment, and ensure proper equipment fit.

OT/DRSs can help vendors stay aware of new equipment and be sure that they are certified for the installation of that new equipment. They also can do a final check of their client's equipment (and make sure that the client can use it) before leaving the vendor's shop. OT/DRSs generally complete the client's training in the client's vehicle after it is adapted, because vehicles vary slightly in equipment feel and placement.

The relationship with the vendor also will help the OT/DRS obtain accurate information on what equipment can be installed in particular vehicles. Vendor and OT/DRS collaboration will help answer all questions before the decision is made to obtain particular equipment. It also will help ensure that prescriptions are written accurately for the equipment that is needed. Vendors should understand that, when a prescription is written for a certain piece of equipment, no substitutions can be made without the approval of the OT/DRS. A good working relationship between the vendor and the DRS will ensure that the vendor asks questions or obtains additional information if anything about the prescription is not clear or if problems with installation arise.

OT/DRSs should stay up-to-date on what equipment is available and how it works so that they can provide proper training. Free or discounted samples of equipment may be available from vendors or manufacturers. Manufacturers have information on equipment materials and components, design purpose, guidelines for maintenance and repair, crash and other tests, and compatible vehicles. A good relationship with the manufacturer can ensure that needed information is conveyed to the client and vendor and help the OT/DRS recommend the best equipment match for the client.

The OT/DRS should not work for a manufacturer or vendor. Doing so creates a conflict of interest, because as a vendor or manufacturer, the OT/DRS may be tempted to recommend the piece of equipment that would bring in the highest profit, which may not be the most suitable piece of equipment for the client. The OT/DRS needs to be able to recommend the equipment that is best for the client, not the equipment that is made by the manufacturer the OT/DRS represents or that provides the best commission.

Adaptive equipment installation and payment for the equipment is rarely covered by medical insurance; however, sometimes workers' compensation or the state division of vocational rehabilitation services will cover costs if the client meets certain requirements. Occasionally, associations such as the Multiple Sclerosis Association of America (www.msaa.com) or the Muscular Dystrophy Association (www.mdausa.org) provide funds for people facing financial hardship. The cost of the equipment and who the vendor is able to bill may be a deciding factor for the client, which the OT/DRS needs to keep in mind. If the equipment is being paid for privately, the client may not be able to afford the equipment. If the OT/DRS has a working relationship with the vendor, the vendor may be willing to provide similar, more cost-effective options for the client. The price of the installation may vary from vendor to vendor, which could also save the client money.

Clients need to know the cost of the equipment and its installation along with how much training is required and the cost of the DRS training. Some people may not realize that training entails additional charges.

Personal Experience 8.1. Incorrect Installation

An elderly client with multiple sclerosis received a prescription for a hand control from her physician. After the control was installed, the client drove with her feet on the way home because she had no training. She tried to use the control but could not do so and was not safe. She called the vendor back in frustration and was given an OT/DRS referral.

My evaluation found that the hand controls should have been installed on the right, not the left. Once the client realized that additional training would be required to properly use the controls, she decided that she could not afford to proceed; she had the controls removed, and she chose not to drive any longer. Had she had all the information from the start, she could have made a decision before she had to pay for equipment that did not work for her.

In another case, a client had hand controls but no accessory controls installed. He managed to teach himself how to drive with the controls, but he could not use the turn signals or windshield wipers, had trouble steering straight with one hand, and could not reach the horn. A policeman pulled him over for not signaling and fined him for not having the equipment listed on his license. (The vendor had not been aware of the state's requirement for road testing for adaptive equipment.) He also mandated that the client have a road test.

After my evaluation, I trained the client in using hand controls and prescribed a spinner knob with a touch control pad. The client could then safely use the steering and accessory controls.

Helping Vendors Understand the Role of the OT/DRS

Some vendors do not understand the difference among a physician's order, an occupational therapist generalist's prescreening recommendations, and the OT/DRS prescription. The vendor needs to understand this difference to take the appropriate action. If a vendor's customer has not been evaluated for the desired equipment, a referral to the local OT/DRS is in order. If the client has a prescription from a DRS along with a plan for training, proceeding with installation of the equipment is appropriate. Vendors are starting to realize the dangers of adapting vehicles without the client first seeing an OT/DRS for evaluation and training. Increasingly, vendors are requesting that clients bring referrals or prescriptions from OT/DRSs that show that the client has had an evaluation. Some vendors receive what looked like prescriptions from physicians and occupational therapist generalists and, not knowing the difference between the disciplines, follow those prescriptions, even though no driver evaluation or training has been conducted and neither the people prescribing the equipment nor the customer has consulted an OT/DRS.

The occupational therapist generalist's prescreen identifies risks for driving and what adaptive equipment a client might need to drive. The prescreen is based on clinical assessment tools and does not involve an in-vehicle evaluation with adaptive equipment or an on-the-road evaluation. It is a precursor to the OT/DRS's driver evaluation. Vendors' understanding of the differences in types of evaluations is

Personal Experience 8.2. Equipment Prescription

A customer went to a vendor with a physician's prescription for a left-foot accelerator. The customer did not know how the equipment worked and ran into a stop sign as he left the parking lot.

The vendor was confused as to why the customer did not know how to use the control. Because I had a good working relationship with the vendor, he called me to figure out what had happened. In discussing the situation, I realized that the prescription from the medical professional looked the same as a prescription from an OT/DRS. The vendor was unaware that a physician's prescription did not mean that the equipment had been evaluated or that training had been completed. I explained the physician's role and told the vendor that a prescription from a physician was a starting point for client involvement with an OT/DRS. It did not mean that the customer had already been seen and trained by the OT/DRS.

critical to meeting clients' needs and keeping them safe. If a vendor has a working relationship with an OT/DRS, any questions about the source of a referral or prescription can be answered immediately.

It can be helpful for OT/DRSs to develop a prescription form for use with vendors, including recommended equipment, skills of the professional evaluating the client, and a signed agreement from the client stating that he or she will learn how to use the equipment before driving the adapted vehicle. The form should have the OT/DRS's company name on it, the plan for training, and the OT/DRS's and client's signatures. The vendor will then know immediately that the customer is involved with an OT/DRS. On the prescription form, it is important to list the client's specific equipment needs, the vehicle make and model that will be adapted, the amount of training that the client has had, whether the OT/DRS will be present for the final fitting, and whether the client is safe to drive the vehicle home from the vendor's shop. A contact person who can answer the vendor's questions about the client and his or her training should be listed on the form. If the customer will need additional training, it can be helpful to outline the training needed and the follow-up that the OT/DRS will provide.

Summary and Conclusion

Working collaboratively will help clients get the right equipment and stay safe as they proceed. If the vendor and the OT/DRS work as a team, each will value the role of the other and work together to best meet the needs of the client. OT/DRSs must continue to inform physicians and occupational therapist generalists about the value that OT/DRSs add to the driver rehabilitation process.

Appendix 8.A. Consumer Guide to Accessible Vehicles

Kathy Woods, OTR/CDRS

Home, work, doctors' appointments, family, friends, grocery store . . . and the list goes on of the places that we travel to throughout our daily lives. For persons who have disabilities, these trips can be made difficult when a personal vehicle is not accessible. On the next page is a grid to help determine vehicle adaptations that may be helpful in making traveling easier (Table 8.A.1).

Starting on the left side of the grid, determine whether the person who has a disability will be a *driver* or a *passenger* in the vehicle. Second, decide if he or she will *ride in the vehicle seat* or *ride in his or her wheelchair* in the vehicle. Next, use the top of the grid to select a vehicle option. The corresponding box will be a list of potential adaptations. Please note: This grid is intended for use as a guideline. There may be unique exceptions.

Other considerations in choosing the best accessible vehicle include how to access secondary driving controls (e.g., wipers, cruise control, gearshift, lights), the vehicle's "garage-ability" (whether the vehicle will fit in the garage), and potential funding resources for the modifications (e.g., state vocational rehabilitation programs, MS Society, Veterans Administration, civic groups).

Ultimately, the goal is to identify what a person's abilities are and what equipment is available to match his or her abilities and to obtain proper training in the use of modifications to promote safe community mobility. If someone is unsure of his or her ability to drive or what equipment may be needed, a certified driver rehabilitation specialist should be consulted. Before purchasing a new wheelchair, scooter, or vehicle, it is highly recommended that a vehicle accessibility specialist be contacted to ensure that the application will work best for the situation.

The author is an OT/DRS with Complete Mobility Systems, www.completemobility.com.

Table 8.A.1. Vehicle Adaptations Grid

Driver	Car	Full-Size Van	Minivan	Pickup Truck/Sport Utility Vehicle
Drive from wheelchair	*Limited option* (PT Cruiser) Lowered floor Ramp Power tie-down	Wheelchair lift Lowered floor Lowered floor in driver/midsection area Gas and brake controls Steering aid Power tie-down	Wheelchair lift or ramp Power door opener Lowered floor Gas and brake controls Steering aid Power tie-down	Not an option at this time
Drive from vehicle seat	Car topper or trunk lift Gas and brake controls Steering aid	Mobility aid lift Power door opener Lowered floor midsection or raised roof and doors Power seat base Gas and brake controls Steering aid	Mobility aid lift or ramp Power door opener Lowered floor or raised roof and doors Power seat base Gas and brake controls Steering aid	Mobility aid lift Power seat base Gas and brake controls Steering aid
Passenger				
Ride in wheelchair	*Limited option* (PT Cruiser) Lowered floor Ramp Tie-down	Wheelchair lift Lowered floor in midsection or raised roof and doors Tie-down	Wheelchair lift or ramp Lowered floor or raised roof and doors Tie-down	Not an option at this time
Ride in vehicle seat	Car topper *or* trunk lift	Mobility aid lift or lowered floor midsection or raised roof and doors Power seat base	Mobility aid lift or ramp Lowered floor or raised roof and doors Power seat base	Mobility aid lift Power seat base

Working With State Departments of Motor Vehicles

9

Occupational therapist driver rehabilitation specialists (OT/DRSs) should strive to cultivate a collaborative relationship with their state department of motor vehicles (DMV). Each state has its own policies, procedures, and DMV structure (see Appendix C). Some states have a medical evaluation unit that is staffed by state driving evaluators; in other states, medical professionals head the unit. For example, Minnesota uses state driving evaluators to staff the medical evaluation unit, and Wisconsin has a nurse heading its medical evaluation unit. Many states have a medical advisory board that provides advice to the medical evaluation unit as needed. The DMV medical evaluation unit should be aware of OT/DRS programs in that state and understand the services that they provide. A collaborative relationship can go a long way toward ensuring that DMVs make appropriate referrals to OT/DRSs, or at the least understand the role that OT/DRSs play in working with seniors and people with disabilities.

In addition, each state has policies and procedures for reporting who should not drive or who should have restrictions on their driving and the appeals process for drivers who disagree with the outcome. In some states, the DMV will take a physician's written information and respond to it without gathering more information (see Wang, Kosinski, Schwartzberg, & Shanklin, 2003, for specific state regulations). The physician may be the only person who can get the patient's license reinstated, and even then the state may require written and road tests. OT/DRSs should be aware of the consequences of physicians reporting their patients to the DMV. Occupational therapist generalists and OT/DRSs can best serve clients and their families if they understand the state regulations governing reporting. They need to know who is required to report, what they are mandated to report, and how to get information reported quickly if they are not a mandated reporter.

State departments of motor vehicles may provide information to legislators about proposed legislation related to driving. OT/DRSs should be aware of such legislation. In some cases, they may want to get involved in furthering legislative changes.

State Regulations Governing Driving Programs

Each state has its own rules and regulations governing driving programs. Some states, including Minnesota and Wisconsin, mandate that anyone providing driver evaluations or driving training be a licensed driving instructor working for a driving school. Other states, such as New York, allow OT/DRSs to evaluate licensed drivers as long as they do not work with new drivers or provide training. DRSs should know the current regulations so that they can ensure that they and their clients are in full compliance.

DMVs have driving school requirements that relate to matters such as space provided, vehicle and business liability insurance, and instructor qualifications. Violation of the regulations could result in large fines, and insurance may not cover an accident if it occurs while violating state rules regarding driving schools. Licensed driving schools receive updates on changes in regulations and laws related to driving. These updates are provided by the DMV. OT/DRSs may find it worthwhile to become a licensed driving school or licensed driving instructor working for an existing school. State DMVs all have different requirements for driving schools and for driving instructors. Some, such as in Minnesota, require instructors to be a high school graduate, receive a certain amount of training, pass a written test, and complete a road test. Others have various combinations of these requirements. Becoming a licensed instructor or school can give OT/DRSs additional protection against liability because the training and credentialing demonstrates that they are able to provide driver training.

Working With State DMVs

A good working relationship with the state DMV is essential. Such relationships are good marketing tools for

Personal Experience 9.1. Driver's License Status

The driving program I worked for covered two states, both of which required that the company be a licensed driving school and abide by the regulations governing licensed schools. Driving schools could be licensed just for the driving portion of driving lessons or for the classroom and driving portion. One state allowed us to work with new drivers; the other state allowed us to work with all licensed drivers older than age 18 but not with new drivers.

It was important to know the driver's license status of each client or whether the client had ever been licensed:

- If the client had a current license, we were allowed to do evaluations and training in a parking lot and on the road.
- If the client had an expired license, he or she first needed to renew it.
- If the client had a cancelled license, which usually happened as the result of a disability, then he or she needed to get relicensed. In one state, the client could get a limited license that allowed us to drive with him or her to evaluate driving potential or to provide training. Some states require such clients to appear before a medical review board to decide the route to license renewal; other states require a physician's letter stating that the driver is fit to drive, after which the client must complete written and road tests.
- If the person's license had been revoked, it was usually the result of a legal issue, such as driving while intoxicated or receiving moving violations. Clients with revoked licenses must resolve their legal problems to obtain a license and work with a DRS.

OT/DRSs and can affect how the state works with people with disabilities who want to drive. The DMV may refer someone with a disability directly to a program or may provide a list of programs from which to choose. If the DMV road testers value the services of OT/DRSs, they may refer drivers directly to OT/DRSs when they test drivers who appear to need driver rehabilitation.

DMVs screen and road test drivers every day. DMV staff, however, are not trained to work with people with many types of disabilities, nor are they familiar with all types of adaptive equipment that a driver may have. Some DMVs have hired OT/DRSs to provide training for DMV employees and act as a consultant on disability-related issues. In such cases, the DRS has helped employees learn about which testing approaches work with different disabilities and how to ensure that people with different disabilities are safe drivers.

Most states treat certain types of adaptive equipment, such as hand controls, as a restriction on the equipment user's driver's license. OT/DRSs should therefore ensure that their clients have their adaptive equipment listed as a restriction on their driver's license, if the state requires it. Obtaining such a restriction usually requires a road test. In some cases, insurance companies will not cover drivers who use adaptive equipment unless they have it listed as a restriction. Most state DMVs provide guidelines for how long a driver can wait between installing adaptive equipment and completing road testing.

Comparison of DMV Employees and OT/DRSs

The DMV is the branch of state government that regulates and tests people's ability to drive. DMV employees work with drivers of all abilities, disabled and nondisabled. They are driving instructors and evaluators; they do not have medical backgrounds. They have the final word as to what a person needs to do to obtain a permit, get a license, and be tested for safe adaptive equipment use. They work with drivers but do not have specialized knowledge of the issues related to older drivers or people with disabilities.

In contrast, OT/DRSs evaluate a client's ability to drive from a medical and driving perspective. They complete clinical and road evaluations to determine a driver's skill. They then review the state requirements for drivers like their client to find out what the client must do to comply with the regulations. An OT/DRS can make recommendations but cannot revoke a person's license, impose restrictions, or give someone the right to drive; only DMV employees can do that. If the DMV requires a road test, the driver must take it, even if the DRS tested the client. The OT/DRS's evaluation is written for the physician so that he or she can provide a report to the DMV, if necessary. DMV testing is designed to assess safety and adherence to state rules of the road. Many people do not understand the distinction, so it is important to explain it to both the client and the referral source (e.g., physician, nurse, occupational therapist).

OT/DRSs understand how to challenge their clients while ensuring safe driving. They may have a standard testing route, but they vary it as necessary to accommodate

Personal Experience 9.2. DMV Road Tests

In the states in which I practiced as an OT/DRS, I would meet with the DMV medical evaluation unit several times each year. I also provided training to DMV employees on topics such as how to work with someone with aphasia or how to assess people with Alzheimer's disease. I frequently traveled to test sites, especially those in rural areas; many employees in rural areas did not feel comfortable working with people with disabilities or testing drivers who use adaptive equipment. The training I provided helped the DMVs provide the best service they could and taught them to value the contributions that an OT/DRS could make to their work.

In one state, the road testing was on a closed course. Many drivers could pass this road test but were not necessarily safe to drive. Raising DMV employees' awareness of such a situation was critical to their providing better driver testing. I worked with the DMV to help the staff understand the needs of certain populations so that they could provide the right type of testing and refer would-be drivers to a specialist, if necessary. In some cases, the DMV could ask that the driver have a special evaluation near his or her home, especially for restrictions based on mileage from the driver's home or low vision.

At one point, I noticed that people with aphasia were not passing the state's tests on the rules of the road. The tests often involved speaking the answers, which is difficult for people with aphasia. I met with DMV officials and provided information on aphasia, emphasizing that people with aphasia often are cognitively intact. The DMV eventually implemented a test that was not language based; the new computerized test uses pictures and text, and the person taking the test selects the correct answer on a touch screen. Evaluators learned to limit their questions to those that could be answered with a simple yes or no and to focus on performance, not language skills, during the road test.

New equipment options can confuse DMV evaluators. Their lack of understanding about how the equipment works can result in negative consequences for people with disabilities seeking driver's licenses. For example, in one state a person who was taking a road test using an electronic accelerator and brake and mini-steering wheel was not fully trained in the use of the equipment and inadvertently accelerated instead of using the brake, nearly causing an accident. Because the advanced equipment was new to the evaluator, he blamed the equipment and worked hard to get it outlawed in that state. Our company had a working relationship with the DMV, and state officials came to us for advice about the equipment. After we consulted with the DMV, the evaluators started to ask about the driver's training and skill before the road test to avoid additional incidents involving drivers who are not trained in adaptive equipment use.

the needs of individual drivers. DRSs generally have a vehicle with dual brakes and adaptive equipment. DMV evaluators, however, complete a standard road test for each driver, either on a closed course or on an open road with limited traffic. The test is virtually the same for everyone. The DMV evaluator's vehicle does not have dual brakes.

Monitoring Legislative and Regulatory Changes

OT/DRSs can influence pending legislation that would affect driving regulations. For example, if a state is considering banning or allowing a piece of equipment, OT/DRSs can help teach regulators and legislators about the equipment so that the regulations governing its use make sense. Another example is that of elderly drivers; rather than ban everyone over a certain age from the road, legislators and DMV officials need to understand that many seniors who drive do so safely. OT/DRSs may find it helpful to develop contacts at state and local DMV offices so that they can obtain the most accurate information about pending and final regulatory and legislative changes.

Summary and Conclusion

The relationship between the state DMV and the OT/DRS can be beneficial for both. Working with OT/DRSs allows the state DMV to know they have a resource who specializes in working with seniors and people with disabilities. The state DMV also benefits from training sessions to ensure that they do not overlook people who may have a disability or effects from aging. As their knowledge of these issues increases, state DMVs more frequently consider the needs of these populations and factor these needs into the requirements for safe driving in that state. The OT/DRS also benefits, getting first-hand information on changes the state is proposing regarding rules of the road or adaptive equipment, or on other statutes. The state can look to the OT/DRS as a resource for any legislation being developed regarding driving, and the OT/DRS can ensure that upcoming legislation meets the needs of the population they are trying to serve. This knowledge and a working relationship are key to the success of both the state programs that address driving and the OT/DRS's programs.

Reference

Wang, C. C., Kosinski, C. J., Schwartzberg, J. G., & Shanklin, A. V. (2003). State licensing requirements and reporting laws. In *The physician's guide to assessing and counseling older drivers* (pp. 77–146). Chicago: American Medical Association & National Highway Traffic Safety Administration.

The Physician's Role

The physician is key to any client's goal of driving. The American Medical Association (AMA) recommends that physicians look at the task of driving for all patients and says that the profession requires assessing, referring, and reporting as needed. The AMA and the National Highway Traffic Safety Administration published a free book for physicians to address senior driving issues: *The Physician's Guide to Assessing and Counseling Older Drivers* (Wang, Kosinski, Schwartzberg, & Shanklin, 2003). The book provides information on how to bring up the topic of driving, how to assess for function and limits in driving, and how to refer a patient to a driver rehabilitation specialist. The book emphasizes the important role of the occupational therapist in driver rehabilitation. (For ordering information, see Appendix A.)

Physicians often do not believe that they play a role in the task of driving. They are focused on medical issues and do not always think to ask about all of a person's previous and current functional skills. They may ask about dressing, independent living, and cooking, but driving is not as obvious a task.

The physician sometimes does not wish to address driving out of fear that the patient will not open up if loss of driving privileges is at stake. The physician may worry that the client will go to another physician or that he or she will get a reputation for taking away patients' licenses, driving away potential patients. Many patients do not understand that the physician plays a role in evaluating driving potential and instead feel that the physician is overstepping his or her boundaries. For these reasons, it is important that the physician has support in addressing driving.

Physicians and State Departments of Motor Vehicles

Because of many high-profile accidents involving seniors, many state departments of motor vehicles (DMVs) are focusing time and energy on following up on drivers at risk, particularly senior drivers. If a senior driver has had several accidents in a short time (e.g., 6 months to 1 year) or if a police officer issues a ticket and questions the driver's ability to drive, the DMV asks him or her come in for a screen. Often, information from the physician is required before the person is cleared to drive.

DMVs rely on physicians to provide accurate information about a person's ability to drive and may mandate reporting of unsafe drivers. The DMV medical evaluation unit (if the state has one) or its equivalent usually will request information from physicians. DMV evaluation units generally have full confidence that physicians have the skill to make decisions about driving. They may assume that all physicians discuss driving with their patients and, if the patient is not safe, report him or her or tell the patient not to drive for a certain period of time. DMVs often have a hard time understanding the role of the occupational therapist driver rehabilitation specialist (OT/DRS) and do not realize that physicians often receive their information on patients' driving abilities from OT/DRSs or other occupational therapists.

If the state DMV does not request information on a patient's driving skills, many physicians do not bring up driving. Physicians do not want to sign the state forms regarding a person's ability to drive without gaining information about this task, but they often do not know how to obtain the information they need. Once physicians understand the role of occupational therapists and OT/DRSs, they come to rely on them for the information they need and often become a source of driver evaluation referrals.

It is difficult to get the word out to physicians about the role of occupational therapy in driver rehabilitation. They are busy with the day-to-day work of being a physician. They do not always attend continuing education seminars that discuss driving or have time for in-services during the day. Often, however, the physician's assistant or nurse has time to listen and pass information on to the physician.

Personal Experience 10.1. License Cancellation

A physician cancelled a patient's license without telling him that he was going to do so. He had talked to the patient about not driving and the need to work on skills in therapy first. The patient agreed to do this but 1 week later received a letter cancelling his license.

The person tried to work with the state and the physician to reverse the cancellation but was not successful. He then hired a lawyer to pursue litigation against the state because he did not feel that he had been given due process: There was no way to appeal or overturn the letter of cancellation. The person won the case.

Physicians should involve the patient and his or her family in decisions made about driving. Most states do not expect physicians to cancel a patient's license if the person is not going to drive until the physician has given approval. Only when it appears that an unsafe patient intends to continue driving does the state expect the physician to inform the state.

Communication with the physician's assistant or nurse is therefore important in reaching physicians.

When a physician asks all patients about their ability to drive, he or she can help them understand that they are not being singled out. If questions about driving are asked routinely, the task will not be forgotten and patients will come to expect the questions. If patients compare conversations, they will see that the issue of driving truly is addressed with everyone.

The physician must be honest with the patient in conversations about driving. It is not appropriate for the physician to talk with the patient about driving, discuss a plan to return to driving later in rehabilitation, and then cancel the person's license. The physician needs to be up front with the patient about submitting information to proceed with the cancellation process. The patient should not be surprised by a letter from the DMV revoking driving privileges. If the physician is concerned that the person will drive even after he or she has told them not to, it is appropriate to pursue cancellation of the license, but the patient needs to be aware that the physician is going to do this.

Physicians need to understand the driver evaluation component of driver rehabilitation. They need to know that it includes clinical assessments, on-the-road driver assessment, and evaluation of the need for adaptive equipment and training in its use. They need to value the medical aspect of driver rehabilitation for their patients whose impairments may affect their driving skills. Physicians who do not value or understand what is being provided by the OT/DRS will not refer a person for the service. This is especially true if the person has concerns about paying for the service.

Physicians as Part of the Rehabilitation Team

The occupational therapist generalist and the OT/DRS need to include the physician as an integral part of addressing the goal of driving. The physician will have a full medical understanding of the client, the disability, and prescribed medications but might not relate this information to driving without the lead of the occupational therapist. The physician can give the occupational therapist pertinent information as driving skills are addressed.

Physicians are used to working with occupational therapists in rehabilitation settings but may not understand that they can assist patients with driving. Physicians need to understand the difference between the types of occupational therapists. The occupational therapist generalist will address activities of daily living (ADLs) such as dressing, showering, cooking, taking care of the household, and community skills. Occupational therapists also can address the instrumental activity of daily living (IADL) of driving along with other areas that may be challenging for the client, but they cannot complete clinical testing that may show if a client can drive. They can identify risks and strengths but cannot give a definite yes or no as to the task itself.

The OT/DRS can provide information about the specifics of driving; the information is based on a combination of clinical tests and on-the-road driver evaluation. They also can provide guidance to the generalist as to what skills to focus on in therapy.

Occupational therapy for ADLs and IADLs is usually covered by insurance; however, because driving is not seen as a medical necessity, most insurance, Medicare, and Medicaid will not pay for driver rehabilitation if that is the only skill that is being worked on by occupational therapy. Most clients, therefore, will need to pay for driver rehabilitation services themselves.

Physicians must understand the risks of letting patients who have disabilities that could affect driving skills try to drive on their own. Some physicians tell the patient to try driving in a parking lot with someone else in the car. This approach is unsafe because the other person is not trained to handle the situation if the person trying to drive cannot. People often hit the accelerator instead of the brake, and without a car that has a passenger-side brake, there is no

Personal Experience 10.2. Importance of the Team in License Cancellation Decisions

A 60-year-old man who had had a left-side stroke was referred by his physician to the occupational therapist generalist for a driver evaluation. The generalist spent 1.5 hours with the client completing clinical assessments. The client could not figure out how the tests related to driving; the therapist did not explain and rushed the client to finish the tests. The client's wife was there; she had just driven with him and felt that he drove well. The therapist did not engage her or ask her for information.

The client did not do well on tests of divided attention or memory testing and refused to do the paper-and-pencil tasks he was asked to do. The therapist ended the session by recommending that he not drive anymore and that cancellation of his license would be recommended to the physician. The physician then cancelled the client's license.

The client received this notice in the mail and did not know his options for pursuing driving. He was depressed and angry that he did not know that the tests could take away his ability to drive. He talked to his physician's nurse and found out that an OT/DRS service in the area provided on-the-road evaluations and would come to his house. The client talked to the physician about pursuing this testing, but the physician, thinking the generalist had provided accurate and complete information, refused to let the client do the testing.

The OT/DRS talked to the physician and explained the differences between the services and the value of the on-the-road testing for this person. It was difficult to convince the physician that the client deserved this chance. The client completed both the clinical and on-the-road testing. Although the tests were similar to those given by the generalist, the OT/DRS could explain how the tests related to driving. During the driving test, the client was consistently safe, except for getting on and off the freeway. The recommendation was for him to limit driving to his community and to not use the freeway. The physician was still skeptical because of the generalist's evaluation so she required one more session on the road before following through on the OT/DRS's recommendations. The client was then given the approval to return to driving.

This long process would have been completed more effectively if the professionals had been part of a team that valued each other and referred the client to the appropriate service. The generalist should have realized her limitations in addressing driving. It is important that all players are on the same page so that a client's skills for driving are evaluated in the best way possible.

way to stop the car. Other problems include a lack of insight, in which the driver may not recognize that he or she is driving dangerously or attempting to handle situations that exceed the driver's skill level. Many spouses have called me, as an OT/DRS, because they were helping their disabled spouse practice driving and things did not go well. Incidents include hitting light posts, sideswiping signs, and being unable to cope with unexpected road construction. These situations do not need to happen.

So how can physicians learn about the value of driver rehabilitation services? Occupational therapists can provide in-service training, marketing visits, and educational materials for physicians and their staff. Providing a copy of the AMA guide (Wang et al., 2003) illustrates that the physician's own association values the service. It also is helpful to make sure that the physician gets a copy of the driver evaluation for the patients they refer to the OT/DRS. He or she can then see what was covered, how the patient did in each area, and what the specific recommendations are for that patient. This approach keeps physicians involved as an important part of the team so that they can take the lead in finalizing recommendations, reinforce the results of the evaluation with the patient, and efficiently report information to the DMV. More information on marketing to physicians is presented in Chapter 11.

OT/DRSs can help physicians understand the importance of a complete driver evaluation. Some occupational therapy practices attempt to evaluate driving skills and make recommendations on the basis of clinical testing and, sometimes, driving simulation. This approach is confusing and misleading. This information cannot replace the complete driver evaluation, and physicians need to understand that. If the generalist and OT/DRS work together, it will help the physician understand this role delineation, and patients will get services that meet their specific needs.

Many people fail the clinical driver assessment but pass the road test, and vice versa. This can happen for a variety of reasons:

- Some people are not good at taking tests and do best with hands-on evaluations.

Personal Experience 10.3. OT/DRS and Generalist Roles

In my practice, one method utilized in a rural area as the protocol was for the occupational therapist generalist to complete the clinical assessment and for the OT/DRS to complete the road assessment. After several months, the generalist started to use the clinical testing to make recommendations to a client as to driving situations he or she could start back to, radius restrictions, and possible equipment needs. Those recommendations looked like the recommendations from the OT/DRS, so the physician approved the client for driving.

The client lived in the country, so the generalist and physician were not as worried about the driving situations that he would encounter. However, as soon as the client tried driving, his wife said that he was unsafe. He did not check for traffic, did not watch his speed, and would pass farm equipment without checking for oncoming traffic. The client's wife found out about the OT/DRS services through the generalist and called to set up an appointment. Her husband did not pass, and the recommendation was that he retire from driving. Driving on the basis of the generalist's recommendations could have had serious consequences.

This scenario was used as a learning tool for the team. The OT/DRS needs to be clear that restrictions should be based on what is seen on the road, not just on clinical testing. The generalist needs to understand that clinical testing cannot replace the road evaluation, and the physician needs to understand the difference between clinical testing and on-the-road testing.

This situation strengthened the program and solidified the importance of the driver evaluation process and expertise required. In this practice, the generalist and physician now know how to explain the need for both types of testing and to ensure that the full testing is completed before clients resume driving.

- Some people do not value clinical tests and do not try hard to do well. They do not see how this will affect driving.
- Some people do not understand that what is being tested will affect their ability to drive. This confusion over why they are there can get in the way of them doing their best at the task.
- Sometimes the tests are so far from the task of driving that the person being tested becomes angry and will refuse to perform (e.g., leather lacing).
- The occupational therapist generalist giving the screen or clinical assessment may not have analyzed the task of driving and the tests they are using. They may make inferences that are not true because of their lack of understanding of the tests themselves or how the tests apply to driving.

Similarly, if the physician does not understand how the tests relate to driving, he or she will not be able to explain their importance to the patient so as to motivate the person to do his or her best on the tests. If the physician is rushed and does not explain what the patient needs to do for the test, the results may not be accurate. If the physician does not feel comfortable talking to the patient about driving, he or she may not explain why the patient must take the tests and what will be done with the results. If the physician does not feel comfortable with the driver evaluation process as a whole, he or she may make abrupt decisions regarding driving, such as sending cancellation reports to the DMV for people who actually have the skills to drive, requiring equipment for the patient so that he or she can continue to drive but it is not right for the client, or letting someone drive who is unsafe.

Many physicians tell people that they can practice driving before taking the OT/DRS driver evaluation because they do not fully understand the driver evaluation process. An OT/DRS can look for skills and work through any rustiness the patient may have after not driving for several months or years. The road assessment starts out slowly and builds gradually, in part because clients are often out of practice driving. Practicing before working with the OT/DRS is too risky.

Penny Wise, Pound Foolish

Generalists, to help curb expenses, sometimes are reluctant to identify and refer clients who need driving services; they feel that many people do not need to pay this extra cost. They may feel that the clinical testing is covered under insurance and that they can provide the needed information to the physician.

To their credit, generalists can be very creative in creating clinical services to replace on-the-road testing. These elaborate testing sessions sometimes take 3 to 8 hours to complete or involve several sessions over several days, sometimes with simulators. Few clinical tests correlate with driving ability; nevertheless, the tests are used to gauge driving ability. Generalists may call their services an IADL evaluation, even though the only focus is driving. (This approach will eventually backfire because if the intervention description is so overused as to become meaningless, it may run the risk of not getting reimbursed at all.) Moreover, if the costs for IADL evaluation billed to insurance are three to four times the cost of a driver evaluation, is that really a good use of this money?

Summary and Conclusion

Occupational therapists need to understand the components of driver evaluation and what the best context is for providing this service delivery model. Occupational therapists and OT/DRSs need to include the physician in the process of screening or evaluating driving. We in the profession need to meet the needs of the client, even if the best way to do this means some payment on the client's part.

Driving is a dangerous and expensive activity that is a privilege, not a right. We need to treat it as such and take measures to evaluate people appropriately before they drive again. Physicians who value the services of OT/DRSs often do not hesitate to tell the person that this would involve a private-pay fee, and they and many clients often feel that the fee is worth the services provided.

Close collaboration with physicians can only strengthen individual driver rehabilitation programs and the occupational therapy profession as a whole. It is a valuable part of successful driver rehabilitation.

Reference

Wang, C. C., Kosinski, C. J., Schwartzberg, J. G., & Shanklin, A. V. (2003). *The physician's guide to assessing and counseling older drivers.* Chicago: American Medical Association & National Highway Traffic Safety Administration.

Driving Program Marketing and Funding Options

Driver rehabilitation programs must meet the needs of the clients who use their services. Occupational therapist driver rehabilitation specialists (OT/DRSs) considering the creation of such programs must research their market so that the program is developed correctly. What type of population will need the services? Are they primarily elderly or have physical disabilities? Are they new drivers? Answering questions such as these will help identify the equipment that is needed and the expertise that is required. If the program is developed to meet the needs of a facility or the OT/DRS professional, the likelihood of its success will be questionable. If the program is designed around the needs of the clients, it is more likely to satisfy those clients and succeed.

Driver rehabilitation is a new and growing field. In creating a new program, it is important to consider planned or existing programs. Does the city or town support several driving programs? Are each of the programs meeting a unique need in the area? Do the programs collaborate with each other, or are they fierce competitors? Competition can be good, because it keeps a program sharp. However, it also can limit the services or quality if the programs compete so much that they lose their focus on the clients. Programs that exist in the same city often have learned to work together and respect each other, sometimes referring clients to another program if that program will best meet their needs.

When programs in the same city do not collaborate or coordinate their services, it does a disservice to clients. They might inappropriately provide second opinions, test clients even though another program might have equipment or procedures that are better suited to the client, or make clients wait for appointments even if referral means the client can be tested more quickly. In such cases, programs do not thrive the way they might if they focused on client needs to a greater degree.

Driving companies can build their skills through collaborative relationships and can add to the services available in the area by working together. Staff for each program can use each other as resources, particularly when a site has only one staff person working at a time. By collaborating, companies can develop their own unique delivery style or service type so that each will have a niche that they can serve. This approach can actually help both companies stay busy.

The state department of motor vehicles (DMV) will be confused if multiple competitive programs each maintain that they are the best for working with clients with disabilities. The DMV staff will be hesitant to refer people if they do not value the programs in their area. If the driving programs work together, they can have a large impact at the state level and provide business for both programs. The field of driver rehabilitation will grow too, because the value will be seen.

Marketing and Education

Continuing professional education helps a company and a profession grow. The American Occupational Therapy Association is developing educational programs on driver rehabilitation. The attention they are giving to the role of occupational therapy in driver rehabilitation will help occupational therapists, the field of driver rehabilitation, and other rehabilitation professionals involved in the field. Focusing on the task of driving and the skills of the professional that will best meet the needs of each client is important, not artificial walls of expertise. This client-focused approach will allow the driver rehabilitation field to grow, generate research to better the profession, and meet client needs.

Many forms of education can be used to market driver rehabilitation programs. Target audiences include physicians, other occupational therapists, and other rehabilitation professionals.

Education of Physicians

Physicians can be a key referral source if they value the need for driver evaluation. They have the most influence in getting a person to either get a driver evaluation or give up driving (see Chapter 10). Physicians need to understand what the field of driver rehabilitation is and what programs are in their area. They also need to understand the need for referrals and how to make the most appropriate referral. Physicians are busy, and it can be hard to get time with them. One creative approach is to invite physician residents to ride along on driver rehabilitation sessions or evaluations. Doing so educates future physicians about what driver rehabilitation is and why it is important. If the physician needs to contact the program to schedule the resident, it provides time for the OT/DRS to give the physician information about the services too. Residents often are excited by what they learned and tell the physician, which reinforces the benefits of driver rehabilitation programs.

Physicians' offices often host health fairs or have days when vendors or therapy services can bring breakfast or lunch to them and explain their services. In my experience, I often received 45 minutes to present information on driver rehabilitation and take questions. The OT/DRS can bring brochures, business cards, and referral forms to make it easy for the physician or the office staff to complete the referral. Questions usually focus on the importance of the on-the-road evaluation, the cost for the services, and driver evaluation outcomes. Physicians also like to know what research has demonstrated the need for such services or the increase in safety for clients completing driver rehabilitation and training.

Education of Occupational Therapists

Getting information to other occupational therapists is important. Occupational therapist generalists need to know what driver rehabilitation is and why a client would need the service. They also need to understand the process of the driver evaluation, so that they can explain to clients what to expect and the benefits of the service. The generalist and other rehabilitation professionals need to understand the liability issues around allowing clients to return to driving without completing a driver evaluation, especially if adaptive equipment is needed for the client to drive.

OT/DRSs and occupational therapist generalists serve clients best when they work as a team. In this way, they can learn to understand and value each other's work and how it relates to client outcomes. Generalists understand the value of screening at regular intervals and learn when it is best to refer a person to the OT/DRS. They also can coordinate with the OT/DRS to better work on tasks in therapy. The generalist and OT/DRS can work together to advocate with the physician for clients to receive driving services or present a consistent message to the client as to the need for alternative community mobility options. The development of such relationships is the best model for service delivery.

Finally, the generalist and OT/DRS can work together to educate physicians, reimbursement sources, and clients as to what occupational therapists at various levels of expertise can provide. With both working together, twice as much marketing can be completed.

Education of Other Rehabilitation Professionals

Education of other rehabilitation professionals is important to broaden awareness of driving as an instrumental activity of daily living and of the field of driver rehabilitation:

- The nurse is at the front lines of getting information to the physician and ensuring that the referral for driver rehabilitation is complete.
- The psychologist working with a person with a mental health condition can be aware of how it will affect driving and the best way to evaluate this skill.
- The pediatric therapist can inform the parents of a small child with a disability about the importance of addressing skills that will affect the child's ability to drive in the future.

All rehabilitation professionals play a role in identifying the need for driver rehabilitation and having the appropriate referral networks, but if they do not have the information they need, the client will not receive appropriate services. It is important to educate all relevant professionals through team meetings, marketing visits, continuing education, mailings, and case examples. Educating professionals will improve the way driving is addressed.

Other Opportunities for Education

Other venues provide opportunities to educate potential sources of referrals:

- Visiting various disability support groups is a good way to get information out about driving services.
- Having a booth at health fairs helps potential clients become aware of available driving services and gives them the opportunity to ask questions.
- Visiting developments that house many elderly people, such as retirement homes, can educate staff, residents, and families about OT/DRS driving services. Materials can be distributed for families to review at their leisure.
- Providing professional in-service training on safe driving, defensive driving, or aging issues in driving is generally popular and offers the chance to provide information on OT/DRS services.

- Having a booth at state conferences for rehabilitation professionals is a good way to get information to a variety of sources and generate future marketing leads.
- Offering internships, mentoring, or opportunities to visit and see what the OT/DRS does can help to get the word out to students about the program and what it offers.

For in-person marketing efforts, it is important that an OT/DRS take the lead, so that the services, delivery model, and driver evaluation can be discussed in detail.

Other Marketing Strategies

It is important to create a variety of avenues for referrals to maintain the number of ongoing referrals as well as the types of people who are referred. This goal ensures the referral of clients with a variety of types of disabilities, availability of funding sources, and program stability. In addition, marketing throughout the year, in busy times as well as slow times, is important to establish a stable flow of clients. People forget about things quickly if they don't hear about them; they need information consistently over time for it to stick in their memory.

Providing driver rehabilitation services in the community rather than on a closed course can help get the name of the company out in the area and provide residents with opportunities to ask questions about driver rehabilitation. It is a good idea to keep a supply of business cards and brochures in the training vehicle. Satisfied clients pass the word to others, generating referrals by word of mouth.

Direct marketing can be the most effective marketing strategy. Bulk mailings increase name recognition of the company and provide information about driving services, but the follow-up after the mailings can do the most to gain attention and increase referrals. The frequency of direct marketing in a community can correlate with the number of referrals that are received.

Payment Sources

Driver rehabilitation services are primarily paid for by the client. Third-party reimbursement options are limited and are as follows:

- Some states provide Medicare reimbursement for driver rehabilitation services.
- Many state agencies that administer vocational rehabilitation services will help fund driver rehabilitation services if the program will enable a client to drive himself or herself to work or school. Helping clients achieve independence saves the state money in the long run because it will not have to provide transportation.
- Workers' compensation will sometimes fund driver rehabilitation if the client's injury or disability is directly related to a work injury.
- Some states have required private insurance and HMOs to pay for driver evaluation. Learning what insurers will cover and what information they require on claims may be helpful in getting insurers to cover driver rehabilitation services in additional states.

When reimbursement options are not available, creative ways exist to obtain funding, but the rehabilitation team or OT/DRS should help the client get started. Clients have been known to organize fundraisers to pay for their driver evaluation and needed equipment. Sometimes, local social clubs will help pay for the services.

Clients who have to pay for the services themselves are more apt to find help with payment if they are able to explain clearly what the OT/DRS is and does. They need to be able to explain what driver rehabilitation services are, what the results of the evaluation mean, and where the results will go. If they value the skill of driver evaluation, the amount they pay may not seem as expensive or they may be more open to finding alternative payment options.

Summary and Conclusion

It is important for the occupational therapy generalist and OT/DRS to work as a team, both to best serve the client and to market the need for occupational therapists to address driving. There is a growing need for driver evaluations to maintain skills, to assist in being able to drive longer, and to make driving adaptations when appropriate. If the marketing is in place, this profession will continue to grow and meet the needs of clients who want to drive and or who need to stop but do not understand why.

Occupational therapists are the right people to address driving as an IADL, both as generalists to get the process started and as specialists to provide comprehensive driving evaluations. The involvement of occupational therapists helps the client have his or her needs met, safety maintained, and independence preserved. Occupational therapist involvement also helps the rehabilitation team know where to refer clients and gets physicians involved in the process as therapists bring this IADL to their attention. As the knowledge of the occupational therapist's role in driving becomes more known to clients, families, rehabilitation professionals, and physicians, the need for OT/DRS services will increase, improving the possibility of funding.

Marketing for a program can be, and often is, educational in nature. Marketing can involve the teaming of a generalist with a specialist who not only work together to treat a patient, but also work together to market each other's services. Another marketing idea is to increase community awareness of the resources available for people with disabilities and seniors.

As a profession, we can look for new, creative ways for funding needed driving evaluations and lobby for medical funding options. This may result in companies that insure clients with disabilities or seniors looking at funding options to keep drivers safer.

Marketing and funding options will help this specialty grow. Not only will more occupational therapists become skilled in the area of driving, but it will also ensure that a client's particular driving needs are addressed accurately and fully.

12

Research and Driver Rehabilitation Program Business Models

Driver rehabilitation presents a new array of screening and treatment options about which occupational therapist generalists and other rehabilitation professionals should be aware. Driving is such a dangerous instrumental activity of daily living that it cannot be taken lightly. For occupational therapists, the task of evaluating driver rehabilitation services and styles of service delivery is critical in selecting a program that best meets a client's needs. For the field, formal evaluation is needed to develop programs that are appropriate for a given target population.

Research to back the methods that are being used is lacking, however. Programs are sometimes created on the basis of need or interest but with little concrete evidence to support use of the selected training or testing methods. No standards have been set for driving, for tests that measure driving skills (either clinically or on the road), or for service delivery. Research is needed before any standards can be set.

Research plays a large role in establishing high-quality driver rehabilitation services. Only research can answer questions about the best way to practice in the field of driver rehabilitation, which models are effective in serving people who are aging or have a disability, what the most cost-effective way is to deliver the best service for the client, and what measures should be used when evaluating driving. Research will help develop the best tools and practices for driver rehabilitation. It will provide evidence on which to base driving services and support for the importance of the occupational therapist in driver rehabilitation. Ultimately, it will help keep all drivers safe by improving the skills of those who can drive and by removing from the behind the wheel those who cannot drive.

This chapter highlights some ongoing and completed research, although it is by no means an exhaustive list. It also presents ideas for future research. Funding sources are included for readers who are seeking ideas for funding their own research projects.

Cynthia Owsley

The research of Cynthia Owsley and her colleagues at the University of Alabama at Birmingham focuses on a wide range of topics related to vision and driving. They have addressed visual deficits that affect driving among elderly people and those with disabilities. Their work adds much to our knowledge of which vision deficits have the greatest impact on driving. Below are selected published papers containing their work.

- Ball, K., & Owsley, C. (1991). Identifying correlates of accident involvement for the older driver. *Human Factors, 33,* 583–595. Funded by National Institutes of Health (NIH) grants, a grant from the AARP Andrus Foundation, and a development grant from Research to Prevent Blindness to the University of Alabama's Department of Ophthalmology.
- Ball, K., Owsley, C., Sloane, M., Roenker, D., & Bruni, J. (1993). Visual attention problems as a predictor of vehicle crashes in older drivers. *Investigative Ophthalmology and Visual Science, 34,* 3110–3223. Funded by the National Institute on Aging, the National Eye Institute, the AARP Andrus Foundation, the Rich Retinal Research Foundation, and the development grant from Research to Prevent Blindness.
- Owsley, C. (1997). Clinical and research issues on older drivers: Future directions. *Alzheimer Disease and Associated Disorders, 11*(Suppl. 1), 3–7. Funded by NIH grants and by Research to Prevent Blindness.
- Fisk, G., Owsley, C., & Pulley, L. (1997). Driving after stroke: Driving exposure, advice, and evaluations. *Archives of Physical Medicine Rehabilitation, 78,* 1338–1345. Funded in part by an NIH training grant and the Edward R. Roybal Center for Research in Applied Gerontology.
- Ball, K., Owsley, C., Stalvey, B., Roenker, D., Sloane, M., & Graves, M. (1998). Driving avoidance and functional

impairment in older drivers. *Accident Analysis and Prevention, 30*, 313–322. Funded by the Edward R. Roybal Center for Research in Applied Gerontology at the University of Alabama at Birmingham, the National Institute on Aging and other NIH grants, Research to Prevent Blindness, and the Rich Retinal Research Foundation.
- Owsley, C., Stalvey, B., Wells, J., & Sloane, M. (1999). Older drivers and cataract: Driving habits and crash risk. *Journal of Gerontology, 54*A, M203–M211. Funded by NIH grants, the Edward R. Roybal Center for Research in Applied Gerontology, the Rich Retinal Research Foundation, and Research to Prevent Blindness.

Linda Hunt

Linda Hunt, herself an occupational therapist, has focused her research on elderly drivers and the role of the occupational therapist. Below is a list of her research projects:

- Mobility Assessment Program. Funded by Maryville University.
- Rehabilitation Options for Enhancing Older Driver Safety. Funded by the National Highway Traffic Safety Administration (NHTSA).
- Attention, Cognition, and Driving Performance in Senile Dementia/Alzheimer's Type. Funded by the National Institute on Aging.
- Remediation Through Adaptive Equipment and Training. Funded by the General Motors Corporation.
- Effects of Dementia on Driving Ability: The Development of a Valid and Objective Driving Evaluation for Individuals with Alzheimer's Disease. Funded by the University of Missouri.
- Duchek, J., Carr, D., Hunt, L., Roe, C., Xiong, C., Shah, K., et al. (2003). Longitudinal driving performance in early stage dementia of the Alzheimer type. *Journal of the American Geriatrics Society, 10*, 1342–1347. Funded by National Institute on Aging grants.

Simulator Development

William K. Durfee, Erica Stern, and colleagues at the University of Minnesota are developing a driving simulator to assess the driving skills of people with impaired cognition caused by brain injury. The project includes a clinical trial to help determine the device's efficacy and to assess whether use of the device can improve the user's appraisal of his or her own driving skills.

National Older Drivers Research and Training Center

The work of the National Older Drivers Research and Training Center (NODRTC) at the University of Florida focuses on older driver assessment and approaches to remediation of conditions or environmental factors that contribute to unsafe driving. The center also counsels people who are contemplating driving cessation. The goal is to help seniors drive longer and more safely. NODRTC's research focuses on examining roadway conditions that might be especially challenging for older drivers, the reliability of clinically administered tests for predicting on-road driving performance, use of driving simulation for evaluating driver skills, and sensitivity of the American Medical Association's screening protocol for older drivers. Projects receive funding from the Centers for Disease Control and Prevention, the Federal Highway Administration, NHTSA, and the Florida Department of Highway Safety and Motor Vehicles. NODRTC collaborates with the University of Florida Transportation Research Center and the Rehabilitation Engineering Research Center on Aging. The center offers a variety of driver assessment and remediation services using instrumented vehicles and a simulator.

Research Ideas for the Future

Although the researchers listed above are looking at key issues in the area of driver rehabilitation, many other questions remain unexplored.

- Does the participation of an occupational therapy professional affect the outcome of driver evaluation? How does it affect the quality and cost of the service?
- What is the accident rate for young drivers with attention deficit disorder? Is there a higher rate of accidents, speeding, or other errors with that population? Does having an occupational therapist driver rehabilitation specialist (OT/DRS) as an instructor improve outcomes more than using driving instructors or driving educators? Does this population have a more difficult time passing the written knowledge test and road test?
- Does having elderly people take classroom refresher courses regularly decrease accident and injury rates? Would these rates decline, and would older drivers be able to drive longer if they had a road evaluation and training to update their skills?
- What alternative transportation options work best for seniors and people with disabilities?
- What tests, both clinical and on the road, most closely reflect the task of driving? Can these tests be standardized, or will doing so not capture the unique driving needs of that individual?
- Is the road evaluation more effective if done at the client's home driving area, or can these skills be simulated and then generalized to their driving demands?
- What specific differences are there in the demands of rural and urban driving? What specific skills does a driver need for each setting?

- What is the injury rate following accidents involving drivers with disabilities and their passengers? Do they have a higher risk because of their disability, and if so, how can they protect themselves further?
- Do the "well elderly" appropriately self-restrict their driving as their skills decline?
- Do families understand the risks of allowing their loved one to continue to drive with declining skills? Do they know how to get information about the available options for addressing their loved ones' driving? Do they know the reporting process in their state and the state statutes related to driving? Do they know that identification cards are available for people who cannot drive?
- Are the existing driver rehabilitation programs sufficient to meet the current demand? If not, what would help develop such programs, and in what areas of the United States are they needed?

Researchers seeking funding to pursue these and other questions might start by contacting the American Occupational Therapy Association, the Association for Driver Rehabilitation Specialists, AARP, or NHTSA to obtain more information and ideas.

Program Business Models

A wide variety of driver rehabilitation programs exist. Their experience can be helpful to those who want to develop or realign an existing occupational therapy program to meet the evolving demands of the profession.

For-Profit Occupational Therapist DRS Program; Community-Based Services

This type of program can be owned and operated by an occupational therapist or business professional. It has low overhead because the OT/DRS will travel to the person, so bricks-and-mortar facilities are not required. Gas and vehicle wear-and-tear costs are higher than for a fixed-site program, but those costs can be factored into the price charged for services.

One benefit of this type of program is that the client is seen in his or her own driving environment, so the OT/DRS can understand the demands of the driving task specific to that person. The client's vehicle can be inspected to ensure a proper fit and upkeep. A downside to community-based service is that the OT/DRS will need to get used to a variety of geographic areas and create standards for testing clients, even though the driving environment changes each time. In addition, the OT/DRS will need to maintain professionalism despite conducting business on the road. Fortunately, devices such as cell phones and personal digital assistants make doing so much easier than in the past.

If the business is owned by the occupational therapist, the medical perspective will be emphasized. If the business is owned by a business professional, the strengths will be in the business side of the company, but the owner nevertheless needs to value the medical perspective to provide high-quality services.

Free-standing Nonprofit or For-Profit Program With Certified OT/DRS; Facility-Based Program

This type of program employs a full-time occupational therapist who may be a certified driver rehabilitation specialist and may have a driving educator available on an as-needed basis for some clients. Some programs may be able to offer training either at the facility or at the client's home.

One advantage of the program model is that it can offer the entire driving package (e.g., clinical, behind the wheel, vehicle modification); it also can take advantage of a variety of payer sources, including insurance and worker's compensation. A disadvantage is that if the program is not affiliated with a hospital or other large rehabilitation institution, it may have difficulty expediting referrals.

Nonprofit or For-Profit Program With Occupational Therapist and Licensed Driving Instructor; Facility-Based Services

This type of program is housed within a large medical institution or has referral arrangements with specialists of all kinds. It is staffed by occupational therapists who may have been certified as DRSs and may be brain injury specialists; it also uses driving educators or instructors who have training in working with people with disabilities and adaptive equipment. This program can provide driver evaluations and driving training services.

One strength of this type of program is the many resources at its disposal. It has options for referring clients to other in-house therapists, including neuropsychiatrists, behavior specialists, community-based therapists, independent living skills specialists, vocational counselors, rehabilitation services specialists, and psychologists (particularly to counsel clients who do not pass the driver evaluation). In addition, sometimes these types of programs have a pool of volunteers who can help locate possible transportation options for the person in his or her area. They have a wide variety of equipment options and the ability as a nonprofit to get equipment donated. The model combines the medical and driving perspective. Driving is not the only function of this program, so during slow times the other programs can provide revenue.

One limitation of the model is that, because it is just one component of a larger corporate entity, decisions must be made through a formal process and cannot be made immediately. In addition, such programs may be limited in their ability to serve clients in their local community.

Conclusion and Summary

Researchers have done much work in the field of driving and driver rehabilitation, but there is much left to be done. A majority of the current research relates to the older population, where those funding grants have focused their time, energy, and dollars. Research on clinical assessment tools is needed for occupational therapy generalists to make the appropriate referral (whether to an eye specialist, a neuropsychologist, a social worker, or driver rehabilitation specialist) in a timely manner. Research on driver rehabilitation assessment tools is needed to develop correlations between driving and consistencies in practice. Research on the road assessment portion of the driver evaluation is needed to determine the best structure for this assessment and a consistent outcome. Results from clinical and road portions of the evaluation need to be weighted to measure safe driving skills.

There are many types of driver rehabilitation models, and each offers different services. It is important to research the model that will best fit the client's needs. Having the right professional, with the right training and equipment, will mean success versus failure with the driving evaluation and outcome. Research into types of models and their rates of success with clients is another area for each generalist and specialist to investigate and also would be a good research project.

The future of research in driver rehabilitation is crucial for occupational therapists and their clients, to ensure that this IADL is addressed with the utmost accuracy and the best practice techniques available.

Appendix A. Resources

General Driving Rehabilitation

American Occupational Therapy Association. (2002). Occupational therapy practice framework: Domain and process. *American Journal of Occupational Therapy, 52,* 609–639.

Mottola, F. (2003). *Your car is a monster! Ten habits will keep it caged! Do you have them?* Cheshire, CT: Interactive Driving Systems. (Available PO Box 98, Cheshire, CT 06410)

Mottola, F. (2004). *Partnership for driver excellence: Teen–parent–teacher, teen's in-car lessons for low-risk habit formation* (5th ed.). Cheshire, CT: Interactive Driving Systems. (Available PO Box 98, Cheshire, CT 06410)

Peli, E., & Pely, D. (2002). *Driving with confidence: A practical guide to driving with low vision.* River Edge, NJ: World Scientific.

Stav, W. (2004). *Driving rehabilitation: A guide for assessment and intervention.* San Antonio, TX: PsychCorp.

Wang, C., Kosinski, C., Schwartzberg, J., & Shanklin, A. (2003). *Physician's guide to assessing and counseling older drivers.* Chicago: American Medical Association and the National Highway Traffic Safety Administration (Available: www.nhtsa.dot.gov).

Low Vision

American Occupational Therapy Association
4720 Montgomery Lane
Bethesda, MD 20814
Phone: (301) 652-2682
Fax: (301) 652-7711
www.aota.org

BiOptic Driving Network
Susan Baillely
7775 Ivygate Lane
Cincinnati, OH 45242
Fax: (413) 638-6941
www.biopticdriving.org

Chuck Huss
Division of Rehabilitation Services
West Virginia Rehabilitation Center
P. O. Box 1004
Institute, WV 25112-1004
Phone: (304) 766-4803
Fax: (304) 766-4816
www.wvdrs.org

Harcourt Assessment
19500 Bulverde Road
San Antonio, TX 78259
Phone: (800) 211-8378
Fax: (800) 232-1223
www.harcourtassessment.com

Low Vision Centers of Indiana
Dr. Richard L. Windsor, OD, FAAO
Dr. Laura K. Windsor
Free video on bioptic can be retrieved from
www.eyeassociates.com

Optisource (Snellen Eye Charts)
40 Saw Grass Drive
Bellport, NY 11713 USA
Phone: (800) 678-4768
Fax: (631) 924-8375
www.1-800-optisource.com

Pro-Ed Inc.
8700 Shoal Creek Boulevard
Austin, TX 78757-6897
Phone: (800) 897-3202
Fax: (800) 397-7633
www.proedinc.com

Reitan Neuropsychology Laboratory
PO Box 66080
Tucson, AZ 85728-6080
Phone: (520) 577-2970
Fax: (520) 577-2940
reitanlabs@aol.com

Richmond Products
4400 Silver Street
Albuquerque, NM 87108
Phone: (505) 275-2406
www.richmondproducts.com

Stereo Optical Company
3539 N. Kenton Avenue
Chicago, IL 60641
Phone: (800) 344-9500
Fax: (773) 777-4985
sales@stereooptical.com
www.stereooptical.com

Vision World Wide
5707 Brockton Drive, Suite 302
Indianapolis, IN 46220-5481
Phone: (317) 254-1332
Fax: (317) 251-6588
info@visionww.org
www.visionww.org

Seniors and Driving

AAA Foundation for Traffic Safety. (1993). *Drivers 55 plus: Check your own performance* [Brochure]. Available online at www.aaafoundation.org.

AAA Foundation for Traffic Safety. (2000). *How to help an older driver: A guide for planning safe transportation* [Brochure]. Available online at www.aaafoundation.org.

AAA Foundation for Traffic Safety. (2005). *Carfit: Helping mature drivers find their perfect fit* [Brochure]. Available online at www.seniordrivers.org.

East Metro Seniors Agenda for Independent Living Project. (n.d.). *A key to choice for seniors: Open the door to services* [Brochure]. Available to members from the Minnesota Health and Housing Alliance (MHHA) Web site at www.mhha.com.

The Hartford. (n.d.). *We need to talk . . . Family conversations with older drivers* [Brochure]. Available online at www.thehartford.com/talkwitholderdrivers.

LePore, P. (2000). *When you are concerned: A guide for families concerned about the safety of an older driver* [Brochure]. Albany: New York State Office for the Aging. Available online at www.aging.state.ny.us.

Other Products

BiOptic Driving Network
Susan Baillely
7775 Ivygate Lane
Cincinnati, OH 45242
Fax: (413) 638-6941
www.biopticdriving.org
Products offered: Driving courses, research, lenses

Braun Corporation
Phone: (800) 843-5438
www.braunlift.com
Products offered: Scooters, wheelchair lifts

Delta Integration
23 Howard Avenue
Lancaster, PA 17602
Phone: (712) 392-2701

Handybar
301-284 Helmcken Road
Victoria, British Columbia
Canada V9B 1T2
Phone: (888) 738-0611
Fax: (250) 658-3008
www.handybar.com
Product offered: Sit-to-stand transfer aid

Maryville University
Occupational Therapy Program
Attn: Driving Program
13550 Conway Road
St. Louis, MO 63141
Product offered: Mobility Assessment Program (MAP)

Mobility Products & Design
P.O. Box 7
7346 West 400 North
Leiters Ford, IN 46945
Phone: (800) 488-7688
Fax: (888) 638-1902
www.mobilityproductsdesign.com
Products offered: Hand controls, extension mirrors

Mobility Transfer Systems
P.O. Box 253
Medford, MA 02155
Phone: (800) 854-4687
www.mtsmedequip.com
Product offered: Life easy-exit handle

Stereo Optical Company
3539 N. Kenton Avenue
Chicago, IL 60641
Phone: (800) 344-9500
Fax: (773) 777-4985
sales@stereooptical.com
www.stereooptical.com
Product offered: Optec vision testers

Sure Grip
Howell Ventures Ltd.
4850 Route 102
Upper Kingsclear, New Brunswick E3D 1P8
Canada
Phone: (888) 370-5050
Fax: (506) 363-2391
www.suregrip-hvl.com
Product offered: Hand control

Tip Top Mobility
Phone: (800) 735-5958
tiptop@minot.com
www.minot.com/~tiptop
Product offered: Car top carriers

Vericom Computers
14320 James Road, Suite 200
Rogers, MN 55374
Phone: (800) 533-5547
www.vericomcomputers.com
Product offered: In-vehicle reaction timer

visAbilities Rehab Services
Mary Warren, OTR/C
210 Lorna Square #208
Birmingham, AL 35216
Phone: (888) 752-4364
Fax: (205) 823-6657
www.visabilities.com
Products offered: Continuing education, Dynavision, assessments

Visual Awareness
2100 Southbridge Parkway, Suite 650
Birmingham, AL 35209
Phone: (205) 335-3701
Fax: (818) 780-5352
www.visualawareness.com
Product offered: Useful Field of View

Training

Adaptive Mobility Services, Inc.
1000 Delaney Avenue
Orlando, FL 32806-1228
Phone: (407) 426-8020
Fax: (407) 426-8690
help@adaptivemobility.com
www.adaptivemobility.com
Courses offered: OT/DRS courses for a variety of levels (e.g., vehicle assessment)

ADED Train the Trainer Programs
711 S. Vienna Street
Ruston, LA 71270
Phone: (800) 290-2344
Fax: (318) 255-4175
www.aded.net
Courses offered: Training in driver's training, not specific to occupational therapy

Online Resources

AAA Foundation for Traffic Safety:
www.aaafoundation.org/home/
ADED, Association for Driver Rehabilitation Specialists:
www.aded.net
Alzheimer's, Dementia, and Driving:
www.thehartford.com/alzheimers/index.html
American Association of Motor Vehicle Administrators:
www.aamva.org
American Association of Retired Persons:
www.aarp.org
American Medical Association:
www.ama-assn.org/go/olderdrivers
American Parkinson's Disease Association:
www.apda.parkinson.org
American Society on Aging
Web seminars and online learning:
www.asaging.org/webseminars/
AOTA Special Interest Section Driving Network Listserv:
www.aota.org (Click on AOTA e-mail lists, then on Driving/Driver Rehabilitation. AOTA also has a link for driving that has resources, fact sheets, and marketing materials related to seniors and driving.)
Brain Injury Association of America:
www.biausa.org
Christopher Reeve Paralysis Foundation:
www.christopherreeve.com
Community Transportation Association:
www.ctaa.org/

Eldercare locator, U.S. Department of Health and Human Services: www.eldercare.gov/eldercare/public/home.asp

Frederik R. Mottola, Driving Educator: www.skidmonster.com

Multiple Sclerosis Association of America: www.msaa.com

National Highway Traffic Safety Administration: www.nhtsa.gov

National Mental Health Association: www.nmha.org

National Multiple Sclerosis Society: www.nmss.org

National Spinal Cord Injury Association: www.spinalcord.org

National Stroke Association: www.stroke.org

Transportation Research Board: www.nas.edu/trb/

Appendix B. AOTA Statement on Driving and Community Mobility

The purpose of this paper is to describe occupational therapy's contribution to driving and community mobility to practitioners within the profession and to referral sources outside of the occupational therapy profession.

Community mobility, an instrumental activity of daily living (IADL), is defined as "moving self in the community and using public or private transportation, such as driving, or accessing buses, taxi cabs, or other public transportation systems" (American Occupational Therapy Association [AOTA], 2002, p. 620). Community mobility or transportation is essential for independence and access to engagement in other everyday life activities (occupations). Community mobility, specifically driving, contributes to quality of life (U.S. Department of Transportation, 2003b), autonomy (Hunt, 1993), fulfillment of life roles (Cox, Fox, & Irwin, 1988), access to leisure pursuits (Cobb & Coughlin, 1997), and engagement in other meaningful activities (Gillins, 1990). Loss of the fundamental role of driving and community mobility in adult life is exemplified by feelings of loneliness and isolation and by depressive symptoms that often arise when one suddenly loses the ability to drive (Marottoli et al., 1997).

Driving and community mobility are included within the domain of occupational therapy (AOTA, 2002) and in the profession's *Scope of Practice* (AOTA, 2004b). Table B.1 illustrates some of the aspects of driving and community mobility within the domain of occupational therapy practice and describes the complexity and influence of this critical instrumental activity of daily living.

Service Provision

Populations Served

Occupational therapists and occupational therapy assistants address driving and other aspects of community mobility with clients of all ages. Intervention may address the following:

- Passenger safety by helping individuals access and ride safely in vehicles (e.g., designing mechanisms to help children with disabilities get on and off the school bus, securing wheelchairs or car seats)
- Community mobility, including walking, biking, and riding as a passenger in a motor vehicle or on mass transit to enhance independence and prevent injury
- Evaluation, education, and training of people with learning disabilities, attention disorders, developmental disabilities, and acquired disabilities such as brain injuries and amputations, in preparation for acquiring a first driver's license
- Evaluation and training of experienced drivers who have impairments or age-related changes that interfere with driving and community mobility
- Exploration of alternative transportation options with older adults and drivers of other ages who must temporarily abstain or retire from driving.

In addition to assisting individuals in engaging in driving and community mobility, occupational therapists and occupational therapy assistants work with communities, agencies, and groups to facilitate successful participation of all individuals. Efforts with community planners, school systems, governmental agencies, aging agencies, transit companies, community businesses, and health care organizations raise awareness of driving and community mobility issues and foster the implementation of alternatives to increase participation throughout the community by all community members.

Knowledge and Skill of Occupational Therapy Practitioners in Driving and Community Mobility

All occupational therapists and occupational therapy assistants possess the education and training necessary to address driving and community mobility as an IADL. Throughout the evaluation and intervention process, all practitioners recognize the impact of clients' aging, disability, or risk factors on driving and community mobility. Through the use of clinical reasoning skills, practitioners use information about client strengths and weaknesses in performance skills, performance patterns, contexts, and client factors to deduce potential difficulties with occupational performance in driving and community mobility.

Some occupational therapy practitioners specialize in driver rehabilitation and community mobility. These occupational therapists and occupational therapy assistants administer assessments specific to the requirements involved in driving and community mobility, including clinical assessments of vision, cognition, motor performance, reaction time, knowledge of traffic rules, and behind-the-wheel driving skill. They have additional training and expertise that enables them to recommend vehicle modifications and provide driver retraining. Many states require that occupational therapy driver rehabilitation specialists become licensed as professional driving instructors to be able to serve novice drivers or people whose driver's licenses have expired. AOTA asserts that occupational therapists and occupational therapy assistants are required to have additional specialized training in driver rehabilitation prior to working directly in the area of driver assessment and intervention with clients who have health- or aging-related concerns.

Occupational therapists addressing community mobility assess clients as well as their communities to determine the client's ability to access transportation alternatives and utilize available resources and equipment. Individual assessments may include clinical testing similar to that in the area of driver rehabilitation. However, the focus of assessment is to determine the client's ability to access and utilize transportation resources. Assessment of the community context may involve analysis of available community resources, location of supplemental agencies, accessibility of transportation alternatives, and policy.

The nature of evaluation and intervention are different, depending on the role of the occupational therapist and the occupational therapy assistant. Consistent with the AOTA supervision guidelines (AOTA, 2004a), the occupational therapist carries the overall responsibility for the evaluation and intervention process. While the occupational therapist oversees the evaluation process, specific assessments may be delegated to the occupational therapy assistant if the occupational therapy assistant has demonstrated competency in administration of the individual assessment. The occupational therapist may delegate, on an individual client basis, any of the assessments in the driving evaluation, including clinic-based tests of vision, cognition, and motor performance or the behind-the-wheel assessment. The occupational therapist is responsible for interpreting the results of any assessments administered by the occupational therapy assistant and for incorporating the results into the analysis of the entire evaluation. The occupational therapist may also delegate to the occupational therapy assistant the responsibility of implementing the intervention in accordance with the occupational therapist's plan and the client's treatment goals (AOTA, 2004a). The *Guidelines for Supervision, Roles, and Responsibilities During the Delivery of Occupational Therapy Services* (AOTA, 2004a) recommends that the occupational therapist and the occupational therapy assistant develop a collaborative plan for supervision, which would be put into action during assessments and the intervention process. The supervision must follow state and federal regulations, as well as the policies of the workplace and the *Occupational Therapy Code of Ethics* (AOTA, 2000).

Both federal and state laws, as well as the activities of key professional organizations, influence delivery of and payment for occupational therapy services related to driving and community mobility. In the United States, the individual receiving services most often pays for driver evaluation and intervention. In general, specialized driver rehabilitation services are not currently considered covered services under Medicare benefits; however, in a limited but growing number of states, Medicare carriers will reimburse for all or part of driver rehabilitation services. The Veterans Administration system provides driver rehabilitation services to veterans at select locations nationwide. State vocational agencies, Medicaid, workers' compensation, and private insurers may cover driver rehabilitation services and vehicle modification. See Table B.2 for a summary of external influences on service delivery.

Case Studies

The following case studies illustrate the ways in which occupational therapists and occupational therapy assistants contribute to driving and community mobility in a variety of practice settings.

Rehabilitation Clinical Setting With Client-Centered Goal: To Return to Driving

During the occupational therapy evaluation, a 78-year-old gentleman, Mr. Smith, has expressed a desire to return to driving. Prior to a mild stroke that resulted in a fall and a right ankle fracture, Mr. Smith lived alone and needed his car for grocery shopping, access to medical appointments, transportation to his favorite fishing location, and visits with friends at the community clubhouse. The occupational therapist identifies residual impairments in ankle mobility that are likely to be permanent, affecting Mr. Smith's driving ability and safety. The occupational therapist communicates her concern about Mr. Smith's driving to the physician and recommends a driving evaluation. Throughout the therapeutic process, the therapist educates Mr. Smith regarding the impact of a right ankle fracture on driving performance safety and the need to participate in a thorough driving evaluation before driving again. Mr. Smith and the occupational therapist collaborate to identify options for alternative transportation until it is determined that Mr. Smith can safely resume driving.

Prior to discharge, the therapist makes a referral for a comprehensive driving evaluation. An occupational therapist who specializes in driver rehabilitation reviews Mr. Smith's discharge information. The occupational therapist performs a comprehensive driving evaluation, discusses various modifications for driving, and evaluates the client's ability to use these modifications in an equipped vehicle. An occupational therapy assistant trains Mr. Smith in the use of a left-foot gas pedal until he is competent, confident, and safe with the new equipment. The occupational therapist writes a prescription for the necessary equipment to be installed by a reputable equipment dealer. After installation, Mr. Smith returns to the occupational therapist so she can inspect the installation and ensure that Mr. Smith is able to use the equipment as it is installed in his own vehicle.

Specialized Occupational Therapy Driver Rehabilitation With the Novice Driver

An occupational therapist who specializes in driver rehabilitation has a contract with a local school system and receives referrals of young adults with disabilities as they approach driving age. Gary, a 16-year-old with a diagnosis of attention deficit disorder, has expressed a desire to obtain a driver's license as he and his classmates reach this all-important milestone. An evaluation of his driving potential reveals the following strengths in performing this occupation: a strong determination to learn to drive, good upper- and lower-extremity coordination, and satisfactory visual and perceptual skills. Barriers include impulsivity, distractibility, and difficulty sustaining mental effort. During the behind-the-wheel evaluation, Gary demonstrates good beginning basic vehicle control skills, but he has a tendency to speed and has decreased visual scanning. His driving skills are observed to decrease sharply following approximately 30 minutes of driving. The occupational therapist prescribes a home program of exercises to improve visual scanning and sustained attention and discusses Gary's medication schedule with the physician. Additionally, the occupational therapist provides behind-the-wheel training to teach Gary safe driving skills and improve his communication with other road users and reinforces Gary's need to maintain a consistent medication regimen. Concurrently, Gary attends driver education classes at a local driving school as required by the state department of motor vehicles. Upon completion of all state requirements and the successful completion of the driving test, Gary is issued his license without restrictions.

Community Mobility for the Adult Client

Mrs. Jones, age 33 years, woman with a psychiatric disability, is concerned about driving after her medications have been changed. She has reported to her physician that the antipsychotic medications are making her very drowsy and that she has become lost several times while driving. Mrs. Jones is referred to occupational therapy for community mobility training. The initial occupational therapy assessment reveals strengths in Mrs. Jones's motor performance, vision, and desire to be independent in moving around her community. Barriers to independence appear to be her impaired time management skills, fluctuating arousal and concentration levels, and periodic confusion. After the occupational therapist collaborates with Mrs. Jones to explore possible alternative modes of transportation, they determine that door-to-door service would be the safest transit for her in her community. The occupational therapist also collaborates with the transit agency regarding sensitivity training for schedulers and drivers. After successfully meeting the comprehensive community mobility goals, Mrs. Jones not only completes her therapy program but also is able to maintain her community involvement by using transportation systems to continue her employment, attend religious activities, and go shopping.

Summary

Attention to driving and community mobility is a growing area of concern because of the implications across the life span, association with occupational engagement, and relevance to other organizational entities (see Table B.2). The skills, knowledge base, and scope of practice of occupational therapy enhanced by additional training in driver rehabilitation place the profession of occupational therapy in the forefront of driving and community mobility services. The focus on injury prevention, engagement in occupation, and intervention strategies used in driver rehabilitation and community mobility services are consistent with the *Philosophical Base of Occupational Therapy* (AOTA, 1995) and, therefore, warrant attention in all areas of occupational therapy practice.

References

American Medical Association, Council on Ethical and Judicial Affairs. (1999). *Impaired drivers and their physicians* (No. 1-I-99). Chicago: Author.

American Occupational Therapy Association. (1995). The philosophical base of occupational therapy. *American Journal of Occupational Therapy, 49,* 1026.

American Occupational Therapy Association. (2000). Occupational therapy code of ethics. *American Journal of Occupational Therapy, 54,* 614–616.

American Occupational Therapy Association. (2002). Occupational therapy practice framework: Domain and process. *American Journal of Occupational Therapy, 56,* 609–639.

American Occupational Therapy Association. (2004a). Guidelines for supervision, roles, and responsibilities during the delivery of occupational therapy services. *American Journal of Occupational Therapy, 58,* 663–667.

American Occupational Therapy Association. (2004b). Scope of practice. *American Journal of Occupational Therapy, 58,* 673–677.

American Occupational Therapy Association. (2005). *About AOTA.* Retrieved March 25, 2005, from http://www.aota.org/general/about.asp.

Association for Driver Rehabilitation Specialists. (2004). *Association for driver rehabilitation specialists.* Retrieved January 29, 2004, from http://www.aded.net.

Cobb, R. W., & Coughlin, J. F. (1997). Regulating older drivers: How are the states coping? *Journal of Aging and Social Policy, 9,* 71–87.

Cox, J. L., Fox, M. D., & Irwin, L. (1988). Driving and the elderly: A review of the literature. *Physical and Occupational Therapy in Geriatrics, 7,* 7–12.

Gillins, L. (1990). Yielding to age: When the elderly can no longer drive. *Journal of Gerontological Nursing, 16,* 12–15, 39–41.

Hunt, L. (1993). Evaluation and retraining programs for older drivers. *Clinics in Geriatric Medicine, 9,* 439–449.

Marottoli, R. A., Mendes de Leon, C. F., Glass, T. A., Williams, C. S., Cooney, L. M., Jr., Berkman, L. F., et al. (1997). Driving cessation and increased depressive symptoms: Prospective evidence from the New Haven EPESE. Established populations for epidemiologic studies of the elderly. *Journal of the American Geriatrics Society, 5,* 202–206.

National Highway Traffic Safety Administration. (1999). *Safe mobility for older people notebook* (No. DOT HS 808 853). Springfield, VA: Author.

U.S. Department of Transportation. (2003a). *Model driver screening and evaluation program final technical report, Volume I: Project summary and model program recommendations* (No. DOT HS 809 582). Washington, DC: Author.

U.S. Department of Transportation. (2003b). *Safe mobility for a maturing society: Challenges and opportunities.* Washington, DC: Author.

Wang, C. C., Kosinski, C. J., Schwartzberg, J. G., & Shanklin, A. V. (2003). *Physician's guide to assessing and counseling older drivers.* Chicago: American Medical Association & National Highway Traffic Safety Administration.

Authors

Wendy B. Stav, PhD, OTR/L, CDRS
Susan Pierce, OTR/L, CDRS
Carol J. Wheatley, OTR/L, CDRS
Elin Schold Davis, OTR/L, CDRS
for
The Commission on Practice
Sara Jane Brayman, PhD, OTR/L, FAOTA, *Chairperson*

Adopted by the Representative Assembly 2005C216.

Table B.1. Domain of Occupational Therapy Specific to Driving and Community Mobility

Areas of Occupation	Community mobility is critical to performance of instrumental activities of daily living, education, work, leisure, and social participation.
Performance Skills (Motor, Process, Communication/Interaction Skills)	• Driving and community mobility require one to possess and execute adequate performance skills. Individuals must use motor skills, including posture, mobility, coordination, strength and effort, and energy to maneuver the body through the environment, manipulate equipment, maintain a position, and sustain the activity through completion. • Driving and community mobility require sufficient process skills to form knowledge, temporal organization, organization of space and objects, adaptation, and energy while moving through the dynamic, unpredictable environment of the community. • Communication/interaction skills are used as individuals need to exchange information, relate, and physically communicate to move through a community in which other individuals also are mobile.
Performance Patterns (Habits, Routines, Roles)	Driving and community mobility involves performance patterns that use habits to operate equipment and routines to travel on an established route. Individuals fulfill the duties and responsibilities of life roles by engaging in community mobility.
Contexts (Cultural, Physical, Social, Personal, Spiritual, Temporal, Virtual)	The context in which driving and community mobility takes place is critical in understanding who, what, where, when, how, and why individuals move through the community. The physical context relates to travel in urban or rural settings, on different types of roadways—over a street, sidewalk, or path—or using underground, waterway, air, or land travel. The cultural context may dictate who operates an automobile, while the social context influences independent versus group travel. An individual's personal context indicates whether travel will be performed as a passenger or operator based on age or socioeconomic status. Temporal context affects community mobility based on the stage of life, time of day, season of year, and duration of driving. Recent technologies permit virtual engagement in community mobility through the use of computers and simulators.
Activity Demands	Driving and community mobility have many activity demands, which consist of the objects and properties of tools used, space and social demands, sequence and timing, required actions, required body functions, and required body structures.
Client Factors	Individuals use their body functions—mental, sensory (including vision), neuromusculoskeletal, voice, and speech—as well as related body structures, to effectively and safely move about in the community.

Table B.2. External Influences on Occupational Therapy Practice Related to Governmental Influences on Driving and Community Mobility

Governmental Influences		
Federal Government	National Highway Traffic Safety Administration (NHTSA)	NHTSA's mission is driver safety, with funding for programs and research on occupant protection specific to safety belt use, air bags, child passenger safety, graduated licensing, new drivers, vehicle modifications, and impaired driving due to alcohol or illegal drug use. A recent focus on older driver safety has generated programs such as a Model Driver Screening and Evaluation Program (U.S. Department of Transportation, 2003a). Reports developed from NHTSA's initiative include *Safe Mobility for Older People Notebook* (NHTSA, 1999) and *Safe Mobility for a Maturing Society: Challenges and Opportunities* (U.S. Department of Transportation, 2003b). The latter report states the need to evaluate and improve driving skills, acknowledges the value of driver rehabilitation, and recognizes the contributions of AOTA to this field.
State Government	State licensure laws	Laws related to driving and community mobility vary by state and jurisdiction with regard to vision standards, medical reporting, legal immunity, and licensure laws. Therefore, occupational therapists and occupational therapy assistants must become knowledgeable of the statutes and guidelines specific to the state or jurisdiction of practice.
Professional Organizations		
American Medical Association (AMA)	• The AMA believes that older driver safety is a public health issue and that physicians play an important role in ensuring the safety of older drivers (Wang, Kosinski, Schwartzberg, & Shanklin, 2003). The AMA has recently dedicated efforts to a safe driver initiative, resulting in a physician training program and several publications. • The AMA collaborated with aging, driver rehabilitation, and transportation experts nationwide to write guidelines for physician practice related to older drivers (Wang et al., 2003). The book advises several alternatives that physicians might pursue, such as referring older drivers to driver rehabilitation specialists. • On December 7, 1999, the AMA's Council on Ethical and Judicial Affairs adopted a report outlining physicians' ethical obligation to address driving issues with their clients (AMA, Council on Ethical and Judicial Affairs, 1999). The report included seven recommendations for physicians to recognize impairments and act on that knowledge when a patient's driving posed a strong threat to public safety.	
Association for Driver Rehabilitation Specialists (ADED)	ADED (2004) is a multidisciplinary group composed of occupational therapy practitioners, driver educators, vehicle modification manufacturers and dealers, rehabilitation engineers, physical therapists and kinesiotherapists, and rehabilitation specialists. ADED provides certification for driver rehabilitation specialists (CDRSs) by means of a portfolio review and standardized exam. ADED recently released *Best Practice Guidelines* for the CDRS.	

(continued)

Table B.2. External Influences on Occupational Therapy Practice Related to Governmental Influences on Driving and Community Mobility, *cont.*

American Occupational Therapy Assocation (AOTA)	AOTA provides standard setting, advocacy, education, and research of the profession of occupational therapy to advance the quality, availability, use, and support of occupational therapy (AOTA, 2005). AOTA has created an Older Driver Initiative to coordinate multiple projects related to awareness and professional training. Projects include • An evidence-based literature review specific to driving and community mobility • Practice guidelines for driver rehabilitation and community mobility for older adults • Older Driver Microsite (www.aota.org/olderdriver) • Specialty certification in driver rehabilitation and community mobility, targeted for availability by March 2006.

Appendix C. Driver's License Renewal Policies in the United States

State	Renewal Cycle (Years)	Accelerated Renewal for Older Drivers	Other Renewal Provisions
Alabama	4	No	None
Alaska	5	No	No mail renewal for ages 69 and older; no more than one mail renewal in a row for all ages; vision test required at renewal for all ages
Arizona	Until age 65	5 years for ages 65 and older	No mail renewal for ages 70 and older; vision test verification required for mail renewal for ages 65 and older; vision test required every 12 years for all ages
Arkansas	4	No	Vision test required at renewal for all ages
California	5	No	No mail renewal for ages 70 and older; no more than two successive mail renewals for all ages
Colorado	10	5 years for ages 61 and older	No mail renewal for ages 66 and older or electronic renewal for ages 60 and older; no more than one mail/electronic renewal in a row for all ages
Connecticut	4 or 6	Ages 65 and older may choose 2 or 6 years	Mail renewal for ages 65 and older only if able to show hardship; vision test required at first renewal and then every other renewal for all ages
Delaware	5	No	None
District of Columbia	5	No	Physician certification of physical/mental driving competency, vision test, and possible reaction test required at renewal for ages 70 and older; written and road tests may be required at renewal for ages 75 and older
Florida	6, 4 (bad record)	No	Vision test required at renewal for ages 80 and older; no more than two successive mail/electronic renewals for all ages
Georgia	4	No	Vision test required at renewal for all ages; mail/electronic renewal every other renewal for all ages
Hawaii	6	2 years for ages 72 and older	Vision test required at renewal for all ages
Idaho	4	4 or 8 years for ages 21–62; 4 years for ages 63 and older	Vision test required at renewal for all ages

State	Renewal Cycle (Years)	Accelerated Renewal for Older Drivers	Other Renewal Provisions
Illinois	4	2 years for ages 81–86; 1 year for ages 87 and older	Road test required at renewal for ages 75 and older; vision test required for in-person renewal
Indiana	4	3 years for ages 75 and older	Vision test required at renewal for all ages; electronic renewal every other renewal if meet eligibility criteria
Iowa	5	2 years for ages 70 and older	Vision test required at renewal for all ages
Kansas	6	4 years for ages 65 and older	Vision test required at renewal for all ages
Kentucky	4	No	None
Louisiana	4	No	No mail renewal for ages 70 and older; no more than one mail renewal in a row for all ages
Maine	6	4 years for ages 65 and older	Vision test required at every other renewal for ages 40–61 and at every renewal for ages 62 and older
Maryland	5	No	Vision test required at every renewal for ages 40 and older; ages 70 and older, new licensees must show proof of prior safe car operation or physician's certification of fitness; age alone not grounds for reexamination
Massachusetts	5	No	Age discrimination with regard to licensing prohibited
Michigan	4	No	Vision test required at in-person renewal for all ages; no more than one mail renewal in a row for all ages
Minnesota	4	No	Vision test required at renewal for all ages; age alone not grounds for reexamination
Mississippi	4	No	None
Missouri	6	3 years for ages 70 and older	Vision test required at renewal for all ages
Montana	8 (4 by mail)	4 years for ages 75 and older	Vision test required at renewal for all ages; mail renewal for all ages only in areas with no driver license services—no more than one in a row
Nebraska	5	No	Vision test required at renewal for all ages
Nevada	4	No	Medical report required at mail renewal for ages 70 and older; no more than two successive mail/electronic renewals for all ages; age alone not grounds for reexamination
New Hampshire	5	No	Road test required at renewal for ages 75 and older
New Jersey	4	No	Vision test may be required at renewal for all ages
New Mexico	4 or 8	4 years if turn 75 in 2nd half of 8-year renewal cycle	Vision test may be required at renewal for all ages
New York	5	No	Vision test required at renewal for all ages
North Carolina	5	No	Parallel parking not required in road test for ages 60 and older; Vision test required at renewal for all ages

State	Renewal Cycle (Years)	Accelerated Renewal for Older Drivers	Other Renewal Provisions
North Dakota	4	No	Certification of vision required at renewal for all ages
Ohio	4	No	Vision test required at renewal for all ages
Oklahoma	4	No	License fees reduced for ages 62–64, waived for ages 65 and older
Oregon	8	No	Vision screening required every 8 years for ages 50 and older
Pennsylvania	4	Ages 65 and older may choose 2 or 4 years	Vision test may be required at renewal for all ages
Rhode Island	5	2 years for ages 70 and older	None
South Carolina	10	5 years for ages 65 and older	Vision test required at renewal for ages 65 and older; beginning Oct. 1, 2008, vision test required every 5 years for all ages
South Dakota	5	No	Vision test required at renewal for all ages
Tennessee	5	No	No expiration for licenses issues to ages 65 and older; no more than one mail/electronic renewal in a row at all ages; fees reduced for ages 60 and older
Texas	6	No	Vision test required at renewal for all ages
Utah	5	No	Vision test required for ages 65 and older; vision test required every 10 years for all ages; no more than one electronic renewal in a row for all ages
Vermont	4	No	None
Virginia	5	No	Vision test required at renewal for ages 80 and older; no more than one mail/electronic renewal in a row for all ages
Washington	5	No	Vision test required at renewal for all ages; no more than one mail/electronic renewal in a row for all ages
West Virginia	5	No	None
Wisconsin	8	No	Vision test required at renewal for all ages
Wyoming	4	No	Vision test required at renewal for all ages; no more than one mail renewal in a row for all ages

Note. From L. J. Molnar & D. W. Eby (2005, Spring), A brief look at driver license renewal policies in the United States, *Public Policy and Aging Report, 15*(2), 1, 13–17. Copyright © 2005, Gerontological Society of America. Reprinted with permission.

Appendix D.
Sample Vendor Forms

The following forms were developed to help occupational therapist driving rehabilitation specialists (OT/DRSs) and the funding source obtain vendor bids for installation of adaptive products. The forms were developed with input from OT/DRSs, vendors, driver educators, the Minnesota Department of Vocational Rehabilitation Services, and the Minnesota Department of Motor Vehicles. In Minnesota, completed forms are submitted to the Minnesota Department of Vocational Rehabilitation Services (when the client is eligible to have the department pay for the adaptive equipment), which selects a vendor based on its bid. These forms can be adapted for use in other states.

Vehicle Modification Specifications (page 1 of 2)

MAPS Requisition # ____________________

Client name and address

(To be provided to the vendor on the authorization only; will not be printed on bid solicitation document.)

Name ____________________

Phone (______) ____________________

Address ____________________

City ____________________ State __________ Zip __________

This section to be completed by Evaluator

Evaluator Name ____________________

Phone # ____________________

Note: When there is a question about the least costly alternative, please create two sets of specifications. These will be used to determine the least costly alternative and cost difference for the consumer.

Type of Vehicle Currently Owned (if any)

Year __________ Make ____________________ Model ____________________

Mileage ____________________

Vehicle Information: Vocational Rehabilitation Services does not purchase the following items. Check all the options the consumer needs to order when purchasing a vehicle or to help the consumer determine whether a current vehicle will meet his or her needs.

- ❑ Automatic transmission
- ❑ Air conditioning
- ❑ Cruise control
- ❑ Rear heat and A/C
- ❑ Power brakes
- ❑ Power windows
- ❑ Power door locks
- ❑ Power mirrors
- ❑ Power driver's seat
- ❑ Tilt steering column
- ❑ Power steering
- ❑ Rear power hatch
- ❑ Extended wheelbase
- ❑ Power sliding passenger door
- ❑ Load-leveling suspension
- ❑ Other

Wheelchair/Scooter Information

Type

Brand ____________________ Model No. ____________________

Power ____________________ Manual ____________________

Folding ____________________ Rigid ____________________

Special Seating/Power ____________________

❑ Power seating ❑ Power recline ❑ Headrest ❑ Power standing

Size

Width ____________________

Height ____________________

Length ____________________

–continued–

Vehicle Modification Specifications (page 2 of 2)

Consumer in Wheelchair/Scooter Measurements

Ground to top of head ______________________

Ground to top of knee ______________________

Footrest height ______________________

Approx. weight of consumer and chair/scooter ______________________

Was the vehicle used in the assessment the same as the one being recommended for modification?

❑ Yes ❑ No

If no, please list differences: ______________________

____

Will the vehicle with the required modifications fit in client's garage? ❑ Yes ❑ No

If no, how has this issue been resolved with the client? ______________________

____

I told the consumer the following options may make a vehicle ineligible for conversion and should **not** be ordered on a new vehicle: ______________________

____

____

The consumer needs the following training to operate the modified vehicle: ______________________

____

____

We discussed possible upgrade options the consumer may want to purchase at his or her expense.

❑ Yes ❑ No

We discussed the availability of rebates for conversions.

❑ Yes ❑ No

I have completed specifications for the following:

❑ Sedan/SUV/Truck ❑ Full-size van ❑ Minivan

I certify that the attached specifications fulfill the minimum requirements that will allow the consumer to drive safely or to ride as a passenger if he or she will not drive the vehicle. I am either ADED-certified or meet the ADED certification requirements.

Evaluator's Name (please print) ______________________ Phone ______________________

Evaluator's Signature ______________________ Date ______________________

Specifications for Sedan/SUV/Truck (page 1 of 2)

Vehicle modifications *required* to allow consumer to drive a sedan, SUV, or truck.
(*Evaluator:* Check only minimally required.)

Acceleration/Braking

❑ Original manufactured effort
❑ Reduced effort (50%) with backup
❑ Zero effort (85–95%) with backup

❑ Mechanical
  ❑ Left ❑ Right
  ❑ Right angle
  ❑ Push/pull (column-mounted)
  ❑ Push/pull stock control
  ❑ Vertical grip style hand control
  ❑ Twist

❑ Left-foot accelerator
❑ Pedal extensions _______________ (size)
❑ Power emergency brake
❑ Gas or brake pedal block

Seating Options

❑ Swivel seat
  ❑ Driver ❑ Passenger
  ❑ Manual ❑ Power
❑ Removable front seat

Extensions

❑ Ignition key
❑ Toggle switch
❑ Climate control
❑ Shift lever
  ❑ Left ❑ Right
❑ Headlight
❑ Dimmer
❑ Parking brake
❑ Turn signal lever
  ❑ Right side
  ❑ Left side
  ❑ Incorporated in hand control
❑ Wiper

Interaction Mechanisms

❑ Turn signal
❑ Wipers/wash
❑ Horn/dimmer
❑ Cruise on/set
  ❑ Right side ❑ Left side
❑ Other positioning details: _______________
❑ Power gear shift
  ❑ Right side ❑ Left side
  ❑ Other _______________
❑ Touch interaction mechanism
Function _______________
  ❑ Dome switch ❑ Pin switch ❑ Tri-pin
  ❑ Other _______________

Steering

❑ Original manufactured effort
❑ Reduced effort (50%) with back-up
❑ Zero effort (85–95%) with back-up
❑ Steering aid
  Position on wheel _______________
  ❑ Spinner knob
  ❑ Tri-pin
  ❑ V-grip
  ❑ Palm grip
  ❑ For hooks
❑ Steering column extension _______________ (size)

Miscellaneous

❑ Wide-angle mirrors _______________
❑ Scooter or wheelchair lift
  ❑ Trunk ❑ Side ❑ Rear
  ❑ Driver/passenger mount
  ❑ Bed of truck
❑ Chair top carrier
❑ Remote start option
❑ Chest straps
❑ Stanchion seat belt
❑ Additional seat belt receptacle
❑ Air bag on/off switch

–continued–

Specifications for Sedan/SUV/Truck (page 2 of 2)

Additional Bid Specifications

*Vendor must agree to adhere to National Mobility Equipment Dealers Association (NMEDA) guidelines.

*Final inspection by driver evaluator is required after modifications are complete, before client acceptance.

*The vendor is responsible for pickup of vehicle from client, and client will pick up for fitting when modifications are complete:

❑ Yes ❑ No—Client will accept responsibility for pickup and delivery after final inspection.

*Other considerations and comments: ______________________________

____

____

____

Specifications for Full-Size Van (page 1 of 2)

Vehicle modifications required to allow consumer to drive a full-size van. (*Evaluator:* Check only minimally required.)

Drop Floor

❏ 4"
❏ 6"
❏ 8"
❏ Midsection only
❏ Midsection and driver
❏ Midsection and passenger
❏ Midsection to firewall

Lift

❏ Rigid platform
❏ Folding platform
❏ Power folding platform
❏ Swing-away lift
❏ Side mount
❏ Rear mount
❏ Single arm
❏ Dual arm

Raised Roof and Doors

❏ Raised fiberglass top ______ inches with certified roll cage
❏ Raised door
  ❏ Rear ❏ Side cargo ❏ Side sliding

Seating Options

❏ Manual swivel seat
❏ Power seat base (4 way)
  ❏ Driver ❏ Passenger
❏ Power seat base (6 way)
  ❏ Driver ❏ Passenger
❏ Interchangeable front seats
❏ Removable front seat
  ❏ Driver ❏ Passenger
❏ Other ________________________________

Power Doors

❏ Passenger side door
  ❏ Cargo ❏ Sliding
❏ Rear/cargo door

Switches for Lift/Door

❏ Toggle exterior controls
❏ Magnetic exterior controls
❏ Dash toggle
❏ Remote control
❏ Pendant control

Wheelchair Securement

❏ Certified manual 4-point tie-downs
  ❏ Passenger ❏ Midsection
❏ Certified retractable tie-downs
  ❏ Passenger ❏ Midsection
❏ Certified power tie-down with deactivation switch:
  ❏ Driver ❏ Passenger ❏ Midsection
  ❏ Alarm ❏ Antitrip device

Acceleration/Braking

❏ Original manufactured effort
❏ Reduced effort (50%) with backup
❏ Zero effort (85–95%) with backup
❏ Pneumatic
  ❏ Left ❏ Right
❏ Electronic
  ❏ Left ❏ Right
  ❏ Gas forward ❏ Gas backward
  ❏ Tri-pin ❏ T-handle ❏ Hand splint
  ❏ Other ________________________________
❏ Mechanical
  ❏ Left ❏ Right
  ❏ Right angle
  ❏ Push/pull (column-mounted)
  ❏ Push/pull stock control
  ❏ Vertical grip-style hand control
  ❏ Twist
❏ Left foot accelerator
❏ Pedal extensions ____________________ (size)
❏ Power emergency brake
❏ Gas and/or brake pedal block

Interaction Mechanisms

❏ Right side ❏ Left side
❏ Other positioning details ______________
  ❏ 2-function touchpad
    Functions: ________________________
    ____
  ❏ 8-function touchpad
    Functions: ________________________
    ____
  ❏ 16-function touchpad
    Functions: ________________________
    ____

– *continued* –

Specifications for Full-Size Van (page 2 of 2)

❑ Power gear shift
  ❑ Right side ❑ Left side
  ❑ Other

❑ Voice-activated
  Functions: ______________________
  ____

❑ Touch interaction mechanism
  Function: ______________________
  ____

  ❑ Dome switch ❑ Pin switch ❑ Tri-pin
  ❑ Other ______________________

Extensions

❑ Ignition key
❑ Toggle switch
❑ Climate control
❑ Shift lever
  ❑ Left ❑ Right
❑ Headlight
❑ Dimmer
❑ Parking brake
❑ Turn signal lever
  ❑ Right side ❑ Left side
  ❑ Incorporated in hand control
❑ Wiper

Steering

❑ Original manufactured effort
❑ Reduced effort (50%) with backup
❑ Zero effort (85–95%) with backup
❑ Secondary steering
  ❑ Left ❑ Right ❑ Center
  Model/style ______________________
Orthotic
  ❑ Tri-pin ❑ 1-knob ❑ 2-knob
  ❑ Hand splint ❑ Swivel pin
  ❑ Other ______________________
❑ Steering aid
  Position on wheel ______________________
  ❑ Spinner knob
  ❑ Tri-pin
  ❑ V-grip
  ❑ Palm grip
  ❑ For hooks
❑ Steering column extension ______________________
❑ Joystick driving
  ❑ Left ❑ Right ❑ Center
  ❑ Orthotic: ______________________

Miscellaneous

❑ Wide-angle mirrors ______________________
❑ Scooter or wheelchair lift
  ❑ Trunk ❑ Side ❑ Rear
  ❑ Driver/passenger mount
  ❑ Bed of truck
❑ Chair top carrier
❑ Remote start option
❑ Chest straps
❑ Seat belt
  ❑ Lap belt
  ❑ Three point
  ❑ Stanchion seat belt receptacle
  ❑ Additional receptacle
❑ Air bag on/off switch
  ❑ Other ______________________

Additional Bid Specifications

*Vendor must agree to adhere to National Mobility Equipment Dealers Association (NMEDA) guidelines.

*Final inspection by driver evaluator is required after modifications are complete, before client acceptance.

*The vendor is responsible for pickup of vehicle from client, and client will pick up for fitting when modifications are complete:
  ❑ Yes ❑ No—Client will accept responsibility for pickup and delivery after final inspection.

*Other considerations and comments: ______________________
____

The following full-size vans (year, make, and model) can be modified to meet the required specifications: ______________________
____
____

The consumer wants the bid to be made on the following full-size van; include year, make, model (and mileage, if vehicle is used): ______________________
____
____

Specifications for Minivan (page 1 of 2)

Vehicle modifications *required* to allow consumer to drive a minivan. (*Evaluator:* Check only minimally required.)

Side-Entry Drop Floor

❏ 10 (Dodge, Chrysler, Ford)
❏ 12 (GM)

Rear-Entry Drop Floor

❏ Short cut (lowered through rear bench area)
❏ Standard cut (lowered to right behind the front seats)

Lift/Ramp

❏ Power ramp
❏ Manual ramp
❏ In-floor ramp
❏ Folding ramp
❏ Power folding lift
❏ Power solid platform lift

Raised Roof and Doors

❏ Raised fiberglass top _____ inches with certified roll cage
❏ Raised door
  ❏ Rear
  ❏ Side sliding

Power Doors

❏ Passenger side
❏ Driver side
❏ Rear hatch

Seating Options

❏ Manual swivel seat
❏ Power seat base (4 way)
  ❏ Driver ❏ Passenger
❏ Power seat base (6 way)
  ❏ Driver ❏ Passenger
❏ Interchangeable front seats
❏ Removable front seat
  ❏ Driver ❏ Passenger ❏ Midsection
  ❏ Other ____________________
❏ Kneel suspension

Switches for Lift/Door

❏ Toggle exterior controls
❏ Magnetic exterior controls
❏ Dash toggle
❏ Remote control
❏ Pendant control

Wheelchair Securement

❏ Certified manual 4-point tie-downs
  ❏ Passenger ❏ Midsection
❏ Certified retractable tie-downs
  ❏ Passenger ❏ Midsection
❏ Certified power tie-down with deactivation switch
  ❏ Driver ❏ Passenger ❏ Midsection
  ❏ Alarm ❏ Antitrip device

Acceleration/Braking

❏ Original manufactured effort
❏ Reduced effort (50%) with backup
❏ Zero effort (85–95%) with backup
❏ Pneumatic
  ❏ Left ❏ Right
❏ Electronic
  ❏ Left ❏ Right
  ❏ Gas forward ❏ Gas backward
  ❏ Tri-pin ❏ T-handle ❏ Hand splint
  ❏ Other ____________________
❏ Mechanical
  ❏ Left ❏ Right
  ❏ Right angle
  ❏ Push/pull (column-mounted)
  ❏ Push/pull stock control
  ❏ Vertical grip-style hand control
  ❏ Twist
❏ Left foot accelerator
❏ Pedal extensions __________ (size)
❏ Power emergency brake
❏ Gas and/or brake pedal block

Interaction Mechanisms

❏ Right side ❏ Left side
❏ Other positioning details ____________________
  ❏ 2-function touchpad
  Functions: ____________________
  ____

  ❏ 8-function touchpad
  Functions: ____________________
  ____

  ❏ 16-function touchpad
  Functions: ____________________
  ____

– continued –

Specifications for Minivan (page 2 of 2)

- ❏ Power gear shift
  - ❏ Right side ❏ Left side
- ❏ Other ____________________
- ❏ Voice-activated
  Functions: ____________________
  ____
- ❏ Touch interaction mechanism
  Function: ____________________
  ____
  - ❏ Dome switch ❏ Pin switch ❏ Tri-pin
  - ❏ Other ____________________

Steering

- ❏ Original manufactured effort
- ❏ Reduced effort (50%) with backup
- ❏ Zero effort (85–95%) with backup
- ❏ Secondary steering
  - ❏ Left ❏ Right ❏ Center
  - Model/style ____________________
  - Orthotic:
  - ❏ Tri-pin ❏ 1-knob ❏ 2-knob
  - ❏ Hand splint ❏ Swivel pin
  - ❏ Other ____________________
- ❏ Steering aid
  - Position on wheel ____________________
  - ❏ Spinner knob
  - ❏ Tri-pin
  - ❏ V-grip
  - ❏ Palm grip
  - ❏ For hooks
- ❏ Steering column extension __________ (size)
- ❏ Joystick driving
  - ❏ Left ❏ Right ❏ Center
  - ❏ Orthotic: ____________________

Extensions

- ❏ Ignition key
- ❏ Toggle switch
- ❏ Climate control
- ❏ Shift lever:
  - ❏ Left ❏ Right
- ❏ Headlight
- ❏ Dimmer
- ❏ Parking brake
- ❏ Turn signal lever
  - ❏ Right side
  - ❏ Left side
  - ❏ Incorporated in hand control
- ❏ Wiper

Miscellaneous

- ❏ Wide-angle mirrors ____________________
- ❏ Scooter or wheelchair lift
  - ❏ Trunk ❏ Side ❏ Rear
  - ❏ Driver/passenger mount
  - ❏ Bed of truck
- ❏ Chair top carrier
- ❏ Remote start option
- ❏ Chest straps
- ❏ Seat belt
  - ❏ Lap belt
  - ❏ Three point
  - ❏ Stanchion seat belt receptacle
  - ❏ Additional receptacle
- ❏ Air bag on/off switch

Other

- ❏ ____________________
- ❏ ____________________

Additional Bid Specifications

*Vendor must agree to adhere to National Mobility Equipment Dealers Association (NMEDA) guidelines.

*Final inspection by driver evaluator is required after modifications are complete, before client acceptance.

*The vendor is responsible for pickup of vehicle from client, and client will pick up for fitting when modifications are complete:

❏ Yes ❏ No—Client will accept responsibility for pickup and delivery after final inspection.

*Other considerations and comments ____________________

____

____

The following minivans (year, make, and model) can be modified to meet the required specifications: ____________________

____

____

The consumer wants the bid to be made on the following minivan; include year, make, model (and mileage, if vehicle is used): ____________________

____

Occupational Therapist Screening Tool for Referral to a Driving Program (page 1 of 3)

Driving Pre-driving Screen Report

Client Name: ______________________ Physician Name: ______________________

Date of Birth: ______________________ Physician Phone: ______________________

Client Phone: ______________________ Physician Fax: ______________________

Driver's License Number: ______________________

❑ Current ❑ Expired ❑ Cancelled ❑ Revoked ❑ Permit ❑ Never licensed before

Endorsements and Restrictions: ______________________

Medical History: (History of seizures and vision problems, epilepsy, diabetes, age, do they meet state statutes)

____

____

____

❑ Aphasia ❑ Expressive ❑ Receptive

____

❑ Compensation Techniques: ______________________

____

Medications: ______________________

____

____

Driving History and Needs (e.g., Where do they drive to? What times of day?): ______________________

____

____

– continued –

Occupational Therapist Screening Tool for Referral to a Driving Program (page 2 of 3)

Physical Skills for Driving:

	Right	Left		Right	Left
Neck rotation AROM (WFL or BFL)			Lower-body ROM (record in degrees)		
Upper-body ROM (record in degrees)			Hip flexion		
Shoulder flexion			Hip extension		
Shoulder extension			Internal rotation		
Horizontal abduction			External rotation		
Horizontal adduction			Knee flexion		
Elbow flexion			Knee extension		
Elbow extension			Plantar flexion		
Upper-body strength (in muscle grade)			Dorsi flexion		
Shoulder flexion			Lower-body strength (WFL or BFL)		
Shoulder extension			Lower-body coordination (WFL or BFL)		
Horizontal abduction			Lower-body proprioception (WFL or BFL)		
Horizontal adduction			Balance (WFL or BFL)		
Elbow flexion			Sitting		
Elbow extension			Standing		
Upper-body coordination (WFL or BFL)			Grip strength (WFL or BFL)		
Upper-body proprioception (WFL or BFL)			Pinch strength (WFL or BFL)		

Note. ROM = range of motion; AROM = active range of motion; WFL = within functional limits; BFL = below functional limits.

Mobility: ❑ Ambulatory ❑ Walker ❑ Cane ❑ Wheelchair ❑ Other ______________________

Transfer into/out of a motor vehicle:
❑ Independent ❑ 1 Person ❑ 2 Person ❑ Total assist ❑ Other ______________________

Functional mobility for community (e.g., ability on uneven surfaces, curb cuts, getting gas, use of alternative transportation):

____

____

Alternative transportation options in patient's community: ______________________

____

Vision Skills for Driving:

	WFL	BFL		WFL	BFL
Contrast sensitivity			Convergence/divergence		
Visual field (need 105γ peripheral)			Visual pursuits		
Distance acuity (need 20/40 in one eye for no restrictions)			Saccades		
Color discrimination			Accommodation		

❑ Yes ❑ No glasses for reading ❑ Yes ❑ No glasses for distance ❑ Yes ❑ No double vision reported

Describe visual concerns: ______________________

Referral needed: ❑ Optometrist ❑ Ophthamologist ❑ Other eye specialist: ______________________

Request: ______________________

– continued –

Occupational Therapist Screening Tool for Referral to a Driving Program (page 3 of 3)

Cognitive & Perceptual Skills for Driving:

Short Blessed Test
Score __________ (Result should be 7 or less.)

or Mini-Mental Short-Term Memory Screen
Score __________/30

MVPT (Motor Free Visual Perceptual test)
Score __________
Areas of strength: ______________________________________
Areas of deficit: ______________________________________

Dynavision Performance Assessment Battery
Mode A Score __________ (Result should be 45 or higher.)
Mode B Score __________ (Result should be 35 or higher.)
One-minute apparatus paced with one-digit test score __________ (Result should be 30 or higher.)
Four-minute self-paced endurance test score __________ (Result should be 175 or higher.)

Weintraub Unstructured Array (for facilities with no Dynavision)
Scan pattern: ❑ Organized ❑ Random ❑ Field cut/neglect
General comments regarding other cognitive tests performed, if any: ______________________________

For dementia or Alzheimer's patients
ACL Score: __________ CPT Score: __________

Other assessment tools used/score

Assessment Tool Name	Score	Area Tested (e.g., memory, planning, problem solving)
1.		
2.		
3.		

Therapist Completing Pre-Screen:

____

Name Phone Date

❑ Referral to specialist before driving evaluation recommended:
Specialist ______________________________ Reason ______________________________
Referral information provided/contact made with OT/DRS.
❑ Based on the results of this pre-screen, the client is suitable and ready for a driving evaluation.
❑ Hospital staff will coordinate scheduling of driving evaluation.
❑ Client will call to schedule a driving evaluation.
❑ Please contact the client to set up a driving evaluation (phone number: ____________________).
❑ Client did not meet state criteria for driving. Referral for specific testing to gain more detail if applicable (e.g., optometrist for specific vision test).

Copy of pre-screen faxed to referral.

Please feel free to call with any questions

Therapist Name: ____

Phone: ____

Developed by Sue Redepenning, Occupational Therapy Solutions.

Index

C

D

E

F

G

H

I

J

K

L

M

N

O

P

Q

R

S

T

U

V

W

About the Author

Sue Redepenning, OTR/L, CDRS, is a licensed occupational therapist and certified driver rehabilitation specialist. She has more than 15 years of rehabilitation experience. Over her career, Sue has worked as a staff occupational therapist and in administration and management in a variety of rehabilitation settings, as well as with a variety of age groups and disabilities. She has owned and operated her own occupational therapy companies and has worked in marketing as a private consultant in the area of driving for a for-profit company. She has taken a variety of continuing education seminars on vision and spinal cord injury and is certified in neurodevelopmental treatment techniques for adults.

Sue currently owns and operates Occupational Therapy Solutions, Inc., which offers driving consultation services to assist in driver rehabilitation and professional presentations. During the 3 1/2 years she consulted in driving for a for-profit driver rehabilitation company, she has worked hard to build the medical side of a driver rehabilitation business in Minnesota and Wisconsin. She currently works full-time in home health rehabilitation (both in traditional and nontraditional settings) and operating her company. She has presented at the local level on occupational therapy's role in driving in Minnesota and Wisconsin and nationally for the American Occupational Therapy Association (AOTA) and the Association for Driver Rehabilitation Specialists (ADED).

In working with her home health clients, Sue discusses driving during the initial evaluation, presents appropriate referral information, and provides education to the client's physician and team to address the important issue of driving throughout the rehabilitation process. Sue's understanding of driver rehabilitation from the inside has been key to her ability to explain the process to the client and team so that they understand its value.

Sue is a member of AOTA, the Minnesota Occupational Therapy Association, and ADED.